PRAISE FOR *AGILE MA*

There is an ongoing debate about whether the principles of marketing itself have changed. But what should be clear to all is that *how* marketing is executed has changed and agile is key to that. Somewhat surprisingly, though, marketers have been slow to really understand what agile means for marketing. This book should be required reading for any marketer who wants to learn how marketing needs to operate now.
Ashley Friedlein, CEO, Guild, and Founder, Econsultancy

Neil is able to articulate the essential elements of agile ways of working in a truly engaging way using easy to understand models, great storytelling and relevant examples.
Christel Kinning, Chief Transformation and People Officer, Oatly

This book is packed full of amazing insights and pragmatic advice for marketers who are looking to transform the way that their team works. Essential reading.
Fiona Spooner, Managing Director, Consumer Revenue, *Financial Times*

The greatest opportunity in modern marketing is the need to embrace agile methodology to fuel growth and accelerate scale. Neil Perkin has forensically written the blueprint for every marketer to follow with rigour, candour and thankfully the odd bit of humour too.
Richard Robinson, Managing Director, Oystercatchers

Prepare to be challenged! Neil Perkin cracks the code for successfully applying an agile mindset and methods at scale to marketing.
Paul Duxbury, Global Repeatable Growth Model Programme Lead, GSK Consumer Healthcare

Superbly researched and articulated throughout this book is full of inspiring stories and practical frameworks. Neil has written the definitive guide on how to apply agile principles at scale in marketing.
Iain Noakes, Head of Marketing Strategy, Planning & Effectiveness, Samsung Electronics

In the modern flux of culture, marketing can be confusing for brands, agencies and customers. Neil has written the essential playbook for shaping your marketing organization to be as agile as culture requires.

Faris Yakob, author of *Paid Attention: Innovative Advertising for a Digital World*

Agile Marketing

*Unlock adaptive and data-driven marketing
for long-term success*

Neil Perkin

KoganPage

First published in Great Britain and the United States in 2022 by Kogan Page Limited

2nd Floor, 45 Gee Street	8 W 38th Street, Suite 902	4737/23 Ansari Road
London	New York, NY 10018	Daryaganj
EC1V 3RS	USA	New Delhi 110002
United Kingdom		India
www.koganpage.com		

Kogan Page books are printed on paper from sustainable forests.

© Neil Perkin, 2022

The right of Neil Perkin to be identified as the author of this work has been asserted by him in accordance with the Copyright, Designs and Patents Act 1988.

ISBNs

Hardback	978 1 3986 0512 1
Paperback	978 1 3986 0510 7
Ebook	978 1 3986 0511 4

British Library Cataloguing-in-Publication Data

A CIP record for this book is available from the British Library.

Library of Congress Control Number

2021062027

Typeset by Integra Software Services, Pondicherry
Print production managed by Jellyfish
Printed and bound by CPI Group (UK) Ltd, Croydon CR0 4YY

CONTENTS

PART ONE

The agile marketing opportunity

01

Marketing in the digital age

Changing marketing – how the 4 Ps are evolving

Marketing can often be obsessed by the shiny and the new. Sometimes this can be helpful since it can help us to challenge our assumptions, focus on innovation and find new ways to engage customers and achieve our objectives. Yet it can also be unhelpful when we forget the fundamentals of marketing strategy and practice in our rush to embrace the latest technology trend or fad. Digital technologies have revolutionized multiple industries, business models, customer behaviour and routes to market. It has disrupted incumbent businesses, rewired the way in which entire markets operate and changed competitive environments for good. It has empowered consumers in ways that were unimaginable 30 years ago. Now, everyone with a smartphone has the answer to just about any question right there at their fingertips.

Yet great marketing is still great marketing. Among all this change the core fundamental elements of marketing have not changed. According to the UK's Chartered Institute of Marketing (CIM):

> Marketing is the management process responsible for identifying, anticipating and satisfying customer requirements profitably.[1]

Let's break that definition down. As a process, marketing is a way of generating value from and organizing activities around customers and their needs. In his classic book *The Practice of Management* Peter Drucker famously declares:

> Because the purpose of business is to create a customer, the business enterprise has two – and only two – basic functions: marketing and innovation...
> Marketing and innovation produce results; all the rest are costs. Marketing is the distinguishing, unique function of the business.[2]

This process revolves around identifying customer needs, which is based on research, observation and insight. Marketing has always placed the customer at its heart, has long been the voice of the customer in business and enabled the organization to focus its activities to generate customer value. Marketing brings customer orientation to the company. Marketing also anticipates customer needs by spotting opportunities and gaps, meaning that it can be customer led but also customer leading. It's also concerned with satisfying customer needs, which means having a clear, customer-focused purpose for products and services and executing that purpose in ways that deliver to and exceed customer expectations. The final part of this definition is profitability which is, of course, about serving the needs of the business. To paraphrase American marketing theorist Richard Bagozzi, marketing is an organized system of exchange – the business gains revenue, profit or some other gain in exchange for the benefits that are provided to customers by the product or service.[3] However, the context for *how* we deliver these essential elements *has* changed. And changed dramatically. From a fragmentation of channels and touchpoints to a revolution in the role that data and technology plays in the discipline, to powerful shifts in customer experiences, targeting and measurement. Digital has changed how we identify, anticipate and satisfy customer needs. It has changed the way in which we derive benefit and profit through new models and new ways of understanding the value and return of the activity we are delivering.

The impact of these long-term shifts has been compounded by rapidly changing, increasingly complex and uncertain environments. Many organizations were undergoing significant digital transformations in response to the need to rapidly digitize capability and become more agile and responsive to changing contexts. The COVID-19 pandemic served to dramatically increase this requirement for transformation as consumers moved rapidly to online channels and companies struggled to adapt to swiftly evolving customer behaviour. McKinsey research has shown that between the start of the pandemic in December 2019 and July 2020 the average share of customer interactions that are digital grew from 36 per cent to 58 per cent globally. This triggered a rapid acceleration in digitization with the number of propositions, products and services that were partially or fully digital growing from 35 per cent to 55 per cent over the same period.[4] Respondents to the survey were three times more likely than before the crisis to say that at least 80 per cent of their customer interactions are digital in nature. A survey of 2,500 enterprise decision-makers from around the world by cloud communications platform Twilio found that 97 per cent of respondents believed the pandemic sped up their company's digital transformation and that it had accelerated companies' digital communications strategy by an average of six years.[5] Data from digital, marketing and e-commerce specialist Econsultancy and Adobe revealed that a majority of businesses in their research (63 per cent for B2C and 57 per cent for B2B) had seen unusual growth in digital customers but also that around half of companies had seen unusual buying behaviour from existing customers.[6] The McKinsey survey also showed that the largest changes (including changing customer needs and requirements) were also the most likely to stick through the recovery period.

With such significant change it has become essential for marketers to respond with greater agility and adaptability to these shifts in both customer behaviour and expectation. And yet while expertise, roles, the use of technology and elements of practice have evolved, my argument in this book is that much around the structure, process and mindsets that marketing teams deploy to execute marketing strategy and realize objectives has not fully kept pace with this change. This book is not about challenging or rehashing classic marketing theory. It is instead a pragmatic view on how marketing teams can apply key principles and practice from methodologies that have grown up with digital to facilitate greater responsiveness and adaptability. It is about how data can be placed right at the heart of marketing practice to support better decision-making, continuous iteration and optimization. It is about marketing execution that is fit for purpose for a rapidly changing world.

But first, let's begin with what's NOT changing.

What's not changing

> I very frequently get the question: 'What's going to change in the next 10 years?'... I almost never get the question: 'What's not going to change in the next 10 years?' And I submit to you that that second question is actually the more important of the two, because you can build a business strategy around the things that are stable in time.[7]

This quote from Jeff Bezos speaks to the importance of paying attention to fundamental customer needs that largely don't change over time. In Amazon's case this might be low prices, ease of purchase, fast delivery and a huge range of products to select from. This, he says, enables a business to be truly exceptional at what is fundamentally important and focus on long-term success and not just short-term profit.

There is much around classic marketing theory and practice that has not changed. The importance of marketing strategy and positioning, and of understanding the market, competitive propositions and how this can shape objectives. The importance of insight into customer needs, motivations and behaviours and how these can shape our segmentation of customers, the identification of who we want to target and the messaging that we want to use. The significance of brand and how this creates disproportionate value for organizations. The need to combine brand building with sales activation. The value that comes from creativity. The need to integrate, plan and measure activity against clear goals. The need to optimize the mix of our activity to ensure the best possible returns. All these things are just as important now as they have ever been.

Taking this into marketing communication, marketing and advertising strategist Tom Roach has defined seven key principles of effectiveness that will always be true, since they relate to the fundamentals of not just marcomms, but how the human brain works.[8] These are a good reminder of essential principles that don't change:

1 **Reach:** Research has consistently shown that brand growth is driven by new and light buyers in the category. In his seminal marketing book *How Brands Grow*, Byron Sharp demonstrates that brands succeed through building mental and physical availability and through reaching new customers, which means reach is fundamental.[9]

2 **Attention:** Reach is of little use if you can't then gain attention from customers and prospects. This means standing out, earning attention and cutting through all the noise.

3 **Creativity:** Work by the Institute of Practitioners in Advertising in the UK and by Peter Field has shown that creativity is a powerful driver of sales and profitability.[10] More powerful than media and targeting.

4 **Distinctiveness:** Distinctive brand assets can help create the memory structures that help customers to recall your brand in buying situations. US ad executive Rosser Reeves famously argued as long ago as the early 1960s that marketing communication should display a unique proposition (a USP), but research by the Ehrenberg Bass Institute for Marketing Science has shown that brand distinctiveness (standing out with impact through assets like name, colours, messaging) is a more effective driver of impact than brand differentiation (setting yourself apart from the competition). In order to be chosen, brands need to come to mind easily.[11]

5 **Consistency:** It's not enough to just be distinctive. Brands need to be consistently distinctive. Roach references an analysis of 1,500 campaigns by Ebiquity that found that long-running distinctive brand campaigns delivered returns that were 62 per cent higher than the rest. Ebiquity also found that second and third bursts of campaigns on average generate ROIs 30 per cent higher than the first burst, as they build on the brand recognition scores initially achieved.[12]

6 **Emotion:** Multiple studies have shown that a consumer's emotional response to marketing communication and advertising has a much greater influence on their intent to buy a product than the actual content of that communication. As Roach puts it: '*Communications evoking emotional responses have better attention, deeper processing of the content, better memory-encoding and retrieval.*'

7 **Motivation:** Paying attention to and showing how the brand can help customers to achieve something they want helps turn connection and engagement into action.

Marketing and marcomms has always worked best when it brings together the full potential of technology with human intuition, empathy, creativity and understanding.

Let's go back to that Jeff Bezos quote that opened this section. Alongside designing and creating long-term value around fundamental needs that don't change, the Amazon founder has also talked about how advantage comes from innovating and delivering against these fundamental needs in exceptional ways. In other words, to break open category norms and surprise and delight customers with new propositions that deliver to those needs in ground-breaking ways (Amazon Prime Now is a good example of this). In other words, the fundamentals remain true, but how we deliver them creates real advantage.

This is now the potential that digital technology has brought to marketing. While key principles are as important as they have ever been to build the foundation of good marketing practice, *how* a team delivers against these principles has never been more powerful in delivering advantage. Turning good practice into great practice is increasingly about how a team can build on the foundation of classic marketing strategy in how they think, work, execute and operate. The contexts and environments within which marketing operates have changed dramatically. It's time that the way in which marketing teams work caught up.

What is changing

One of the all-time classic frameworks for marketing is the 4 Ps of marketing: product, price, place and promotion. The origins of the 4 Ps stem from Neil Borden, an advertising professor at Harvard University who first wrote about the concept of the marketing mix. His ideas were built on by E Jerome McCarthy, a marketing professor at Michigan State University, who turned the marketing mix concept into the 4 Ps as we know them today.[13]

Given the new contexts for marketing that have been created by digital technologies, let's consider how the 4 Ps are changing.

- **Product:** How our product meets customer needs. The growth of 'as-a-service' solutions, service design and innovation, and direct-to-consumer propositions mean that a growing number of products are becoming digitized services. A toothbrush was once just a toothbrush, but now it is a connected device that tracks your brushing and an app that provides you with recommendations and notifications. Innovation in razors was once about adding another blade but now it's about a subscription service that knows your shaving preferences and habits. A car was once a metal box on wheels and now it is a connected device that serves up multiple personalized options. As service design and innovation proliferate, the lines between product and service are becoming blurred. With software becoming integrated into an increasing number of products, the lines between product and marketing are also becoming blurred. Customer experiences require modular, personalized, joined-up, on-demand, scalable, networked, adaptable solutions that meet and exceed customer expectations. This brings changes to the role of content, how we understand customer needs and intent, the relationship that brands have with customers and the value that is created by data. It creates opportunities to bake marketing into products, to join up interaction and product usage with marcomms in much more seamless ways, to understand product life cycle and usage in ways that can inform strategy and achieve marketing objectives such as customer acquisition and engagement, to place data from a much wider range of sources at the heart of decision-making. It is both a challenge and an opportunity for marketing but is dramatically shifting the context that product brings to the discipline.
- **Place:** Where customers look for and buy our product. Digital has markedly increased the potential routes to market for products, from

direct-to-consumer propositions to a proliferation of specialist retailers, the growth of marketplaces, affiliate marketing through influencers, content creators and publishers, and the growth of live streaming and social commerce.

- **Price:** What customers pay and the value of the product. Digitization of pricing has brought with it greater visibility and transparency through aggregators and price comparison. It has catalysed the ability to scrape pricing data in fundamentally easier ways. It has enabled dynamic pricing (pricing that responds in real time to surges in demand, competitive pricing or time-based dynamics). It also shifts the strategies that marketers can adopt to create real and perceived value in a customer's mind. It enables new models (like subscription) that can be priced in smart ways to generate longer-term customer value.

- **Promotion:** How we choose to promote, publicize and differentiate our product. The amount of promotion and channel opportunities open to marketers has exploded as a result of digital. Data has transformed how we identify and anticipate customer needs, segment our customers and target them with relevant messaging. Customer experience is now a complex, ever-changing phenomenon that pulls in multiple touchpoints, data signals and opportunities to engage. Advertising is now increasingly bought programmatically in automated ways. The fragmentation of channels brings ever more nuanced ways to reach customers. Real-time measures give us far greater transparency around campaign performance and the ability to adapt and optimize.

These new contexts may not have changed the key principles that underpin good marketing strategy, but they have framed a huge shift in the environment in which marketing operates. A shift that requires different ways of operating, working and delivering to those all-important conventions. This book is about how marketers need to evolve practice and execution to be truly fit for purpose for the digital empowered world.

The impact of data, technology and marketing automation

It can almost go without saying that technology and data have had a profound impact on marketing practice, but let's consider just how profound this is. Renowned marketing technologist Scott Brinker conducts an annual survey that maps the marketing technology landscape. When he began conducting the survey in 2011 there were only 150 different technology vendors in the market. Less than a decade later and there are over 8,000 separate technology solutions for marketers to choose from.[14] The market has exploded, presenting an ever-increasing range of services that marketers can combine into an individualized marketing technology stack but also an ever-heightened level of complexity for them to navigate. The research also reveals that an average large enterprise has up to 120 tools in its marketing technology (MarTech) stack. Gartner found that in 2020 marketing technology already made up 26 per cent of the average marketing budget, and 68 per cent of CMOs were planning to increase their technology spending into 2021.[15]

As marketers look to marshal capability into a cohesive whole, a number of critical shifts have emerged. The rise in automation has enabled far greater efficiency in marketing execution, but also a shift in effectiveness through more sophisticated use of data and optimization. According to a report by Research and Markets, the size of the marketing automation software market was estimated at $6 billion in 2019 and is expected to grow to be worth almost $17 billion by 2025 (a compound annual growth rate [CAGR] of over 19 per cent).[16] Marketers are also increasingly looking towards how combining different technological capabilities can drive compounding benefits. This may relate to establishing a common core to the MarTech stack while also creating a custom suite of apps to augment proficiency in key areas or blending together software and services in ways that allow for greater flexibility and adaptability over time or using data and attribution to drive further into profitability measures rather than just sales and revenues. Marketers are increasingly looking to establish a core data-driven foundation in technology (through CRM systems and customer data platforms), which can then integrate efficiently with multiple other services and systems that can serve specific requirements. As the investment in and significance of data and analytics continues to grow, machine learning and predictive analytics are being baked into systems, catalysing new understanding and learning at speed. This in turn is shifting the dynamics of data, with greater focus on data quality and analysis, first-party data and more sophisticated understanding of customer behaviours and preferences. A growing proportion of customer interaction is happening over digital channels, and these channels account for an ever greater proportion of budgets. In their CMO spend survey Gartner found that digital channels accounted for almost 80 per cent of budgets in 2020, with almost a quarter of the marketing budget going on digital advertising and paid search, and almost 60 per cent going on owned and earned digital channels.[17]

This is resulting in some elemental changes in marketing practice. Adept use and application of technology and data have become ever more essential to marketing and there is far greater demand for specialist expertise in data, a wider need for marketing practice to be far more data-driven and a rise in marketing operations functions and roles that are focused on building and operationalizing the marketing technology stack and optimizing workflow efficiency. The ability to use real-time data and fast customer feedback loops is transforming the ability of marketing teams to make smarter decisions quicker. As I'll discuss in the next section, the need for marketing teams to work in closer alignment with product and technology teams is driving a shift towards more iterative and continuous delivery of value. As an example, the frequency of software release that many technology teams now operate to has dramatically decreased over the past few decades. According to data operations firm DataKitchen, the average frequency of software releases under the waterfall model in the 1980s was around 12 months.[18] Waterfall may have worked well in situations where detailed requirements are understood well in advance and don't change, but in fast-changing environments this becomes problematic. As software teams abandoned waterfall methodologies and adopted Agile development in the late 1990s and early 2000s companies organized technology development around shorter iterations and the average release frequency dropped to about three weeks. Now, as working practices evolve still further and practices such as DevOps are introduced, the average release frequency of software projects has reduced further to increments of days or even minutes. As agile practices have expanded beyond technology teams, the rhythm and cycles at which businesses operate have dramatically shortened.

As the focus on customer experience expands within organizations, there is a parallel opportunity for marketing to expand its impact, enabled and driven through a technology and data revolution that is changing marketing practice forever. Marketers find themselves facing a perfect storm of factors including rapidly changing customer behaviour, shifts in technologies that are reimagining possibilities, the need to be always on in communications, increasing pressures for growth in often low growth environments, volatility in markets and macro-contexts, and heightened demands around accountability and value attribution. Every one of these factors is leading to a re-evaluation of not only competencies and processes but entire ways of operating. CMOs are looking to embed far greater levels of agility, adaptability, responsiveness, efficiency and accountability into the fabric of how their teams work.

Systems and empathy

With data, technology and machine learning changing marketing practice in such fundamental ways it is essential for agile marketers to remain focused on how they can bring technology and human capabilities together in ways that compound benefit and impact.

In 2014, journalist and author Charles Leadbetter was asked to write a paper about the future of cities.[19] Great cities, said Leadbetter, bring together two foundational elements: systems and empathy. Systems 'bring together disparate interacting components to achieve a common purpose'. They act as the oil for cities to function. Yet systems are also ways of doing things, processes, methods that enable scale, efficiency, transparency and reliability. As an example, trains, ticket machines, signalling software, station equipment and escalators are all part of the London Underground system, which is in turn a part of the wider London transport system. Systems are essential. Without them, cities would fall apart.

Yet cities also need human connection, understanding, insight, compassion and rapport so that the people within that city might come together and share, find affinity and common understanding:

> Creative cities depend on a kind of dark matter, something that must be there to make them work, but which cannot be observed directly. That dark matter is empathy, our capacity to connect with other people who are different from us, to find common ground and to engage in sharing and exchange. That is the basis for the collective genius of city life: collaboration, cooperation and civility.[20]

While it is systems that make cities work, it is empathy that makes cities human. A lack of systems may result in chaos and inefficiency but a lack of empathy results in distance and coldness. It is when systems and empathy are brought together (Leadbetter gave the example of the London 2012 Olympics as an experience that defined this combination best) that cities are most able to realize their full potential.

So it is with agile marketing teams. The combination of systems and empathy brings together two foundational elements that between them enable teams to blend the efficiency, control and empowerment of technology with the connection, insight and affinity that can only come from human understanding and perspective. Agile marketing teams are empowered through technology and systems that can help them to work efficiently, communicate well, execute easily, test rapidly and learn fast. Yet they also

FIGURE 1.1   Systems and empathy in agile marketing

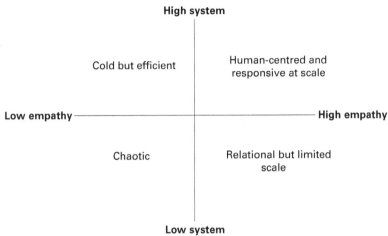

never lose sight of the importance of human insight and understanding, connection and engagement, and creativity. Empathy is what enables a team to be truly customer-obsessed and deliver experiences that are exceptional rather than just functional. Empathy is what enables teams to collaborate and work together in ways that break down silos and realize the true potential that technology facilitates.

If systems are the oil that makes the engine run smoothly, then empathy is the fuel that powers the engine.

The growing impact of product strategy and thinking

As the focus on digitized products and services inside organizations has risen, so has the significance of product strategy and management. These roles have been key in translating business strategy into product strategy, owning the product vision and higher-level roadmap, and understanding how the customer and market environment impacts how the product can best serve both customer and business objectives. With the proliferation of agile practice, product owner roles have also grown in number and importance, typically working closely with agile teams to optimize the development process and the delivery work that the team is doing and oversee the product backlog and its regular reprioritization.

Over time, as environments have become increasingly uncertain and fluid and the digitization of products and services has expanded, there has been a real need for products to be developed and optimized more incrementally and in far more adaptive ways so that development can always take account of the latest known customer and market contexts.

This has resulted in a move away from a situation where product managers could 'throw requirements over the wall' to an IT or development team to work through, effectively turning the latter into a so-called 'feature factory'. This approach may have worked in environments where products were shipped and changed infrequently, but as complexity grew and the requirement for rapid feedback loops, testing and prototyping also grew, the need for more concurrent and closer working became paramount. With increasingly digitized products and services, more frequent release cycles and a wider need for greater agility, businesses now needed to break down functional silos and bring together key disciplines to work together towards common goals. Business strategy needed to be tied more closely to product strategy. Product strategy needed to be coupled better with development. Product development needed to work in a more joined-up way with marketing.

As digitization and product thinking has expanded, it has become ever more important for marketers to consider not only brand, positioning, customer insight and segmentation, but also how the development of the product itself can support marketing objectives (such as customer acquisition, for example) and how marketing strategy and execution can in turn support the development of the product. The huge growth in importance of customer experience is also a force amplifier in bringing product and marketing closer together. Both areas deal with important areas of the customer experience and journey – marketing more focused on brand awareness, driving consideration and purchase or acquisition, and product dealing with post-acquisition product experience, activation, engagement, optimization and customer success. The inability to join the journey up in seamless, customer-focused ways leads to a poor customer experience. A failure to bake marketing into product development (for example, to develop mechanisms where existing customers can support the acquisition of new ones) leads to missed opportunities. A failure of marketing teams to understand how products are used and how customer feedback is shaping development leads to more missed opportunities. A failure to align product and marketing strategy leads to disjointed customer experiences and under-optimized business and customer outcomes. The growth of product marketing has come in response to exactly this need for greater alignment and integration.

The third leg of this three-legged stool is technology. If technology doesn't work closely with product, it will be impossible to develop, experiment, test, prototype and adapt. If technology doesn't work closely with marketing it

FIGURE 1.2   The convergence of product, marketing and technology

will be very difficult to understand needs, derive insight, target, promote, optimize and measure. Technology and development are the critical enablers for both product and marketing. This is a new 'holy trinity' in organizational capability.[21]

Huge opportunity exists from bringing these foundational elements closer together in the service of business objectives and customer needs. As environments become increasingly complex, the need to be adaptive and emergent with all three of these elements is critical. As they become ever more integrated and entwined the opportunity is to align not only strategy and execution but also ways of working, cadence and rhythm to deliver better outcomes for both customers and the organization. *This* is the opportunity for agile marketing.

Endnotes

1   OpenLearn. What is Marketing? Open University. www.open.edu/openlearn/ money-business/understanding-your-customers/content-section-1.2 (archived at https://perma.cc/6QNQ-X2BK)

2   P Drucker (2006) *The Practice of Management*, Harper Business, New York.

3   R P Bagozzi. Marketing as Exchange, *Journal of Marketing*, October 1975, 39 (4), 32–39, www.jstor.org/stable/1250593 (archived at https://perma.cc/ GQ5W-VK5K)

4   McKinsey. How COVID-19 has pushed companies over the technology tipping point – and transformed business forever, 2021, www.mckinsey.com/business- functions/strategy-and-corporate-finance/our-insights/how-covid-19-has-pushed- companies-over-the-technology-tipping-point-and-transformed-business-forever (archived at https://perma.cc/5SZW-PTVM)

  5 Twilio. COVID-19 Digital Engagement Report, www.twilio.com/covid-19-
     digital-engagement-report
  6 Econsultancy and Adobe. The 2021 Digital Trends Report, January 2021,
     econsultancy.com/reports/2021-digital-trends-report/ (archived at https://
     perma.cc/B5BF-SCMP)
  7 J Bezos. Quote about change, Goodreads, 2021, www.goodreads.com/
     quotes/966699-i-very-frequently-get-the-question-what-s-going-to-change
     (archived at https://perma.cc/F32L-9AAU)
  8 T Roach. Seven principles of effective marketing communication, *Marketing
     Week*, October 2021, https://www.marketingweek.com/principles-effective-
     marketing-communication/ (archived at https://perma.cc/NX5K-NWNK)
  9 B Sharp (2010) *How Brands Grow*, Oxford University Press, Oxford.
 10 IPA. New evidence on tangible value of creativity, October 2018, ipa.co.uk/
     news/new-evidence-on-tangible-value-of-creativity (archived at https://perma.
     cc/MBU3-ETBV)
 11 Ehrenberg-Bass. Differentiation vs. distinctiveness, i.e. stand out or be
     distinctive, February 2020, www.marketingscience.info/differentiation-vs-
     distinctiveness-i-e-stand-out-or-be-distinctive/
 12 Ebiquity. Measuring creative effectiveness, June 2020, www.ebiquity.com/
     news-insights/press/measuring-creative-effectiveness/ (archived at https://
     perma.cc/W29C-CC4Q)
 13 E Jerome McCarthy (1960) *Basic Marketing – A Managerial Approach*,
     Homewood, Chicago.
 14 S Brinker. Marketing Technology Landscape Supergraphic (2020): MarTech
     5000 – really 8,000, but who's counting? April 2020, chiefmartec.com/2020/
     04/marketing-technology-landscape-2020-martech-5000/ (archived at https://
     perma.cc/W4HT-7NYR)
 15 R Ramaswami. Gartner CMO Spend Survey 2020–2021: Technology and
     Digital Channels Withstand Budget Cuts, August 2020, www.gartner.com/en/
     marketing/insights/articles/gartner-cmo-2020-2021-tech-digital-channels-
     withstand-budget-cuts (archived at https://perma.cc/YPJ9-ZZ95)
 16 Research and Markets, Marketing Automation Software Market, Growth
     Trends 2021–2027, July 2021 (archived at www.researchandmarkets.com/
     reports/4591293/marketing-automation-software-market-growth (archived at
     https://perma.cc/4B6F-HBW7)
 17 R Ramaswami. Gartner CMO Spend Survey 2020–2021: Technology and
     Digital Channels Withstand Budget Cuts, August 2020. www.gartner.com/en/
     marketing/insights/articles/gartner-cmo-2020-2021-tech-digital-channels-
     withstand-budget-cuts (archived at https://perma.cc/78TT-JBE9)

18 DataKitchen. Releasing New Analytics Every Second, August 2017, medium. com/data-ops/releasing-new-analytics-every-second-fc5fefd92360 (archived at https://perma.cc/B5SP-2Z3D)

19 Centre for London. The London Recipe: How Systems and Empathy Make the City, April 2014, www.centreforlondon.org/publication/london-recipe/ (archived at https://perma.cc/7XJ6-R6RK)

20 Centre for London. The London Recipe: How Systems and Empathy Make the City, April 2014, www.centreforlondon.org/publication/london-recipe/ (archived at https://perma.cc/U339-D4VF)

21 Econsultancy. Organisational Structures and Resourcing Best Practice Guide, March 2020, econsultancy.com/reports/organisational-structures-and-resourcing-best-practice-guide/ (archived at https://perma.cc/V623-7Y82)

02

Defining agile marketing

What it is, and what it's not

Looking at the new through the lens of the old

Entrepreneur and venture capitalist Chris Dixon has described how significant computing waves generally have two eras: one defined by skeuomorphism where the design thinking is predominantly adapted from older domains, which then gives way to the native era where the true potential of the new technology is realized.[1] He gives the example of how the early web saw mainly digital adaptations of pre-internet era activities.

Media and publishing are a great example of this phenomenon. The first digital magazines were PDFs of printed magazines put up online. These were static, hard to read and impossible to navigate on a screen. They were a terrible user experience, lacking any of the true features that are core usability functions of the web: the ability to read/write; to interact, share, post, comment, engage. It took over a decade for publishers to retrain their thinking to enable such functionality. Even then, skeuomorphic applications that allowed users to literally turn the pages of online magazines became briefly popular in a last attempt by some publishers to cling on to outdated principles. Somehow, some very smart people in publishing companies missed the fact that reading PDFs online is a terrible way to consume digital content and that turning pages in an online version of a magazine and having to zoom in and out of the page to actually read it is a whole lot more cumbersome than just reading a web page and clicking on a link.

This kind of skeuomorphic thinking can hold businesses back from progressing towards the native application of the new technology and result in companies looking at the new through the lens of the old. Let's take another example from the media. For years publishers avoided embedding links into their content posted online, believing that doing so would mean that they would 'leak' traffic and that this would reduce the number of unique users on their site. Since early monetization techniques depended largely on the number of users and page impressions that a publisher could generate, they became protective about holding on to users and imagined their media brands to be like walled gardens where the longer they could hold onto users the more impressions and advertising revenue they could generate. The direct relationship between page impressions and ad impressions meant that the more of the former that a publisher could generate, the more revenue they would make. This led to ridiculous tactics like pasting up articles that offered up the '25 best examples of x' but that hosted each example on a separate page and forced a user to click through multiple pages to view the entire piece. In their rush to monetize, many publishers forgot the fundamentals of their profession: if the success of your media is dependent on a terrible user experience, then you are doomed.

Similarly, for many years newspaper publishers placed a disproportionate focus on the importance of their home page at the expense of accepting that any page on their site may be a point of entry for a user. They imagined websites would be read in the way that a printed newspaper might be read, where a reader always begins with the front page and navigates from there. In doing so they underestimated the proportion of traffic that would come into the site from search or social media, deep-linked into specific article pages. For most newspaper sites the home page accounts for a relatively small proportion of the traffic, and it is the article pages that are often the real driver of people coming into the site. This means that every article page needs to be designed in a way that it can offer up other contextually relevant articles that might interest readers that have arrived to read a particular piece of content.

I don't have a particular axe to grind with publishing, but media has been a good example over time of how it can take years to unlearn traditional approaches and thinking and how businesses can cling to outdated models for extended periods of time without challenging their own assumptions. This is the case even when examples of the new native models emerge. Publishers missed a very clear example of how an altogether different approach to user experience can create value for the user and the media owner – Google. Right from their launch in 1998, Google had realized that the quality of their user experience should be dependent on how quickly they can send people *away* from their site rather than how long they *keep* them on their domain. If users could click on a link and find a good answer to the question that they were asking, then they would return to use the site again. Google was not the first search engine of course, but their simplistic interface was brilliant at providing users with exactly what they needed with no complications. Where many other search engines of the era (Excite, Lycos, Yahoo) had become 'portals', which populated their home pages with an abundance of stories, article headlines and images in an attempt to keep users on the site for as long as possible, Google took the opposite approach. Where portals emulated online versions of printed newspapers, the new kid on the search-engine block gave users what they wanted in a way that was native to the web. A lot has been written about how Google upended traditional approaches to user experience and became so successful, but the point is that even when clear examples of the new thinking exist it can take years to reimagine models and move on from the initial skeuomorphic interpretation of technology.

A broader point here is that the same is true of ways of working. Just as companies can take years to move on from simple adaptations from older domain thinking in models, propositions and customer experiences, so they can take years to remake and reimagine the fundamentals of how they operate. Marketing is no different. Many of the assumptions that are embedded in the way that a majority of marketing teams still work need to be sacrificed for a more native approach. For example, many marketing processes are still heavily linear in nature, which results in inefficient hand-offs between departments and teams. A linear, waterfall process like this can easily result in teams being heavily dependent on inputs from another team and great thinking being lost in translation from one team to another. Dependencies can slow teams down and often means that outputs can take too long to emerge, resulting in a lack of agility and missed opportunities. Marketing teams are often structured in functional silos which limits concurrent working, generates inefficiencies and hampers joined-up execution. Data is often utilized at specific stages of a linear process rather than being integrated and informing activity throughout. Fixed ways of working limit flexibility and learning and prevent teams from adapting quickly to changing contexts.

The opportunity here is to move on from skeuomorphic approaches to structures, processes, operations, team behaviours, performance management and any other attribute that is holding your team back from realizing the full potential of modern digital capabilities and technologies.

A definition for agile marketing

We might easily define agile marketing as the process of identifying, anticipating and satisfying customer needs profitably. 'Isn't that the same definition that you used for marketing in Chapter One?' you might well ask, and you'd be right. That's because the fundamentals of what we're trying to achieve with agile marketing are exactly the same. We are still determining and fulfilling customer needs, and we're still doing it in ways that enable a good, profitable return. What has changed is *how* we activate this.

There is no single blueprint for the application of agile principles to marketing practice. In this book I define a set of useful methods, conventions and models that draw from a wide spectrum of agile thinking and provide a pragmatic approach for their application to marketing. Every application of these approaches should be influenced by the unique contexts that exist with individual marketing teams and organizations.

However, it's also just as important to consider the mindset shifts involved in moving away from traditional, linear approaches to marketing to far more adaptive and agile practice. Agile marketing is so much about a mindset that enables a process. Without the right culture and behaviours, the application of these approaches will struggle to thrive and may well not survive. That's why a good proportion of this book is dedicated to the cultural attributes and team norms that can really catalyse these ways of working. The potential of agile marketing principles and mindset lies in their capacity to transform marketing structures, processes and operations to become truly fit for purpose in the unpredictable, uncertain world in which businesses now operate.

The heightened impact of customer experience

It's no secret that organizations of all types have placed a growing emphasis on customer experience (CX) over the past decade. A 2020 survey by consulting firm North Highland of 700 senior business leaders in the US and UK in companies that had more than $1 billion in annual revenues revealed that 87 per cent of those leaders believed that customer experience would be the key engine of growth for their organization. This has been a consistent story for a number of years. Yet challenges remain. The North Highland survey also showed that only around a third of respondents felt that their company was very prepared to address this opportunity. So while customer experience is seen by executives as a critical opportunity to drive advantage, the reality and practicality of joining up data and systems, evolving strategy and processes, and embedding a truly customer-centric culture and behaviours throughout the organization means that this has been, and continues to be, a long-term strategic play.

Marketers have a key opportunity with this realignment of organizational focus. The function has always been a champion of customer understanding in business and now the importance of this has been writ large across fragmented touchpoints and the opportunity to create joined-up customer journeys and seamless omnichannel experiences. Done well, this can bring direct and tangible business benefits. A survey from Econsultancy and Adobe, for example, found that 70 per cent of leaders in CX (which were defined as those businesses that had an advanced approach to CX that aligned strategy and technology) had significantly or slightly outpaced their sector in 2020. This compares to only 43 per cent of businesses that were classified as 'CX mainstream'.[2] The opportunity here is for the importance of marketing practice to grow alongside the increasing strategic importance of customer experience. Marketing should be absolutely central to customer understanding and CX delivery and so it's key that the function prove its value to senior leaders in driving business value through customer-centric approaches and ways of working.

One of the challenges around CX is how customer expectations are continually changing. As the pace of innovation continually creates new ways for consumers to interact with brands, solve their problems and serve their needs, the expectations around service delivery, fulfilment and on-demand value are shifting. The growth of so-called 'quick commerce', which delivers products on demand to customers, often within half an hour, is just one example of this. But as innovation in service levels happens in one industry, customer expectation may well change in other (not directly related) sectors. Salesforce research, for example, has shown that a majority of customers say that their experiences with one industry influence their expectations of others.[3] This means that continuous experimentation and innovation are required to enable teams to keep pace with this evolving competitive landscape and evolving expectation.

How should marketing respond to these important shifts? The two most significant opportunities that marketing has are to double down on customer understanding and to prove the fundamental value that marketing contributes to the organization – to position the function as a driver of growth rather than simply a cost to the business. This means proving the value of both creativity and data-driven decisioning in serving both customer and business needs. It means achieving greater levels of agility through continuous customer feedback and the use of data to optimize and drive both effectiveness and efficiency. Data from Econsultancy and Adobe, for example, has shown that businesses that were strong in their speed to insight (the ability to understand, interpret and action customer inputs and feedback) were more successful in the second half of 2020 and more likely to be able to justify increases to marketing and customer acquisition and retention budgets. Despite many companies being relatively data rich now, only 23 per cent of executives in that survey rated their organization as 'very strong' in their speed of gaining accurate insights.

Clearly there is some way to go here, but the path of opportunity is open to every marketing team. Establishing a strategy for growth that places marketing at the heart of not only customer experience and customer-focused thinking and working in the organization but also at the centre of driving greater agility and growth for the wider business.

Catalysing customer-centricity

Forrester have defined a future-fit technology strategy as:

> a customer-obsessed approach to tech that enables a company to quickly reconfigure business structures & capabilities to meet future customer & employee needs with adaptivity, creativity and resilience.[4]

Their research shows those companies that apply future-fit technology strategies in this way grow 2.7 times faster than their competitors. The key combination in that definition is the bringing together of greater organizational adaptability and agility with customer obsession, and this is an excellent way of thinking about what agile marketing is truly about. While every company likes to believe that they are truly customer-centric, the reality is often that they end up doing things that are distinctly not customer focused. Examples of this might be poor omnichannel experience (sadly all too common), interoperability challenges that get in the way of solving a problem, inconsistent experience across touchpoints, companies that funnel customer service queries into a poorly articulated FAQ page or automated phone menus that don't answer the question that customers have and that then make it hard for them to find a real person to speak to. I could go on. The point here is that great customer experience is really hard to get right, and it typically requires not only joined-up systems and data but a real customer-first culture right through the business that is brought right into the fabric of how teams work. Teams and businesses are frequently organized and structured in ways that make sense for the business rather than the customer. The goals and incentives that teams work to are often business rather than customer focused. The business places greater emphasis on efficiency rather than customer satisfaction or learning.

This needs a fundamental shift in emphasis towards value demand (helping to create more value) rather than failure demand (dealing with the consequences of not getting it right). Forrester uses the phrase 'customer-obsessed' in the definition that I used at the beginning of this section. This phrase has become synonymous with perhaps the most famously customer-centric organization of them all – Amazon. Their very mission begins with this foundational call to arms: 'We aim to be Earth's most customer centric company.'[5] This means, it goes on, continually raising the bar of the customer experience and using technology to help and empower consumers, businesses and content creators. This may be just like any one of a hundred other company mission statements that say they want to be the most customer-centric business in their category, yet the company really lives and breathes this philosophy. Bezos has talked about how the expectation is that everyone in the company is customer-obsessed, regardless of where they work and how their foundational philosophy as a business is 'working backwards from customer needs'. As Bezos himself has put it:

> We start with the customer and we work backward. We learn whatever skills we need to service the customer. We build whatever technology we need to service the customer.[6]

The company finds multiple ways to bring this philosophy to life. Managers and leaders spend time each year in call centres to get a better understanding of customer frustrations and questions. They famously used to have an empty chair in every meeting, which represented the customer as a reminder that they have a voice in every decision that the company makes. Team objectives and performance measures are aligned to customer experience wherever possible (500 measurable goals track performance and 80 per cent of these relate to customer objectives[7]). Data and data-driven decision-making is used throughout the organization to improve and continually optimize around customer outcomes. They maintain an unrivalled pace of innovation in service of customer needs and focus on continually driving greater efficiencies for customer benefit (an example of this is their continual focus on page load time – they believe that a 0.1 second delay in page rendering can result in a 1 per cent drop in customer activity). And, of course, Amazon also has a scaled application of agile principles throughout the business that enable teams to iterate and continuously improve customer-focused metrics.

The point here is that it's one thing saying that you are customer-centric and a whole other thing truly delivering against that. Agile principles and culture place the customer right at the centre of value creation and the way that teams operate. Gibson Biddle, a former VP at Netflix, has described how their version of customer obsession was about not just listening to customers but testing and learning via 'consumer science'.[8] It was about moving beyond understanding customer needs to inventing and delivering against anticipated future needs. About not just customer satisfaction but long-term customer delight. About not just beating the competition but pioneering new frontiers. This is the opportunity with agile marketing – an opportunity for marketers to bake customer obsession into the fabric of how teams work and make decisions.

What agile marketing is not

Transforming a marketing team to becoming truly agile is a serious commitment. The benefits can be significant, but the challenges are also very real. Leaders and organizations need to ensure that they have the appetite for true change to happen. Agile marketing is not about introducing a few agile ceremonies into the team environment and expecting big change to happen. It requires a strong vision, comprehensive understanding of agile principles and the behaviour change required and a learning mindset to adapt deployment in response to shifting contexts. This will not be an overnight fix but rather an ever-evolving journey.

Endnotes

1 C Dixon. Tokens are a new digital primitive, analogous to the website, September 2021, cdixon.mirror.xyz/0veLm9KKWae4T6_H3siLpKF933N SdC3F75jhPQw_qWE (archived at https://perma.cc/AG2R-39UN)

2 Econsultancy and Adobe. The 2021 Digital Trends Report, January 2021, econsultancy.com/reports/2021-digital-trends-report/

3 Salesforce. State of the Connected Customer, 2021, www.salesforce.com/resources/research-reports/state-of-the-connected-customer/ (archived at https://perma.cc/E382-V4PB)

4 Forrester. Customer-obsessed, future-fit firms grow almost 3x faster, TechCentral, 25 May 2021, techcentral.co.za/customer-obsessed-future-fit-firms-grow-almost-3x-faster-forprom/170152/ (archived at https://perma.cc/B24G-2QFR)

5 Amazon. Amazon mission statement, 2021, www.aboutamazon.co.uk/uk-investment/our-mission (archived at https://perma.cc/WJ39-3JQU)

6 D Lyons. Jeff Bezos on Amazon's success, Slate, 24 December 2009, slate.com/news-and-politics/2009/12/jeff-bezos-on-amazon-s-success.html (archived at https://perma.cc/2ZSN-UDMF)

7 G Anders. Inside Amazon's idea machine: How Bezos decodes customers, Forbes, 4 April 2012. www.forbes.com/sites/georgeanders/2012/04/04/inside-amazon/3/#3ec60390650f (archived at https://perma.cc/YUC6-VEFZ)

8 G Biddle. How Netflix's customer obsession created a customer obsession, 17 April 2018, gibsonbiddle.medium.com/customer-obsession-8f1689df60ad (archived at https://perma.cc/A2TU-9E36)

03

Agile process and principles

The 'fifth P' – process

Earlier in this book, I described how the classic 4 Ps of marketing are fundamentally changing as a result of the impact of digital technologies and rapidly changing contexts. This book is focused on the application of agile principles and practices to empower marketing execution in a way that is truly fit for purpose in the modern world. We might describe this as the 'fifth P' of this model – process. Process complements the other 4 Ps since it is an elemental part of marketing practice. It's how we bring the other 4 Ps to life and ensure that strategy and execution are truly customer-focused, adaptive, agile and data-driven.

Agile process and principles

The origins of agile principles and thinking come from the Agile development movement that arose from a meeting of software developers in Snowbird, Utah, in 2001. Frustrated by the rigidity of processes like waterfall development, the engineers came together to discuss how more lightweight development practices could enable better outcomes and learning. More adaptive approaches to development had been around for a few years but the Agile manifesto that resulted from the meeting helped to properly define a new way of working and creating value.[1] Fundamental to the Agile manifesto were four key shifts in value ('while there is value in the items on the right, we value the items on the left more'):

- Individuals and interactions over processes and tools.
- Working software over comprehensive documentation.

- Customer collaboration over contract negotiation.
- Responding to change over following a plan.

These values were captured in 12 key principles that specified more detail on working practices, outlook, approaches and expectations. The essence of these principles can be paraphrased and summarized to provide some foundational principles that should be applied to agile marketing, as follows:

- Satisfying the customer through early and continuous delivery of value is the highest priority.
- Change should be embraced, even late in the process, since it can lead to better customer outcomes.
- Value should be delivered to the customer frequently and iteratively.
- Different disciplines in the business should work concurrently together throughout the project.
- Teams should be supported and motivated, and an environment of trust created to enable them to do their best work.
- Face-to-face conversation and 'productive informality'[2] are efficient and effective ways to share information.
- Teams should be focused on outcomes, and progress can be measured against outputs created to deliver those goals.
- Teams shouldn't be overburdened and should be able to maintain a constant pace.
- Teams pay continuous attention to customer needs, good design and delivering working solutions.
- Simplicity and the art of maximizing the amount of work not done is essential.
- Where possible, teams should organize how best to deliver the work themselves, guided by clear goals from stakeholders.
- The team should reflect on how to become more effective at regular intervals, and then tune and adjust behaviour accordingly.

After the publication of the Agile manifesto, Agile processes rapidly gained traction and soon there were a number of different methodologies (Scrum, Kanban, XP, SAFe) that each sought to apply these foundational principles in slightly different ways. The thinking revolutionized how technology and software teams worked and enabled them to be far more adaptable to changing requirements. Over the years agile principles and practices have expanded far beyond technology teams to encompass a much wider opportunity for businesses to embed greater agility into their strategy and operations. This movement has already presented a clear opportunity for multiple functions to benefit from greater agility through practice and culture. Marketing is no different.

Agile with large 'A', agile with a small 'a'

At the heart of Agile processes is the rapid and continuous delivery of value to customers and the business. The value that the application of agile brings should always reflect both the needs of customers and the goals of the business but at their core, agile processes bring much greater customer focus to everyday working practices. The principles enable a heightened level of adaptation, always taking into account the latest known contexts, inputs and customer feedback. Agile balances vision (a clear goal or outcome) with iteration (adaptive delivery). This avoids the challenge of becoming overly fixed in rigid, linear processes and empowers a team to learn continuously through their delivery and feedback loops.

Agile with a capital 'A' relates to the methodology and process that is defined and utilized. As mentioned previously, there have been a number of different Agile methodologies that have grown up around the movement, but as I'll go on to explain later, in agile marketing there is no single, rigidly fixed methodology that fits every context and team. There are, however, a collection of essential principles that can be applied in ways that take account of the unique contexts in your team. In Parts Three and Four of this book, I'll set out exactly what those principles and approaches are and how you can apply them to strategy and execution. At the highest level, what follows are the key agile marketing principles that I'll be discussing, broken down into strategy and execution.

Agile marketing strategy

- The importance of situational awareness to ground strategy in a clear understanding of contexts, situation and environment.
- The ability to utilize past experience and information, and real-time data, to inform decision-making but also to think big about possible futures.

- Understanding the problems that you are setting out to solve and where more emergent approaches are required.
- Setting a clear vision, goals and an outcome to empower direction and measurement.
- Turning that vision into a coherent strategy.
- How focusing on outcomes (goals) rather than outputs (ways of solving problems) helps a team to stay adaptive, avoid path dependence and bias.
- Breaking down large projects and campaigns into smaller increments and tasks.

Agile marketing execution

- Using agile principles to execute against a strategy.
- Bringing together small, cross-disciplinary teams as the unit of delivery and how those teams might be aligned.
- Using sprint methodologies to deliver value including:
  - Generating backlogs of tasks from broad, overarching projects or objectives.
  - Capacity planning and regular reprioritization.
  - Iterating through fast feedback loops.
  - Tracking velocity of work.
  - Using hypothesis and 'safe to fail' experiments.
  - Learning fast through review and retrospective.
- Measuring outcomes and value.

These principles will provide a blueprint for how you can apply agile methods and thinking to marketing. Following on from this, I'll be setting out how agile can be scaled in realistic and pragmatic ways that mitigate dependencies, align teams and generate workable agile structures for marketing teams. As part of this, I'll be setting out how data-driven decisioning can play a central role in supporting application and execution.

Just as important as the methodology, however, is the culture and behaviour that enables this new way of working to really take shape and become embedded in organizational practice. This is agile with a small 'a'. In this book, as well as setting out the essential principles at the heart of agile marketing, a good proportion of what I've written about here is about how teams can optimize agile with a small 'a'. This brings in team culture, expectation and behaviours. It includes the environments that can enable this way of working to flourish and thrive, and those that can enable true high performance. It incorporates the cultural norms that can facilitate the scaling of agile practice and thinking right across the marketing team and beyond.

Agile as a mindset that enables a process

If agile is as much about mindset as it is about methodology, it's important that we recognize the key mindset shifts and challenges that can act as a brake on agile adoption and scaling. From years of experience and consultancy around the application of agile in multiple organizations, here's my take on the critical mindset enablers and challenges:

- **Uncertainty:** In linear projects and working we are much more used to forecasting exactly where we will be at a particular stage in a project execution (for example, how many customers we will have acquired by a certain date). In reality these forecasts are rarely right, since they are based on existing knowledge or past data and fail to take into account how contexts will change. Transposing this thinking into an agile environment can be problematic since the team will end up focusing on reaching that specific target rather than what they should be doing, which is always looking for what will deliver maximum customer and business value at the earliest opportunity. This can lead to teams slipping back into a linear delivery process and drifting from truly being agile and adaptive. In an agile delivery it's impossible to say in advance exactly where a team will be at a given stage in a process since they will be continually adapting. This level of uncertainty can be problematic for stakeholders to accept, especially when they have been schooled in linear thinking for decades.

- **Risk:** In order to overcome objections around the apparent uncertainty of agile, it can be useful to frame how these processes are essentially about mitigating and reducing risk as the project progresses. An agile approach starts with breaking down a big objective into smaller, manageable tasks. All of these tasks can be treated as assumptions until they are tested with real customers. Testing and learning through the process effectively turns assumptions into validated learning as the process continues, thereby mitigating risk.

- **Failure:** We've all heard the platitudes around embracing failure and failing fast. In many ways this is not helpful since failure in itself is not the objective. This can also create significant cultural challenges in businesses that have grown up for decades around the idea that 'failure is not an option'. Far better to put the emphasis on learning and how teams can learn fast from successes and failures. An openness around learning empowers teams to try things out, experiment and validate assumptions.

- **Perfection:** Organizations are typically used to linear ways of working that involve lots of up-front work to capture inputs and requirements that can inform the design of a solution that is then executed in a relatively fixed and rigid way. The need to make sure everything is perfect or at least as good as it can possibly be, is embedded into this thinking. Agile practice, however, champions the opportunity to balance good with fast. The idea of 'good enough', for example, means that in the right contexts it can be better to move faster with a test that is not perfect, rather than wait until something has been created that everyone in the business is happy with. This doesn't mean that agile processes are synonymous with poor-quality outputs (quite the opposite, in fact), but rather that good judgement around when there is an opportunity to be fast and roughly right and to learn through 'safe to fail' tests is all important.

- **Flexibility:** Teams that are used to linear deployment of initiatives and campaigns can find that it is uncomfortable to shift to more flexible and adaptive ways of working. Teams can easily become path-dependent on particular ways of solving problems (I'll discuss this later in the book), which can reduce flexibility and adaptability.

- **Openness and transparency:** Fast, iterative working requires a culture of open communication and an environment where everyone can contribute and speak up. It also requires good transparency around the work, what everyone is working on and the progress that teams are making. In cultures that are protective and territorial, such transparency can be challenging to scale.

- **Politics:** Internal politics is a reality in many large organizations but it can really slow a team down. Working more concurrently with teammates from other disciplines requires high levels of trust. Adapting and moving fast requires high levels of trust. Highly political environments can be problematic.

While the methods and practices that sit at the heart of agile marketing are all important, they will likely fail if the environment in which they are expected to be applied does not support the critical mindset shifts that enable scaling and adoption. Marketers ignore these shifts at their peril.

Marketing as a continuous flow of work

Agile marketing is not a strategy. Instead, it provides the means to implement marketing strategy more effectively and efficiently. As I'll discuss in Part Three of this book, good marketing still requires good situational awareness, identification of the challenge or opportunity, customer understanding and segmentation, and clear objective setting. Yet the opportunity with agile is to be far more iterative in delivery, to experiment and test more, and to use rapid feedback loops to learn, adjust and optimize. Marketing has undergone a huge shift over the past decades. Channels have fragmented, meaning greater complexity in customer journeys but also greater opportunity to reach customers across a wider set of touchpoints in meaningful ways. As channels have evolved there has been a significant shift from marketing relying on a few bursts of activity in a year, to campaigns being combined with always-on activity that never sleeps. As digitization has proliferated, so has data-driven marketing and the opportunity to use analytics to gain real-time feedback, to improve understanding, measure better and optimize effectiveness.

All of these shifts are converging around an opportunity for marketing to be delivered in a way that brings learning and adaptation into the heart of execution. In other words, to move away from a relatively fixed, linear, 'big bet' model for marketing to one where campaigns and always-on activity can be delivered concurrently and in far more adaptive ways. This requires marketing endeavours to be viewed as a continuous programme of work rather than bursts of activity. It requires big programmes and campaigns to be broken down into smaller increments that can easily be reprioritized based on changing inputs and feedback. It requires a shift away from linear fixed planning so more fluid, iterative delivery.

Agile marketing is therefore a new operating model that redefines the process, structures and mindsets around how a marketing team works and how marketing is executed. It sets out a model for how the organization realizes marketing strategy and delivers the work in a way that embeds continuous learning and improvement. The outcome of implementing agile marketing should be more adaptive and responsive delivery of strategy, more embedded customer-focused ways of working and more effective marketing.

The benefits of agile marketing

There are multiple benefits that applying agile marketing principles can bring to teams and organizations but at its heart this is about embedding truly customer-centric practices into how teams work on a daily basis and doing it in a way that delivers improved marketing effectiveness and efficiency. If we consider the metrics that moving to agile can directly improve, these again will reflect improved customer and business outcomes. A study by McKinsey related to the insurance sector for example, found that insurance businesses that had implemented agile practices at scale had become 5 to 7 times faster in time to market as a result, with productivity gains of 20–30 per cent, an increase in customer satisfaction by 20–30 percentage points and an increase in employee engagement by 20–25 percentage points.[3] Focusing more specifically on agile marketing, a survey conducted by Agile Sherpas and Aprimo found that 53 per cent of agile marketing teams are able to shorten the time to market after implementing agile practice.[4] One of the biggest benefits, of course, is bringing customer feedback and data deeper into the process and the ability to adapt as needs and contexts change. A study by CMG Partners found that around 80 per cent of CMOs in their research said that adopting agile marketing helped them deliver a better and more relevant end product and 93 per cent said that it helped them switch gears more effectively and rapidly.[5] Let's be clear about the benefits that applying agile brings to marketing teams:

- **Time to market:** As we've seen from the studies mentioned above, implementing agile can bring a marked improvement in speed of delivery.
- **Adaptability:** In the modern environment the ability to respond rapidly to changing contexts and manage changing priorities creates competitive advantage.
- **Greater efficiency:** By minimizing hand-offs and through empowered teams.
- **Value delivery and productivity:** Continuously focusing on prioritizing high-value work over low-value work.
- **Improved outcomes:** According to a Standish Group Chaos Study, agile projects are twice as likely to succeed as projects that are run with more traditional project management.[6]
- **Continuous delivery of value:** Releasing early and often. Agile marketing is a very transparent way of working, meaning that stakeholders and teams understand what everyone is working on.

- **Team culture and employee engagement:** Agile teams are motivated. The Agile Sherpas/Aprimo study mentioned earlier found that following an agile transformation 40 per cent of agile marketing teams report improvement in team morale.

- **Alignment and focus:** Clearly defined missions and metrics align agile teams against specific outcomes and support greater accountability.

- **Learning fast at scale:** Supported by continuous feedback and data-driven decisioning.

- **Optimization and innovation:** Agile practice can be applied easily to both optimizing existing propositions and journeys, and generating new value through innovation.

- **Flexibility and swarming problems:** Agile allows for greater fluidity of resourcing and the ability to realign people and focus rapidly to respond to short-term opportunities and challenges.

DELL'S MOVE TO AGILE MARKETING

As a multinational technology business, Dell has around 200 people around the world that work in the marketing team. The business was facing challenges around aligning working practices and approaches across different product lines, meaning that working patterns were not repeatable and were inefficient. The company reorganized its global marketing function around an agile structure, aligning teams to product families to support common ways of working. Everyone in the marketing team was trained on a common approach (based on HubSpot's inbound marketing methods) meaning that the team had a common language and process for how it operated. Operating in 30-day sprint cycles enabled the teams to prioritize regularly, learn and adapt, and empower continuous delivery. The benefits of this shift were realized within seven months, but the team continued to learn about how to improve their agile implementation. Greg Davoll, former senior director of marketing and product GM at Dell said: 'when you are trying to find your product market-fit with a new offering, it's an iterative process. It's nearly impossible to get right the first time but if you iterate, you'll hone what matters most.'[7]

Endnotes

1   AgileManifesto.com. Manifesto for Agile Software Development, 2001, agilemanifesto.org/ (archived at https://perma.cc/PA94-4SMN)

2   M Edgar. Put down all behaviour hurtful to informality! 7 February 2016, blog. mattedgar.com/2016/02/07/put-down-all-behaviour-hurtful-to-informality/ (archived at https://perma.cc/R6YV-79V8)

3   J-T Lorenz, D Mahadevan, B Oncul and M Yenigun. Scaling agility: A new operating model for insurers, McKinsey, 14 September 2020, www.mckinsey. com/industries/financial-services/our-insights/scaling-agility-a-new-operating-model-for-insurers (archived at https://perma.cc/3QQ5-HS95)

4   A Fryrear. Benefits of Agile Marketing: Stats You Need to Know, Agile Sherpas, 2020, www.agilesherpas.com/blog/benefits-of-agile-marketing (archived at https://perma.cc/L5AG-2YAR)

5   Sixth Annual CMO's Agenda. The Agile Advantage, CMG Partners, cdn2. hubspot.net/hubfs/661700/CMOs_Agenda/CMO6/CMG_CMO6_ AgileMethodology.pdf (archived at https://perma.cc/5Q5A-VN3R)

6   A Mersino. Why Agile is Better than Waterfall (Based on Standish Group Chaos Report 2020), Vitality Chicago, 1 November 2021. vitalitychicago.com/blog/ agile-projects-are-more-successful-traditional-projects/ (archived at https:// perma.cc/EQ2C-VZWL)

7   Chris Strom, Interview with Dell Software Product Leader Greg Davoll, Clear Pivot, Sept 2015, https://www.clearpivot.com/blog/dell-software-product-leader-greg-davoll-talks-about-how-his-team-made-the-switch-to-an-agile-inbound-methodology (archived at https://perma.cc/J4FF-HASN)

PART TWO

Agile marketing strategy

04

Understanding context and situational awareness

Sun Tzu's *The Art of War*[1] sets out five key factors that determine victory or defeat in a war and that effectively define the competitive environment. Taking these elements, we can define equivalent principles that can determine success in agile marketing:

TABLE 4.1 Situational awareness in agile marketing

Sun Tzu's five elements		Agile marketing elements	
Element	Description	Agile marketing principle	Description
Principle	the common cause shared by the leader and the public	Vision	the shared vision, purpose and mission for what we are trying to achieve
Heaven	the interaction between natural elements and forces	Environment	the need to understand the context in which we are acting, and any relevant changes in that context that require an adaptation of the strategy
Terrain	the geographical features of the battlefield	Pathway	the understanding we have of our situation, opportunities and risks, the plan we need to navigate them
Generalship	the necessary virtues for good military leadership	Leadership	the need for good leadership in setting direction, and motivating, enabling and inspiring action

(continued)

TABLE 4.1 (Continued)

Sun Tzu's five elements		Agile marketing elements	
Element	Description	Agile marketing principle	Description
System	the structure of the organisation, logistical support, regulations for controlling forces	Method	the tools, methodology and resources that are aligned to execute the strategy

Great strategy and marketing require a solid understanding of direction and how goals will be achieved, along with good leadership to ensure great execution. But it also requires real awareness of the environment in which you are operating and the contextual intelligence that can inform how you can navigate the journey to success.

Situational awareness is essential to good agile strategy and yet is so often overlooked. It's no good setting out a path to achieve a goal if you have no understanding of the position from which you are starting or if you fail to acknowledge how the environment may change along the way. A sensible hiker plans a day's walk by mapping a path from their current position to a destination but also looks at the terrain and the weather reports to know what clothing to wear and considers what they need to take with them to keep them safe in the event of an unexpected change in the conditions. So the agile marketer requires an understanding of their current position and context alongside an appreciation of the environment in which they are working and the potential challenges and opportunities they will encounter. In addition, they are prepared to be adaptable to a changing situation.

Researcher Simon Wardley has long emphasized the importance of understanding position and movement in support of strategy,[2] and the need for situational awareness when considering past and present contexts. Hundreds of years ago, Vikings would navigate by telling stories and by using chants and rhymes that could be easily passed between them. The modern equivalent of this, says Wardley, is the stories that get told within teams and organizations of historical successes that lack any context of the environment or situation at the time. Alongside storytelling, the Vikings used a plethora of other, more current inputs to inform navigation. These included using landmarks and mental maps, the positioning of the sun, moon and stars, the patterns of weather and spotting certain birds and whales (for example, some birds only fly a certain distance from land, and whales tend to stay close to currents where fish can be found).[3] They used a range of senses. They watched for the colour of the sea and the way the waves were moving, they could 'smell' when land was near and feel the directional change of winds.

It was the use of a wide variety of historical and contemporary inputs that led to the Vikings being so successful in navigating the world's seas. So successful in fact that Norse explorer Leif Erikson is believed to have been the first European explorer to have set foot on the continent of North America, around half a millennium before Christopher Columbus.[4] So it is in agile marketing that combining past context and present situational awareness enables a better understanding of position that can inform strategy and direction. An appreciation of the past can bring with it valuable learning. However, we also need to accept that contexts are continually changing, meaning that we need at all times to take account of the current situation. As the nineteenth-century Prussian military commander Helmuth van Moltke is famously quoted as saying:[5]

> No plan of operations extends with any certainty beyond the first encounter with the main enemy forces.[6]

As Simon Wardley notes, we might set out with a game plan to win a game of chess, but it is the moves during the game and the shifting position of the pieces that leads to changes in approach and an adaptation of that strategy. In other words, it is the context-specific gameplay that enables us to win. Given the rapidly shifting contexts in which marketing now operates, this means that it has never been more important to combine an appreciation of the past and an understanding of our base position with rapid adaptation in execution based on latest known inputs and contexts.

In summary, good situational awareness is based on a refined understanding of past, present and future contexts. The past can be used for historical context on current position, as a source of ideas and understanding. The present can be used for contemporary awareness, for context-specific gameplay and to know when we need to adapt or pivot. We can set goals for the future and create new possibilities through our appreciation of how contexts may change. Yet each of these contexts carry with it specific challenges that we must be cognizant of if we are to use them correctly.

Past: walking backwards into the future

> We look at the present through a rear-view mirror. We march backwards into
> the future.[7]

This quote from media theorist Marshall McLuhan expresses his belief that
our futures are often determined by a past that many of us fail to compre-
hend or even acknowledge. History can bring valuable context to the
present. It can enable learning that can inform our understanding of our
current situation and the knowledge to avoid repeating mistakes or poor
decisions. The concept of 'walking backwards into the future' actually
predates McLuhan by several thousand years. In ancient Mesopotamia it
was widely believed that a clear view of the past can inform how best to
prepare for and manage the future.

Similarly in agile marketing, learning from the past can greatly inform
our perspective on how best to solve today's challenges. Much classic
marketing and advertising theory, for example, is as relevant today as it has
ever been. Knowing the historical story of a brand can shape not only brand
positioning and storytelling but also provide useful ideas and examples of
how previous challenges have been overcome. We dismiss the past at our
peril. Yet there are several inherent dangers within this idea of walking
backwards into the future:

- As I discussed earlier in the book it can be all too easy to view the new
  through the lens of the old. When new possibilities are created (for example, through technology) it is often the case that we still apply existing
  assumptions, formats and contexts to those possibilities. Sometimes such
  skeuomorphism can be useful. In graphical user interface design, for
  example, the waste bin icon on our computers enables us to immediately
  know where to put unwanted files. Yet it can often result in us missing
  opportunities to redesign and reinvent.

- When looking to learn from the past, it can be common to undervalue the
  context of specific examples, which can lead to over-generalization or
  misinterpretation of patterns. For example, we might look to derive
  explicit learning from only successful or effective examples without looking to consider the context of unsuccessful ones.

- Learned practice can, of course, be tremendously valuable, but the tyranny
  of best practice can be that it can create a one-size-fits-all approach to
  solving problems. This can mean that best practice approaches are applied

too generically or that teams can become stuck in a process. Our desire for certainty among all the complexity and ambiguity that surrounds us might well result in the over-standardization of process and the under-recognition of the need for more specific context.

It is essential that we learn from the past but also that we remain aware of the lens through which we are observing it and make deliberate and careful choices about how we view those lessons. As Stephen R. Covey said in his famous book *The 7 Habits of Highly Effective People*: 'We must look at the lens through which we see the world, as well as the world we see and (know) that the lens itself shapes how we interpret the world.'[8]

Present: the art of now

In agile marketing a continual stream of inputs can enable a team to understand how contexts are evolving through a process. Situational awareness is not a one-off task that happens at the beginning of the project or campaign, nor an exercise that is undertaken periodically in order to inform a strategy review. Teams need to be focused on how important contexts (like customer action and response or competitive activity, for example) are shifting and how execution and strategy needs to adapt in response. Environments are moving too fast for teams to rely on outdated information or assumptions. Fast feedback loops identify metrics that can be tracked to enable the team to understand current context and how this can inform greater adaptability.

Later in the book I'll discuss the role that data dashboarding and data-driven decision-making can play in helping teams to respond quickly to shifts in context, but it's important to consider the different types of thinking that a team will need to do this well:

- **Inductive reasoning:** This relates to the type of reasoning that can make broad generalizations from specific observations. For example, a team may observe specific behaviour patterns from a few customer responses and identify a theory around a new or changed customer need. The risk with inductive reasoning is that we over-generalize and fail to take account of the nuances of the specific observations that we are making. For this reason, it can be helpful to frame our generalized theories as hypotheses.

- **Deductive reasoning:** Where inductive thinking goes from the specific to the general, deductive goes the other way. Here, we may begin with a general statement and then consider all the different possibilities in order to reach a logical conclusion. Using hypotheses and testing can help us to prove or disprove our theories and the relevant data and logic can be used to deduce the specific reasons for something happening.

It can often be useful when looking at using inputs through a process to have a continuous interplay between these two types of reasoning. For example, inputs may come from specific observations, which generates a theory about customer responses. A team may then form a hypothesis around this general theory and conduct a series of tests in order to deduce the actual reasons behind the responses.

Abductive reasoning is a third approach that may be necessary when a team is working from incomplete or imperfect information. In this instance, the team might look for the likeliest possible explanation for a group of observations and then form hypotheses to test, learn and validate. When operating in an environment that is new or relatively unknown, educated guesses may be needed at the start in order to enable the learning process to begin. As the team forms hypotheses and gains feedback and data, the environment and contexts become more familiar and enables more inductive and then deductive reasoning.

Future: possible futures

Just as the challenge in using examples or information from the past can be that we look at the new through the lens of the old, so the risk in looking into the future can be that we look at the future through the lens of the present. Once again, we can fail to appreciate the shift in contexts which can change what is possible or we fail to apply context to generalized assumptions or predictions. Many maturity models, for example, presume to set out what is universally good to help establish a way of assessing your own capability and plotting a path to improvement. While there may well be more widely applicable rules of thumb, adding a layer of context about your own organizational situation can help improve the usefulness of the model.

Agile marketing teams need to be continuously horizon scanning and experimenting around emerging capability but also thinking big about reimagining possibilities. The risk is that we get stuck in current thinking, forgetting that capabilities evolve continuously and that new possibilities can emerge at any time or that we constrain our ambition by only aiming for incremental improvement. Google famously build what they call '10×' or 'moonshot' thinking into their innovation process, challenging teams to improve something by 10 times rather than by 10 per cent.[9] A 10× goal forces teams to work back from first principles, break open existing assumptions, push beyond existing models and rethink an idea entirely. They also open their focus to ideas beyond their core business to support a continuous push into new territory. A 70/20/10 model introduced in the early days of Google keeps a focus on core needs while also ensuring that there is always a stretch into new areas:[10]

- 70 per cent of our projects are dedicated to our core business.
- 20 per cent of our projects are related to our core business.
- 10 per cent of our projects are unrelated to our core business.

Typically, in organizations we work around future scenarios that are based on current known knowns or scenarios that might be considered to be probable. But in order to avoid constraining our thinking, it's important alongside this to imagine possible futures and scenarios that take account of how elements may change in the future. The concept of projected, probable, plausible, possible and even preposterous futures comes originally from the work of Joseph Voros. His futures cone sets out a range of future scenarios:[11]

- **Projected futures** extrapolate out from the current position and are what will happen if nothing changes and business continues as usual.
- **Probable futures** are still likely to happen, but they may take account of what we know now about current trends and their trajectory.
- **Plausible futures** may still happen based on what we know now but are less likely to happen.
- **Possible futures** may not currently be thought of as probable or plausible but may become so given a change in environment or situation.
- **Preposterous futures** may be currently impossible but can still be a useful provocation for a team to open up new thinking.

In his review of the futures cone, strategy specialist Mike Baxter describes the different level of planning needed.[12] We can plan for probable scenarios by considering the probability of given shifts happening and how much they will impact trajectory. We need less fidelity of planning around plausible and possible scenarios, but it is important to be vigilant to changes in circumstance that increase probability or plausibility of them happening. Considering possible (or even preposterous) futures is a good exercise to stretch team thinking and create greater readiness to respond as contexts evolve. It can help a team to take a possible future scenario and think through what needs to change for it to become plausible and then what the team can do to help that plausible future become probable.

Finally, it's important to be aware of the role that our own cognitive bias can play in these shifts. In *Thinking, Fast and Slow*,[13] Daniel Kahneman noted that the value people place on changes in probability (for example, the probability of winning something) between states varies. People place a high value on changing something from 0 per cent probability to 10 per cent probability or in other words on changing something from impossible to possible. We typically perceive this as a greater gain than the leap from 40 per cent probability to 50 per cent even though the shift is similar. This may be reasonable since we are actually seeing a new possibility emerge, but we need to be cognizant of the risk of undervaluing the shifts from implausible to plausible and from improbable to probable. People tend to place the highest value of all on a change from 90 per cent probability to 100 per cent or, in other words, going from a probable scenario to certainty. Later in the book we'll look at how cognitive bias can lead to poor decision-making in agile marketing and can even derail entire projects. Humans like certainty but again, the risk is that this quest for certainty can reduce our flexibility and adaptability through a process and our willingness to experiment and learn through failure as well as success.

Looking at strategy like we look at the weather

In weather forecasting we are perfectly accepting that the 'spread' of forecast accuracy will widen as we go further into the future. We understand that it's naturally more difficult to forecast whether it will be glorious sunshine or cloudy with showers on a given day one month away than it is tomorrow. Yet somehow in strategy we often expect to be able to predict outcomes with precision even when they are some way off. This may be workable in stable, slow-moving environments but soon falls apart in the contexts of environments that have multiple changing variables, like the weather. It's important therefore, for teams to accept that the further ahead in time that they are looking the harder it will be to define a single truth with precision. Yet teams still need direction and vision.

FIGURE 4.1　Looking at strategy like we look at the weather

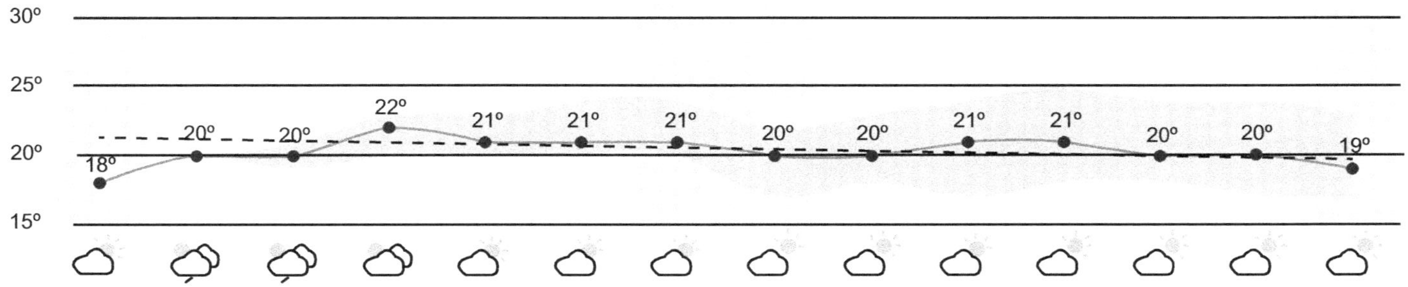

This is a challenging balance for teams to achieve. It's, of course, essential for teams to have clear short-term goals as well as longer-term direction. The level of fidelity that we need around each of these elements is different, however. Many organizations don't have a well-articulated long-term view of the future. Netflix is a good example of setting out a vision for what the future of their category (in their case entertainment) looks like.[14] It's broad enough to frame a direction and a point of view, yet loose enough to allow for flexibility in how that vision will be achieved. As I'll discuss in Part Four of this book, this balance in the fidelity of understanding is key to agile practice. Teams need a long-term direction for where they are headed. This should be a vision that inspires and that is relatable enough to feel stretching but achievable, yet also broad enough to enable teams to find the best way of delivering that vision through adaptation and iteration. Teams also need, however, a much more granular understanding of the work and the short-term goals that are right in front of them. The fidelity of these short-term goals needs to be more specific, more focused and more accountable.

Complexity requires emergent approaches

In agile marketing it's important to understand the context of the work that we are undertaking and the environment in which we are taking decisions. A key part of knowing how best to approach problem-solving is to begin by understanding the type of problems that we are looking to solve.

Dave Snowden's Cynefin model[15] is a particularly useful framework for aligning decision-making with context and it sets out the differences between 'best practice' and more emergent approaches.

- **Simple contexts:** These may be characterized by a clear causal relationship, known situations and responses or stable and slow-moving environments. They are the conditions and circumstances that have been encountered before or are familiar and so the business and team know how to respond. This is the domain of best practice. Teams can develop known and accepted processes or checklists that are followed. The opportunity here is to drive efficiencies over time and agile principles and working can be used in this context to create and iterate improvements (for example, through process innovation). The risk associated with this domain is that teams can become complacent meaning that they miss opportunities to challenge or improve.

FIGURE 4.2   The Cynefin model

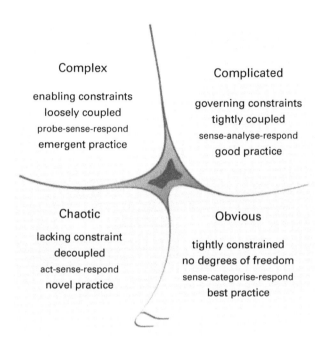

- **Complicated contexts:** These situations will likely have more variables and potential answers than simple contexts and so require more analysis in order to identify the right response. Since there are more possible answers that may not be immediately obvious, good practice rather than best practice is what is required. This is therefore the domain of experience and expertise. In an agile marketing context, complicated challenges require a team to analyse and to learn through experience and expert input. The risks associated with this domain include over-analysing, which can slow teams down, or the possible bias of experts towards certain solutions.

- **Complex adaptive contexts:** These have many variables, but also involve contexts and environments which may be evolving all the time. The challenges that we need to solve therefore are also likely to be constantly changing and the optimal solution needs to be found through emergent approaches that enable teams to test and learn and experiment in 'safe to fail' ways. There is a clear opportunity here for agile approaches to facilitate rapid learning and adaptation. The risk here is that rapidly changing challenges and high unpredictability can often lead to command-and-control responses from leadership teams that are seeking certainty. The ability to learn fast and adapt in these environments is essential.

- **Chaotic contexts:** The fourth categorization in Dave Snowden's model has no discernible or manageable patterns and so clear, decisive action is required to create some degree of order and predictability as soon as possible. Evolving these challenges so that they are complex rather than chaotic then enables an approach where an emergent approach can be adopted.

If simple contexts are known knowns, complicated ones represent known unknowns, and complex adaptive challenges may well be characterized by unknown unknowns. Having a team that is cognizant of the types of challenges and contexts that they are facing means that they can establish the right responses. Best practices and checklists can be useful in situations where a team has to be sure that they are following established procedure but as contexts change the definition of what best practice is may need to change as well. The risk with best practice is that it becomes inflexible, over-simplified or automatic and unchallenged, which can open up unnecessary risk. In the complex adaptive scenarios that characterize many of today's environments and challenges, emergent approaches that enable adaptation and learning have become far more of an imperative.

Endnotes

1 Sun Tzu (2010) *The Art of War*, Tribeca Books, New York.
2 S Wardley. Wardley maps, 7 March 2018, medium.com/wardleymaps (archived at https://perma.cc/R4JS-UB2R)
3 I B Petersen. How Vikings navigated the world, ScienceNordic, 9 October 2012, sciencenordic.com/denmark-history-society--culture/how-vikings-navigated-the-world/1377436 (archived at https://perma.cc/4JFA-UECX)
4 Leif Erikson, history.com, April 2010. www.history.com/topics/exploration/leif-eriksson (archived at https://perma.cc/WEQ5-LE6Q)
5 Quote Investigator. No plan survives first contact with the enemy, 4 May 2021, quoteinvestigator.com/2021/05/04/no-plan/ (archived at https://perma.cc/RM87-S6CV)
6 H Graf von Moltke (1900) *Moltkes Militärische Werke: II. Die Thätigkeit als Chef des Generalstabes der Armee im Frieden* (Moltke's Military Works: II. Activity as Chief of the Army General Staff in Peacetime), *Zweiter Theil* (Second Part), *Aufsatz vom Jahre 1871 Ueber Strategie* (Article from 1871 on strategy), Ernst Siegfried Mittler und Sohn, Berlin. books.google.com/books?id=aHM-AAAAYAAJ&q=%22einiger+Sicherheit%22#v=snippet& (archived at https://perma.cc/MS6B-MTW7)

7 M McLuhan, Q Fiore and J Agel (1996) *The Medium Is the Massage: An Inventory of Effects*, Penguin Classics, New York.

8 S Covey (2020) The 7 Habits of Highly Effective People, 30th anniversary ed., Simon & Schuster, New York.

9 Oliver Franklin-Wallis, Inside X, Google's Top Secret Moonshot Factory, Wired, February 2020, https://www.wired.co.uk/article/ten-years-of-google-x (archived at https://perma.cc/ED33-KMDK)

10 Google Workspace. Creating a culture of innovation, 2021, workspace.google. com/intl/en_uk/learn-more/creating_a_culture_of_innovation.html (archived at https://perma.cc/ED33-KMDK)

11 J Voros. The futures cone, use and history, 24 February 2017, thevoroscope. com/2017/02/24/the-futures-cone-use-and-history/ (archived at https://perma. cc/B2UF-PVZD)

12 M Baxter. Envisioning the future for strategic planning, May 2020, goalatlas. com/envisioning-the-future-for-strategic-planning/ (archived at https://perma. cc/7YXU-25C3)

13 D Kahneman (2012) *Thinking, Fast and Slow*, Penguin, London.

14 Netflix. Long-term view, July 2021, ir.netflix.net/ir-overview/long-term-view/ default.aspx (archived at https://perma.cc/KC8K-PYDG)

15 D Snowden and M Boone. A leader's framework for decision making, *Harvard Business Review,* November 2007, hbr.org/2007/11/a-leaders-framework-for-decision-making (archived at https://perma.cc/98GL-36SG)

16 Snowden, CC BY-SA 3.0, Wikimedia Commons, October 2020, commons. wikimedia.org/wiki/File:Cynefin_as_of_1st_June_2014.png (archived at https:// perma.cc/8E6T-DRQ3)

05

Adaptive strategy

Working customer back

Good situational awareness for a marketing team comes from understanding the market, the competitive environment, positioning and customer types and needs. A marketing strategy is founded on these critical elements and uses this understanding to frame the opportunity and objectives that the team has to deliver against business needs. Agile marketing is no different. Yet as I mentioned earlier in the book, the real opportunity here is in defining a new operating model for how marketing strategy is delivered.

Later in this book I'll discuss the heightened role that data can play in generating situational awareness and customer understanding. Yet there is a powerful principle at play here that begins in strategy and continues right through to execution – the value of working customer back. This means that as well as developing a good understanding of the customer opportunity as a central element of our marketing strategy (customer insight, segmentation and persona generation, messaging and targeting), customer understanding is continuously developed through execution and delivery. Working customer back means that a team is continually working back from their understanding of customer needs, wants and behaviours to always deliver what is of most value to the customer. It means being adaptive to changing customer needs and working back from these needs to evolve execution. It means using customer behaviour, interaction and feedback continuously through the process to optimize and modify.

This requires a balance between vision and iteration. As I mentioned earlier in the book, it was Amazon that originated the phrase 'start with the customer and work backwards' as a way of articulating a foundational philosophy for how teams should work. Amazon have defined five core questions that frame good customer understanding at the start of any project:[1]

1 Who is the customer?

2 What is the customer problem or opportunity?

3 What is the most important customer benefit?

4 How do you know what customers need or want?

5 What does the customer experience look like?

There are strong parallels here with good marketing practice around starting with customer insights, defining customer needs and the opportunity, segmenting customer types and defining the relevant messaging. So these are good questions to ask in order to bake customer understanding into strategy right from the beginning and frame a vision for the customer opportunity and our plan to deliver to that opportunity. Yet if we are to be genuinely iterative in how we deliver to that goal, we also need to allow for the flexibility that is needed to be truly adaptive. The more a linear, rigidly defined succession of steps is laid out to define our plan, the more dependent we will be on delivering to that plan and the more our flexibility and adaptability is reduced.

This balance between vision and iteration is framed well by the Amazon working backwards document, which is an example of how business cases are made in the company. The document can be created by anyone in Amazon that has an idea for a new proposition and is a written narrative that follows the same structure:

- **Heading:** Name the product in a way that the target customer will understand it.

- **Subheading:** Describe who the market for the product is and what benefit they get (one sentence).

- **Summary:** A summary of the product and its benefits (a short description that works on the assumption that the reader will not have read anything about the idea).

- **Problem:** Describe the problem your product solves.

- **Solution:** Describe how your product elegantly solves the problem.

- **Quote from you:** A quote from a spokesperson in your company.

- **How to get started:** Describe how easy it is to get started.

- **Customer quote:** A quote from an example customer that illustrates how they experienced the benefit that the product brings.
- **Closing and call to action:** Wrap up and references for where the readers should go next.

The document is a good example of balancing direction and a clear outcome with adaptive delivery. It starts with a clear definition of the customer problem that is being solved, which ensures that customer understanding and opportunity is baked in from the beginning. It then articulates a vision for how that problem will be solved in an elegant and exciting way, which frames a strong vision or outcome to aim for. Yet unlike many organizational business cases the document does not lay out a linear succession of steps for how the team will deliver the solution. Instead, it frames a starting point and then allows for the team to learn and adapt through delivery to ensure that they can deliver the outcome in the best way possible.

The learning here is that being agile does not mean that a team lacks direction. Agile teams still need a vision and an outcome to aim for. Yet an overly fixed and linear plan will restrict the learning and adaptability that the team is able to deploy throughout the process. It's so important to allow agile marketing teams the flexibility they need to use feedback continuously to iterate and optimize, while still being held accountable to an overall outcome or goal.

Setting goals and outcomes

It should go without saying that a clear articulation of marketing goals is an essential element in marketing strategy. Setting SMART (specific, measurable, achievable, realistic and time-framed) objectives enables a clear definition of relevant measures as well as a coherent direction and target.

Earlier in this section I wrote about the importance of situational awareness and the need to work back from a solid understanding of our position and our customer needs. Later in this section I'll discuss the importance of working back from a vision and how important outcomes are over outputs in staying adaptive and flexible through a process. Yet in order to achieve desired outcomes it's also critical that we are not baking in assumptions that can derail us as we progress through a project or campaign. In agile marketing, the aspiration should be to remove as many assumptions from the process as possible.

Assumptions can be conspicuous or they can often be hidden, meaning that we don't even realize that we are including them in our planning and execution. In unpredictable environments or when uncertainty is high assumptions can be particularly dangerous since they can lead to poor decision-making, wasted time and effort, and even detrimental outcomes. Perhaps the worst kind are 'toxic assumptions', or the kind of beliefs or expectations that go unquestioned perhaps because they are the way things have always been done in the organization.

A useful way of identifying potential assumptions up front in a planning process is to use Rita Gunther-McGrath's concept of discovery-driven planning.[2] This is based on setting a clear outcome for what needs to be delivered at the end of an initiative and then asking a simple question before you start: *what needs to be true for this outcome to happen?* In a stable or slow-moving environment, we might believe that we can reliably extrapolate from past data or events and predict how the project or campaign will play out. When the contexts are more unpredictable or fast-moving however, those assumptions can easily and rapidly become out of date. Agile marketing seeks to acknowledge assumptions up front and then turn those assumptions into validated learning through a process of testing and data-driven decision-making. Such assumptions may relate to customer needs, perceptions and behaviours, the impact of marketing activity or even the systems that will be used and how the team will work to optimize outcomes. Asking the question at the start about what needs to be true to achieve an outcome opens up a team's thinking to *all* the potential assumptions that they have in front of them, which they can then validate through a process of testing and learning. This in turn helps to mitigate risk, minimize wasted resources and focus a team on learning fast around a clear goal.

Turning vision into strategy

A defined organizational vision and goals are essential to lead marketing and product strategy and it should go without saying that a good vision should be clear and well understood in the business. It is, after all, there to provide inspiration and direction. And yet somehow this is often not the case. Interview a random selection of people from a business and ask them what the company vision is and, in the case of many businesses, employees would struggle to articulate what it is. This may well result from the way in which the vision has been communicated, but it could just as well result from how the vision is framed. There can often be a confusion between the vision (which should capture and express a future state of what you want the company of the future to become), the business goals (what the business expects to accomplish and where it needs to be over a given period of time) and the business mission (why a company exists and the purpose that it serves). A good business vision needs to be:

- **Aspirational:** Expressing a future state that is inspiring, imaginative and emotionally compelling.

- **Ambitious:** A future state that is appealing but also stretching.

- **Empowering:** A vision should be broad enough to enable people to take the initiative but also focused enough to be directive.

- **Comprehensible:** Expressed in ways that make it communicable, intelligible and relatable.

Business goals that align with the vision should, of course, be focused, clear and SMART.

Having defined a clear business vision and goals, these should in turn direct a clear business strategy. In his book *Good Strategy/Bad Strategy: The Difference and Why it Matters*,[3] Richard Rumelt describes strategy as '*a coherent set of analyses, arguments and actions that respond to a significant challenge*'. Rumelt saw strategy as deriving from a consideration of many plausible courses of action and then the selection (in a deliberate, reasoned way) of one or more of those courses of action to the exclusion of others. For Rumelt, the 'kernel' of a strategy contains three elements:

1 A **diagnosis** that defines or explains the nature of the challenge.

2 A **guiding policy** for dealing with the challenge.

3 A set of **coherent actions** that are designed to carry out the guiding policy.[4]

There are several important elements in this definition. The need for a strategy to understand position and context, the need for strategy to define direction and the need for strategy to understand progress and the achievement of goals.

The planning cycle, set out in JWT's classic Planning Guide from 1974,[5] attributed to Stephen King, details five key questions that form the planning process. Paraphrasing from these original questions, we can define the essential stages that inform a good strategy:

1 **Where are we now?** Business/brand positioning, competitive situation and market contexts.

2 **Why are we there?** The factors that have contributed to that position including market and customer contexts.

3 **Where could we be?** Defining the desired future position or objective/ goal.

4 **How could we get there?** The strategy and plan.

5 **Are we getting there?** Determining whether the strategy is working and knowing when you have reached your goal.

Let's be clear about this – agile marketing is founded on good strategic direction. Being agile is not an excuse not to plan. Establishing a good strategy gives agile marketing the focus, the direction and the measures to succeed.

At this point we need to consider how the business strategy informs both product and marketing strategy. As mentioned in Part One of this book, product and marketing are more intertwined than ever and both are critical to creating an exceptional and joined-up customer experience. It's of little use having a truly outstanding marketing campaign to acquire customers onto a platform where the product experience falls short. You can have the best product experience in the world, but you will be unlikely to truly capitalize on it unless the marketing does the product justice. And let's not forget that you can have the best designed product and a brilliant marketing strategy, but if the technology is not there to support both, both will suffer.

Businesses therefore need to think carefully about how these elements should be integrated in a way that seamlessly aligns business, product, marketing and technology:

1 Business strategy flows from business vision and goals, and directs marketing and product strategy.

2 Marketing strategy aligns with product strategy in ways that ensures that they can both deliver business strategy *and* customer experience in an integrated way.

3 The technology stack is the enabler of exceptional product and marketing strategy and therefore the wider business strategy.

FIGURE 5.1   Aligning strategy and technology

Process will be the facilitator of this alignment. It starts with business vision and goals, which should be clear and well understood. A business strategy, which is also clear and well understood, is designed to meet those goals. Product and marketing strategies are designed concurrently to achieve the business strategy and integrated and adapted in order to ensure complete alignment.

Adaptive strategy

With agile marketing, a key requirement is that strategy needs to be adaptive and in many ways, this is in itself not new. Good strategy has always evolved. The JWT Planning Guide mentioned earlier describes how their five questions form an unbroken cycle that recognizes that 'there must be a continuous process of learning a modification and responding to changing competitive circumstances'.[6] As soon as we've answered one question we move on to the next. They also acknowledge that the process requires feedback and inputs like research and how answering each question (and trying out each experiment) prompts a re-examination of the question before. The questions themselves are comprehensive and being questions they give people the freedom to look for imaginative solutions ('it's a stimulus, not a straitjacket'). All of these principles are still valuable and valid.

So what's different with agile marketing? The key difference is that with modern, fast customer feedback loops and data inputs we are now able to iterate, optimize and adapt at a far higher frequency and cadence than we could before. This is not to say that strategy should entirely become about rushed, rapidly executed loops. In agile marketing you need to periodically go slowly to then go quickly. In other words, strategy frames the direction and can be revisited and reframed at regular intervals, but within those

FIGURE 5.2   The strategy circle

intervals executional loops enable a team to iterate quickly to deliver, adapt and learn.

Distilling the JWT questions slightly, we might therefore capture the strategic circle as:

- **Where are we now, and why are we here?** This is an opportunity to gather relevant inputs including market information and contexts, competitive activity and positioning, customer understanding, archetypes and insight, relevant product information such as purchase and usage patterns or positioning, an understanding of strengths, weaknesses and assets, product and marketing historical activity.

- **Where do we want to get to?** This is an opportunity to define the goals and objectives that will frame your target state and to also define the measures that relate to them.

- **How do we get there?** Defining the strategy (the overarching how), the plan (the sequence of events) and the execution (for example, RACI – who is responsible, accountable, consulted and informed).

- **How do we know when we've got there?** Measures, review and learning.

Outcomes, not outputs

In agile marketing, it is critical to optimize for outcomes, not outputs. Understanding the difference between these two things may seem like semantics, but it is essential in realizing optimal impact. If the outcome is the end result or goal that the business wants to achieve, then the outputs can be thought of as the particular way of solving the problem or the actions that the team have defined in order to achieve that outcome. In rapidly changing environments contexts can evolve fast, and the optimal way of solving for an outcome can change with them.

As discussed earlier, having a clear goal or outcome to aim for is essential to provide direction, but it is all too easy to become fixated on the methods that we have selected to achieve this result. This in turn can reduce our flexibility and stifle our learning. We can easily become emotionally invested in a certain way of solving a challenge because we don't want to be proved wrong. The more time, effort and budget we put into this course of action the less we want to have to change. While we may believe that we are open to evolving our plans, in reality we are far more likely to earnestly plough on.

In a linear, waterfall marketing world this burgeoning path dependence can reduce our adaptability and lead to poor decision-making. In an agile marketing environment, the key is to maintain good levels of adaptability throughout the process and embrace change, even at a late stage. We can represent these differences in mindset and process in Figure 5.3.

FIGURE 5.3   Flexibility in waterfall and agile approaches

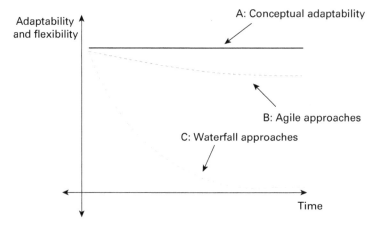

To stay adaptive, the agile marketer needs to be aware of several key biases that we can easily be susceptible to.

Sunk cost fallacy

Sunk costs can easily create bias around being unwilling to change a strategy because the costs of doing so appear to outweigh the benefits. We can easily feel this way when we have invested heavily in a course of action, even when it becomes clear that abandoning the current course would be more beneficial.

This fallacy is a close relative of loss aversion, the tendency we can have to psychologically or emotionally perceive losses as more severe than the equivalent gain. Thus the pain of losing an amount of money feels greater than the happiness we feel at gaining the same amount. Behavioural economist Richard Thaler has described how humans think of value in relative rather than absolute terms, which accounts for why we are more likely to spend more when we pay with a credit card than we are when we pay with cash,[7] and why we are more likely to spend a small inheritance but to invest a large one.[8] When we invest a lot of effort, money and/or personal status in a particular course of action, we can hold those costs in a different mental account to the costs associated with making a significant change in direction. Thus, the cost of change (whether time, money, loss of status or just inconvenience) can seem greater than the benefits of making that change. This can easily result in a desire to determinedly persist when it would be far better to pivot or adapt.

In order to overcome sunk cost fallacy, we need to first admit that it exists and question our reluctance to change whenever we are faced with a decision about persevering or pivoting. Focusing on the current situation and future costs rather than those already committed can help. Relevant data on our current position and progress can help to identify when we do need to make a change but as I'll go on to discuss, even here we can easily be susceptible to other biases that may creep in.

Plan continuation bias

Continuation bias, like sunk cost fallacy, can result in a tendency to maintain a particular course of action even when it becomes evident that that choice will carry with it significant downside or risk. In the airline industry the phenomenon of so-called 'get-there-itis' is used to describe what can happen when a pilot is so determined to reach their destination that they continue on their course and decide to land at the destination even when flying conditions at their destination have worsened considerably and they should really divert to land at another location. A 2004 NASA Ames study that analysed 19 airline accidents that were attributed to human error from 1991 to 2000 found that almost half of these incidents involved plan continuation bias among the pilots and crew.[9] The study highlighted some critical errors on behalf of the pilots involved, including a resistance to divert to an alternative airport. It's worth noting that continuation bias gets stronger the closer we get to our end point or destination.

As marketers, we can easily succumb to continuation bias, meaning that we stick with a strategy or plan well past the point at which we really should have pivoted and moved on. What can make this worse is that technology and data can actually serve to amplify continuation bias in some contexts, exemplified by the tragic story of Alicia Sanchez.

In August 2009 Alicia, a 28-year-old nurse from Las Vegas, set out on an overnight adventure with her 11-year-old son to Death Valley National Park.[10] Following her GPS, she travelled down a remote gravel road in the southern depths of the park until she got a flat tyre. She texted her family to let them know. It would be the last that they heard from her for five days. After changing the tyre, she made the decision to continue to follow her GPS and carry on down the gravel road and even continued when the road became a barely passable track until she'd driven over 30 miles into one of the remotest corners of the park. Eventually, she became stranded, her Jeep Cherokee buried axle-deep in the sand. She had no choice but to wait for help. Five awful days later, a ranger found the car, medical tape spelling out SOS on the windshield. Fortunately, Alicia was still alive but tragically her son was not. What was meant to be a fun trip had turned into a nightmare, and the longer that Alicia followed her GPS the worse her situation became. It wasn't the first time that people in the park had ended up in perilous situations by following their navigation devices in a phenomenon that Death Valley wilderness coordinator Charlie Callaghan began calling 'Death by GPS'. As Micah Alley, one of the search and rescue coordinators in the park, said at the time:

> People are so reliant on their GPS that they fail to look out the windshield and make wise decisions based on what they're seeing.[11]

Sometimes we can become so reliant on technology that we forget to look out of the window and orient ourselves with where we are and question whether we should still be pursuing the path we are taking.

As we can learn from this tragic story, persisting on a course of action beyond when it is wise to do so can have significant consequences. Sometimes, even the failure to make minor course corrections can lead you to a very different, and very unintentional, end outcome. Sometimes, even what might seem to be small errors can lead to significant consequences.

On 28 November 1979, a McDonnell Douglas DC-10 took off from Auckland airport on a sightseeing trip to Antarctica. On board the Air New Zealand Flight 901 were 30 crew members and 227 eager sightseers who had paid for an 11-hour non-stop round trip to fly over the great southern continent. Around noon that day, Captain Jim Collins piloted the plane and made a couple of large loops to bring the plane down out of the clouds and down to a height of 2,000 feet so that the passengers could see the icy landscape below and take their pictures. As the plane emerged from the cloud shortly before 1 pm, instead of seeing McMurdo Sound and the coastline of Antarctica in front of them the crew saw that they were actually about to fly into a mountain. As the proximity alarm rang out, they tried frantically to pull up but it was too late. Flight TE901 crashed into the slopes of Mount Erebus killing all those on board.

The tragedy left New Zealand in a state of shock. For years after the crash there were bitter arguments about the causes and the repercussions of the crash are still felt over 40 years later. A Royal Commission of Enquiry into the crash found that a different flight path had actually been programmed into the flight computer than the one that had been briefed to the pilots. Unknown to the pilots, this flight path had a minor two-degree error in the flight coordinates, which placed the plane 28 miles east of where they believed they were. Even though both pilots on board were experienced, they had no way of knowing that instead of flying over McMurdo Sound with a view of Antarctica on the horizon they were actually over Ross Island and about to fly into the second highest active volcano on the continent.[12] The pilots were not to blame. Instead, a matter of a couple of degrees of error had caused a terrible tragedy.

In air navigation, the '1 in 60' rule of thumb means that for every one degree that a plane veers from its intended course it misses its planned destination by 1 mile for every 60 miles that are flown. What can start out as a relatively minor error can lead to significant divergence from the intended course. After flying 60 miles you may arrive one mile off target and still be able to see your destination and course correct. On a flight from London to Sydney (just over 10,500 miles) a one-degree difference could mean that you arrive in Canberra 177 miles away. A one-degree error flying completely around the world would leave you over 400 miles from your target destination.

Small errors can have big consequences. The further you travel, the further away you can get from your intended outcome. This can be amplified when small errors or poor decision-making is combined with continuation bias that keeps you on an incorrect course. And it can be amplified even further when the reaction to overcoming unexpected obstacles is to throw ever greater resources at the problem in an escalation of commitment (Napoleon's march on Moscow is probably one of the most famous examples of this).

The lesson that we learn from these stories is about adaptation. The need to look out of the window regularly and reassess our situation. The need to course correct and adapt. How small things can lead to big things. Staying adaptive through the process, always using the latest known inputs to inform decision-making as we progress and being open and willing to reprioritize frequently helps to avoid continuation bias and minor errors becoming bigger problems.

Confirmation bias

Plan continuation bias can become even more powerful when combined with other common biases including confirmation bias, the tendency to look for or interpret information and data in ways that support or confirm our existing beliefs or views.

The Wason selection test is a famous task created by University College London cognitive psychologist Peter Wason in 1966. It's a well-known test of deductive reasoning. There are different versions of the test but a simple example (given by author Ian Leslie[13]) is where you might have four cards on a table, each with a number on one side and letter on the other. Participants are tasked with proving whether a statement is true or false: 'All cards with a vowel on one side have an even number on the other side.' The question is, which card or cards do you need to turn over to prove this rule? Think about it now.

FIGURE 5.4   The Wason selection test

If you picked 'E' and '4' then you'll be aligned with about 80 per cent of people who do the same. Yet this is not the right answer. The rule doesn't say that consonants can't be paired with even numbers. So the correct answer is to turn over E and 7 because those are the only two cards that can prove the rule false. If, for example, there is a vowel on the other side of 7 or an odd number on the other side of the E the rule has been disproved. The Wason selection test was designed as an experiment in human reasoning but the fact that so many people get it wrong shows how inclined we all are to look for evidence that confirms our beliefs (and in this case also confirms the rule).

The often cited example of confirmation bias is the proposed armour plating of bomber planes by the US Air Force in 1943. Since the US bombers were at the time flying daytime raids over Germany they were suffering heavy losses. The Air Force conducted research to assess the damage on the planes returning from missions, which had revealed a typical clustering of bullet holes around the tail gunner, the wings and the centre of the fuselage.

The Air Force was proposing to armour plate the bomber planes to better protect them but they could only use a limited amount of plating otherwise

FIGURE 5.5   Example damage to a World War II bomber plane

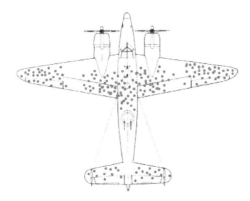

SOURCE Illustration of hypothetical damage pattern on a World War II bomber, dot pattern roughly based on that given at www.motherjones.com/kevin-drum/2010/09/counterintuitive-world derived from: commons.wikimedia.org/wiki/File:PV-1_BuAer_3_side_view.jpg CC BY-SA 4.0

the planes would be too heavy to fly. So they proposed to reinforce the planes in the areas where they had noted the most damage. Renowned mathematician Abraham Wald, who'd been asked by the Air Force to be a part of the project team, pointed out to them that the bullet hole clusters were actually showing where a plane could be hit and still make it back. All the other planes that had been shot and damaged in the other areas had been the ones that had actually been shot down. So Wald's proposal was that the Air Force should do the exact opposite of what they had proposed.

A 2013 study into venture capitalist investing behaviour, based on a survey of 51 VCs from the US, argued that plan continuation bias impacted the proclivity of VCs to provide follow-up rounds of funding to a company based on whether they had already invested in that company at an earlier stage.[14] This bias, say the researchers, can be reinforced by a potentially false assumption that since they invested previously at a time when there was limited information available about the business, now that there is more information at their disposal, they feel more comfortable investing again. In addition, they may well overestimate the benefits of their own contribution and believe that the business stands a better chance of survival now that they're involved. A well-known 2006 study called 'A Hubris Theory of Entrepreneurship' has revealed the tendency we can so easily fall foul of, whether we like to admit it or not, to overestimate the accuracy of our own foresight and interpretation.[15] In other words, the subjective confidence we have in our own judgements is typically greater than the objective accuracy of those judgements. This can potentially lead to the under-valuing of data which is telling us something different than our previous judgement led us to believe.

The lesson from the Wald story is, of course, about how easy it is to misinterpret data or other inputs based on our desire to be right and our eagerness to over-value learning from successes at the expense of learning from failures. In an agile marketing context, we need to be willing to learn from all inputs and results, whether they have been derived from successes or from failures. We need to use data to make smarter decisions, but we also need to be wary of how bias in interpretation can lead us astray. Later in this chapter we will look at the role of hypothesis generation in avoiding confirmation bias and ensuring that teams can learn well through a process, course correct when necessary and validate their learning as they go.

Outputs are a means to an end. As we noted from the story of the Flight TE901 tragedy, relatively small errors or miscommunications can grow to have significant impacts on outcomes. Being overly focused on one way of achieving a goal at the expense of adaptability can derail a team and a project. Not pausing regularly to orient yourself and understand whether you need to change course can lead to poor decisions. Ploughing on when your original plan is no longer optimal leads to poorer outcomes.

Staying focused on the end goal but maintaining flexibility in how you solve for it allows for the correct balance between direction and iteration. An adaptive team can remain flexible and learn better how to achieve the end result that they need. Outcomes, not outputs.

From strategy into execution

In his book *Strategy: A History*[16] Laurence Freedman described how a plan 'supposes a sequence of events that allows one to move with confidence from one state of affairs to another'. Plans, he noted, can easily be thwarted by unpredictable environments and 'different and possibly opposing interests and concerns'. A strategy therefore needs to be adaptive.

When marketing is regarded more as a continuous flow of work, it's necessary to break big initiatives, projects or campaigns down into smaller blocks of work so that this can allow for regular reprioritization and adaptability. In agile marketing it's also important to have a continual focus on the blend between customer and business needs. Traditional focus has really been about serving the needs of the business and considering audiences as large, homogeneous groups. As customer understanding becomes more sophisticated and customer feedback and data more granular, there is the opportunity to bring customer needs much closer into the work process so that they are embedded in the language and processes throughout.

At the same time as embedding customer needs, it's essential to have a clear line of connection from business goals and strategy to marketing and communications strategy, to marketing execution and activity. Isolated activity that is not connected to outcomes that the business is going after remains as isolated activity that likely has little value.

In order to create the clear line of sight from business goals through to marketing activities we can consider how each cascade into, but also feeds from, the other. The top down here, is a cascade of strategy to execution but the bottom up is a feed of continuous customer feedback and data that enables optimization, adaptation and even transformation.

FIGURE 5.6 Linking strategy to execution and execution to strategy

Strategy can therefore define critical areas of focus (initiatives), which can in turn define campaigns/epics and stories/tasks:

- **Initiatives:** These are long-term objectives that flow out of product and marketing strategy. They represent the key ways in which the business will achieve its business goals through product and marketing. They are the broad themes and areas of focus that can shape longer-term work. Initiatives may be more product or marketing focused but will likely define jobs that both areas need to do to be successful, so again it is critical that business/product/marketing are all aligned and integrated. Major initiatives and projects may be managed through QBRs (quarterly business reviews) as they will likely take longer than one quarter to implement, and these may be used to inform a further breakdown of the work into epics.

- **Campaigns/epics:** In agile marketing these are large bodies of work that can be broken down into smaller tasks. Campaigns and/or epics may incorporate several sprints (depending on the sprint cadence of course).

- **Tasks/user stories:** tasks are the smallest units of work. A single sprint may deliver against multiple tasks. Sometimes it can make sense to express a task as a user story that articulates tasks from a customer perspective. User stories can define a requirement and are typically expressed in this way: 'As a (role) I want (goal) so that (benefit).'[17] Not everything the team need to execute will likely need to be expressed as a user story, but it can still be a useful customer-focused lens through which to view tasks.

FIGURE 5.7 Strategy and execution loops

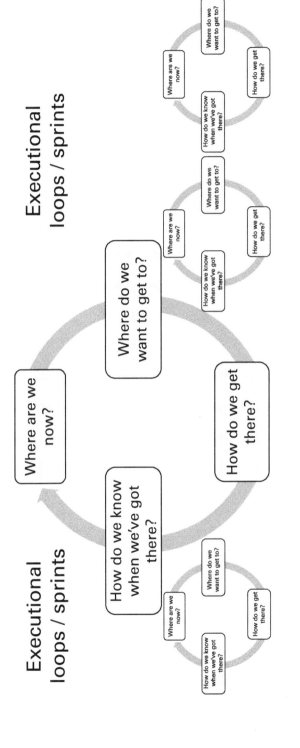

Strategic loop / QBR

Where are we now?

Where do we want to get to?

How do we get there?

How do we know when we've got there?

Executional loops / sprints

Where are we now?

Where do we want to get to?

How do we get there?

How do we know when we've got there?

Where are we now?

Where do we want to get to?

How do we get there?

How do we know when we've got there?

Executional loops / sprints

Where are we now?

Where do we want to get to?

How do we get there?

How do we know when we've got there?

Bearing in mind the importance of outcomes over outputs and the need for strategy to be adaptive and informed by latest known contexts, we might represent the cadence pattern of strategic and executional loops that we mentioned earlier as shown in Figure 5.7.

The larger strategy loops here represent an opportunity to revisit and reassess the broader strategy based on last known inputs and positioning (for example through QBRs). The smaller executional loops are about delivery, doing the work and learning fast, and a single loop will likely be characterized by a single sprint.

Endnotes

1 Working Backwards: Public Sector Hands-On Workshop. Amazon Innovation, October 2020, innovation-amazon.com/wp-content/uploads/2020/10/Working-Backwards-Booklet-WWPS.pdf (archived at https://perma.cc/E99V-FSW9)

2 R Gunther McGrath and I MacMillan. Discovery-driven planning, *Harvard Business Review*, July–August 1995, hbr.org/1995/07/discovery-driven-planning (archived at https://perma.cc/FMQ7-6HLH)

3 R Rumelt (2017) *Good Strategy/Bad Strategy: The Difference and Why It Matters*, Profile Books, London.

4 R Rumelt (2017) *Good Strategy/Bad Strategy: The Difference and Why It Matters*, Profile Books, London.

5 JWT. Planning Guide, March 1974, plannersphere.pbworks.com/f/JWTPlanningGuide.pdf (archived at https://perma.cc/S6TH-NZFB)

6 JWT. Planning guide, 1974. plannersphere.pbworks.com/f/JWTPlanningGuide.pdf (archived at https://perma.cc/4V59-9ZFE)

7 D Prelec and D Simester. Always leave home without it: A further investigation of the credit-card effect on willingness to pay, MIT Sloan School of Management, April 2000, web.mit.edu/simester/Public/Papers/Alwaysleavehome.pdf (archived at https://perma.cc/866C-PL6L)

8 T Garling, N Karlsson and M Selart. The role of mental accounting in everyday economic decision making, January 1999, www.researchgate.net/publication/231641212_The_role_of_mental_accounting_in_everyday_economic_decision_making (archived at https://perma.cc/3BN8-Z7BK)

9 K Dismukes and L Loukopoulos. The limits of expertise: The misunderstood role of pilot error in airline accidents, 2004, humansystems.arc.nasa.gov/flightcognition/article2.htm (archived at https://perma.cc/3M49-QSVB)

10 G Milner. Death by GPS: are satnavs changing our brains? *The Guardian*, June 2016, www.theguardian.com/technology/2016/jun/25/gps-horror-stories-driving-satnav-greg-milner (archived at https://perma.cc/U77Q-9SMU)

11 T Knudson. Death by GPS in the desert, Sacramento Bee, 30 May 2012, www.sacbee.com/entertainment/living/travel/article2573180.html (archived at https://perma.cc/7RGM-NM65)

12 A Illmer. Mount Erebus disaster: The plane crash that changed New Zealand, BBC, 28 November 2019, www.bbc.co.uk/news/world-asia-50555046 (archived at https://perma.cc/HN68-3XCY)

13 I Leslie. Why disagreement is vital to advancing human understanding, Aeon, 2021, aeon.co/essays/why-disagreement-is-vital-to-advancing-human-understanding (archived at https://perma.cc/YW8D-W7DE)

14 D Kahnin and R Mahto. Do venture capitalists have a continuation bias? *Journal of Entrepreneurship*, September 2013, www.researchgate.net/profile/Raj-Mahto/publication/258154232_Do_Venture_Capitalists_Have_a_Continuation_Bias/links/5dba06ce4585151435d6147d/Do-Venture-Capitalists-Have-a-Continuation-Bias.pdf (archived at https://perma.cc/DJ7L-7TS6)

15 M Hayward, D Shepherd and D Griffin, A hubris theory of entrepreneurship, *Management Science*, February 2006, www.researchgate.net/publication/43508500_A_Hubris_Theory_of_Entrepreneurship (archived at https://perma.cc/WN9W-ZNFX)

16 L Freedman (2013) *Strategy: A History*, Oxford University Press, Oxford.

17 Agile Modeling. User Stories: An Agile Introduction, 2021, www.agilemodeling.com/artifacts/userStory.htm (archived at https://perma.cc/4RPX-SY5P)

PART THREE

Agile marketing execution

06

Using sprints

Don't get lost in methodology

Agile is characterized by a plethora of different and quite specific methodologies. Each of these methodologies is in turn characterized by distinct practices and ceremonies, and advocates can sometimes become very passionate in their defence of particular ones. In agile marketing, this can sometimes be unhelpful. It is clearly important to have common approaches, tools and methods. This helps teams to work in similar ways, which supports better understanding, coordination, collaboration and transparency. There is, however, no one methodology that is right for every team and organization.

Each business and each marketing team will have its own unique contexts, which means that a more flexible approach to methodology is more helpful. It's important for teams to find the particular practices and ways of working that work best for them. Defining a broad approach to agile methodology is helpful but a company or team shouldn't feel as though using elements from one methodology should preclude them from making use of practices from others. For example, some marketing teams may adopt sprint working and place elements from common agile methodologies such as Scrum at the heart of their version of agile marketing. Other teams may find that working in a continuous flow of work more akin to Kanban approaches (which are discussed later in the book) is more appropriate. Some agile marketing teams may use prioritization frameworks from specific methods in combination with ceremonies from others. There is no one way, but it's important to understand that most of the value in agile marketing comes from the actual adoption of more inherently iterative and adaptive ways of working rather than the specific methodology that the team adopts. Find your own way. Frame a broad approach that will enable common approaches and then allow for a degree of flexibility to test and learn with attributes, practices and ceremonies to find ones which can have more widespread benefit and application.

Having acknowledged this, we must recognize that there are some fundamental principles drawn from agile methodologies that are both useful and valuable in this context. Let's look at those now.

Working in sprints

Breaking work down into time-boxed sprints is useful, even when teams are not strictly using Scrum methodologies, since it creates a regular cadence of adaptation and learning for teams to work to. The benefits of this are that teams can be aligned to focus on particular outcomes but can also see a regular delivery of value, which is both motivating and also helps to bring the stakeholder on the journey.

As mentioned earlier in the book, it can be helpful to take appropriate elements of different agile methodologies and apply them to suit your own organizational contexts and needs. There are a number of useful aspects and ceremonies from Scrum methodologies that can be helpful in establishing productive ways of working and habits for teams and I'll look at how you can apply each of these in turn, but it's also worth noting that there are several key decisions that need to be made upfront.

Team alignment

How small teams or squads are aligned and focused is an important choice for the business to make in setting up an agile marketing programme for success. It may well be the case that within one large marketing team there will be teams focused on different types of outcomes, but in a scaled application having one dominant philosophy around how teams are aligned helps to manage dependencies and ensure better alignment and common approaches. There are a number of options for alignment, each with its own benefits and challenges to manage:

1   **Customer journey, need state or life cycle**
    Where squads are aligned to focus on end-to-end customer journeys, particular need states or a stage in the customer life cycle. The advantage with all of these approaches is that it allows for good task alignment in ways that are inherently focused on delivering customer value. A team

that is aligned to an end-to-end customer journey (for example, a mortgage acquisition journey for a bank) can focus on opportunities to apply both optimizations and innovation throughout the journey in order to maximize a particular outcome (in the example case it would be mortgage acquisition rate). There can be clear metrics for success, which are both business and customer focused. Aligning to a customer need state (for example, 'I want to move house') can pull in a broader opportunity for a team to provide value to the customer and help product and marketing opportunities to be maximized in an integrated way. Whereas focusing a team on a stage in the journey (for example, conversion) can help place a more targeted spotlight on the optimizations of a particular job-to-be-done with a clear measure of success (conversion rate).

The watch out with these alignment options is the need to manage dependencies well across teams. When multiple squads are working on potentially overlapping customer journeys, needs and required inputs will likely overlap too (for example, a squad aligned to one acquisition journey may want to make a change to one particular part of a website which will in turn impact on what another squad is trying to achieve). We'll discuss strategies for tackling dependencies later in the book. Another watch out for squads that are aligned to particular stages in the customer lifecycle is the risk of creating disjointed customer journeys. Alignment across the different relevant squads that impact that journey is key here.

2 **Product alignment**
In this instance, squads may be aligned to particular product areas. The benefits of this approach are clarity of focus and one that aligns well with how the rest of the business may well be focused. There is an opportunity for continuous improvement and optimizations around individual product areas. The potential downside to this approach is that it is not necessarily very customer-centric, and the risk is that business needs are continually prioritized over customer needs. This can also possibly lead to disjointed customer journeys.

3 **Media or channel**
Where squads are aligned to specific media, touchpoints or channels this can bring good channel focus and optimization but joining up an omnichannel customer experience is again the challenge.

4 **Innovation / development / optimization focus**
Here squads are focused on developing new propositions or on optimizing existing ones. Teams can be aligned to solving particular challenges or

innovating and optimizing around a particular area of strategic importance. It's also possible to align squads around a 'pioneers, settlers, town planners' model, a concept originated by researcher Simon Wardley, which focuses people on stages in the innovation process:[1]

o **Pioneers:** Exploring uncharted territory, generating new concepts and experimenting to create new possibilities. The failure rate is likely to be higher at this stage, but this is all about generating future potential.

o **Settlers:** Commercializing ideas, generating business models around them and making them useful for larger audiences, turning prototypes into products and building understanding.

o **Town planners:** The operationalizing and scaling of new products and services in order to drive efficiencies and economies of scale.

The advantage of this approach is that resource and space is dedicated to innovation and exploration and it can be useful for where a continuous stream of new propositions is needed. The risk with a pioneers, settlers, town planners approach is disjointed hand-overs, the loss of expertise as projects are handed from one area to the next and a lack of consistency.

There is no one right way. Selecting the right approach for the business will depend on the particular contexts that your organization has and, as mentioned above, there is the potential for more than one approach to be adopted across a large team (for example, having a dominant approach that aligns squads to customer journeys but also having several squads focused on innovation and development). However, since the motivation for bringing agile ways of working into the team is often the desire to become more customer-centric, alignment around customer needs or journeys is often a good place to start.

As well as considering the context in which the business is operating (for example, the need for more customer-centric ways of working or the need for greater innovation), it's also important to look at the work that needs to be done and organize teams around achieving outputs and outcomes in ways that are efficient and productive.

As we'll discuss later in the book, running pilot teams can be a useful way to gain learning in advance of a wider roll out of agile. When defining the alignment of pilots, as well as acknowledging the wider objectives of the shift in ways of working it's important to consider:

- **Learning:** The degree to which the pilot will enable the business to learn (for example, about the best application of agile processes, customer-centric ways of working).
- **Feasibility:** Ability to spin up the pilot quickly, minimizing unnecessary disruption.
- **Resourcing:** The ability to commit resourcing, minimize any complexities working with other teams or external inputs and partners (like agencies, for example).
- **Impact:** Does the pilot help to position marketing as a growth driver for the business? What is the potential for commercial value? Can it bring greater efficiencies?

Defining a team mission

Once the decision has been made on how to align teams, it's a good idea to spell out a mission for each squad that defines the team's purpose and brings clarity to the outcomes they are going after.

In an ideal scenario, a team mission should be MECE:

- **Mutually Exclusive:** Overlap with other teams is kept to a minimum. No two teams should be trying to solve the same problem.
- **Collectively Exhaustive:** Missions should cover everything that the team/ organization needs to do – there should be no gaps.

A good mission should answer the following questions:

- Who is your customer/user? What are you doing for them?
- What are the needs of the business?

This brings together a meeting of business and customer needs in a way that is most beneficial. For example, a squad mission could be: 'Design and optimize a simple mortgage acquisition journey that is profitable and scalable, and supports home buyers in finding the right mortgage solution.' The squad need to be working to maximize business benefit while also doing this in a way that brings customer needs right to the heart of the mission, the work and the decisions that the squad make.

Sprint length

Sprints can operate at different cadences. While some teams prefer to work in two-week sprints, others may find that four weeks or even six weeks are better. In setting a sprint rhythm, the key consideration is how long it will take for the team to deliver valuable, working outputs. The full value of working in this rhythmic way won't be realized if the team is not able to generate real outputs in the period of the sprint, but a sprint shouldn't be so long that it is slowing down delivery of value.

The other important consideration is to ensure that teams that are working on similar or closely related missions are aligned to similar cadences. Having a similar sprint length across multiple teams is helpful in creating a common rhythm across a wider area, which can in turn help with tracking progress, alignment and reporting.

Key principles of sprint working

Earlier in the book I described the fundamental principles of agile methodologies and in the next chapter we'll take a closer look at how to individually apply some of the most useful attributes and ceremonies from scrum sprint methodology. To begin with, it's important to recognize the fundamental conventions at play here:

- **A continuous, regular delivery of value:** It's important to define the outcomes that will result from each sprint and that working outputs are delivered at the end. This ensures that value to both the customer and the business is delivered as early as possible and frequently.

- **Reprioritization and adaptation:** Working in sprints opens the opportunity for teams to bake adaptive strategy and delivery into their ways of operating, so it's important to capitalize on this through frequent reprioritization of the backlog and always basing decision-making on the latest known inputs and data.

- **Team capacity and estimation:** It's important to plan the work in ways that don't overburden the team but allow for a continuous flow of outputs and value. This means determining the time and effort that work will take to deliver (sizing the work) and understanding the capacity of a squad.

FIGURE 6.1 Sprint working

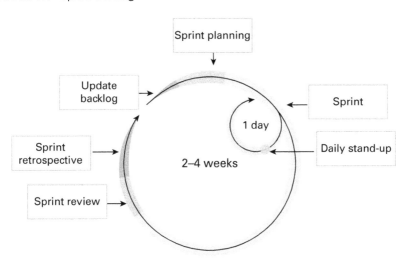

- **Progress and transparency:** It can be really useful for members of the squad to see what other members are working on, to be clear about the responsibilities they have as individuals to get to the required outputs and the progress that the squad is making through a sprint. There should be a high level of transparency around the work.

- **Learning through review and retrospective:** it's critical to bake learning and continuous improvement into squad working and this means regular review and retrospective at the end of sprints. This not only helps to bring stakeholders along on the journey but also enables the team themselves to focus on how they can improve their own ways of working and the way that they work with other teams.

The figure above demonstrates the structure of a typical sprint.

Scaling sprint working enables a team and an organization to embed adaptation into the fabric of how it operates and also to embed learning. As agile ways of working scale, so too does responsiveness and learning. Taking this sprint blueprint into account, we can define how to apply each critical element of the process in ways that will deliver maximum value.

Endnote

1   S Wardley. On pioneers, settlers, town planners and theft, March 2015, blog.
gardeviance.org/2015/03/on-pioneers-settlers-town-planners-and.html (archived
at https://perma.cc/MG5N-FMQW)

07

Applying methodology
to marketing execution

From campaigns into backlogs

Breaking initiatives and campaigns down into a continuous flow of work and into smaller increments enables frequent reprioritization of those smaller tasks and therefore far greater adaptability. Tasks can be gathered onto a backlog, which can be reorganized at regular intervals based on latest known inputs and contexts. The principles of a good backlog are:

- It should be visible to all of the team and to key stakeholders. This transparency helps to set and manage expectations and ensure that everyone is aligned and aware of what work is to be done next. It also helps create an environment of trust. There are a number of virtual project management tools that can visualize backlogs and the flow of work and provide good transparency for stakeholders and the team alike.

- Items on the backlog should be clearly linked through to marketing and business goals and objectives. The team should be undertaking work that is focused on addressing customer needs but also that is contributing to the achievement of marketing objectives.

- Backlog items may be expressed as simple tasks, or it can sometimes help to frame a task as a 'user story'. This involves articulating a task from a user's perspective. As mentioned earlier in the book, an example might be 'As a [persona], I want to [intent] so that I can [goal].' This articulation helps to frame the customer need (and so defines tasks in customer-centric ways) without specifying exactly what the solution looks like. This in turn allows for a degree of autonomy for the team to decide how best to solve for that need. Not every task may be expressed as a user story, but it can be a useful way to encourage a team to continually focus on the value that is being created for customers.

- Agreeing a definition for when each task is complete (sometimes called a 'definition of done' in agile) is helpful in ensuring a common understanding of what the end result of each task should be.

- The backlog should be prioritized based on customer and business value. I'll discuss prioritization methodology in the next section, but the principle should be that teams should always be focused on working on the items that have maximum value for the customer and the business.

- The prioritized list dictates what the team should work on, and tasks are pulled in from the backlog. Stakeholder requests should be considered alongside other items on the backlog for the value that they have to the customer and to the business. The prioritization is agreed in a conversation between stakeholders and the team.

A backlog should be a shared, visible and regularly updated resource that is a common source of truth for both the team and for stakeholders.

Using Scrumban

As discussed before, it can be useful for marketing teams to cherry pick elements from different methodologies and combine them in ways that best suit their particular contexts. An example of this, and a method that has been used by existing agile marketing teams, is Scrumban. This hybrid methodology combines elements of Scrum and Kanban and seeks to bring together the best of both.

Scrum methods are based on the classic sprint cycle and timeboxing work in iterations. However, a team may want to visualize a more continuous flow and find it useful to bring in elements of Kanban. The latter process grew out of manufacturing but involves visualizing the workflow. Large projects are still broken down into smaller tasks and these tasks are represented on a real or virtual board in lanes that can represent steps in the process (for example, work to do, work in progress, work awaiting testing or checking, work shipped and so on). Tools such as virtual Kanban boards can help to visualize work in progress and can be used to track both the pace and progress of the work that is underway. There are many such project management software tools, but the key is to use them primarily as a tool for the team to help them optimize their workflow and easily see what other

FIGURE 7.1   Example of a Kanban board

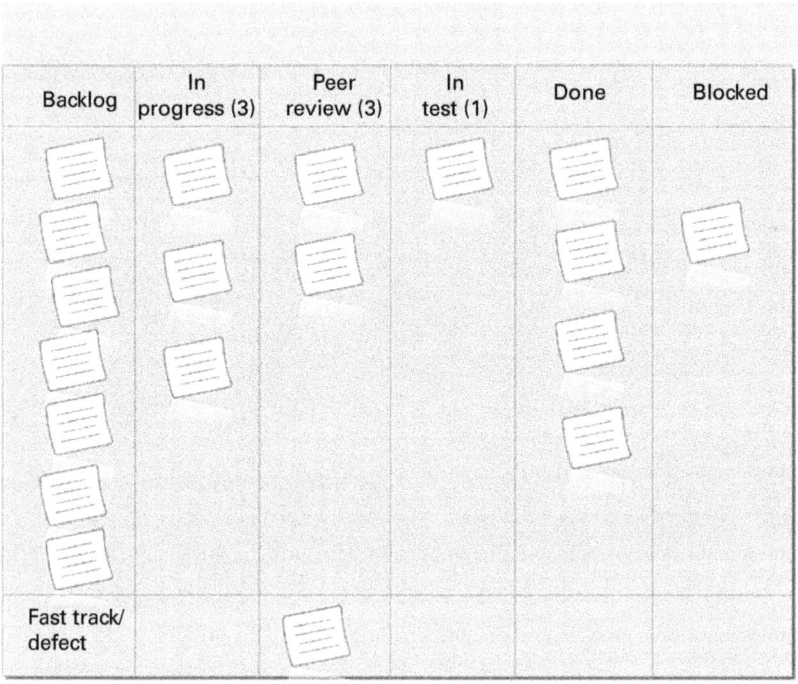

Image: By Dr Ian Mitchell – own work, CC BY-SA 2.5, commons.wikimedia.org/w/index.php?curid=20245783

team members are working on and when the work is completed. At its simplest level the Kanban board has a column with the tasks/user stories the team will be working on, columns that indicate when the tasks are in the process of being in flow and a column that demonstrates when it is finished.

Teams 'pull' tasks into the flow of the team work, and limits are placed on the number of items that are being worked on concurrently (typically using a tool called work-in-process limits) ensuring that the team is not overburdened but is still delivering a continuous flow of value. Teams will often measure the average time from when work is requested to when it is completed (lead time) and work to optimize this. The aim is to create a continuous and predictable flow of value to customers and to the business.

When a team is working in Scrumban it may well be using a board, work-in-progress limits and lead times, but also be using the structured approach of sprint working to regularly reprioritize the backlog based on latest known inputs, plan what will be pulled into the next iteration and then regularly conduct reviews and retrospective. In this way it can effectively combine the best of both, embedding the iterative cycles and reprioritization of Scrum with the flexibility, visualization and transparency of Kanban.

Regular reprioritization and sprint planning

Regular reprioritization of the backlog should be baked into the working of an agile marketing team. When working in sprints this happens at the beginning of every sprint, along with the process of planning and aligning around what the team will actually work on and achieve as outputs at the end of the sprint. Where work is set up to be more of a continuous flow, frequent and systematic reprioritization and planning is also essential.

In order to manage the flow of work properly, teams will need to size and estimate the work and also know the capacity of what they can realistically achieve over a given period of time. It's important in estimation that the full team take part in order to ensure that as complete a picture as possible is built into the sizing process. Estimation may take the form of an evaluation of time to complete individual tasks, or it may be helpful to score tasks using points that take account of complexity and effort required. The risk with time-only estimations is that you are subject to planning fallacy (the tendency we all have to under-estimate the time it takes to complete a task). Using a points system based on difficulty keeps the team focused on solving and shipping work rather than simply spending time on work. The team should all then be able to input into the estimation process using techniques like planning poker. In this informal process, items from the backlog are discussed and then each team member scores the item individually before everyone reveals their scores. If the scores are wide apart then additional discussion may be needed before a consensus is reached, but if they are close together this can be minimized. The benefit of estimation exercises like planning poker are that they are inclusive, democratic and take account of different perspectives and inputs. This can help ensure a more realistic view of the amount of work that can be achieved which can then inform what the team will work on.

A key principle of this planning process is that the team is not unnecessarily overburdened. Since the team have agreed what they will work on and all been involved in the estimation process, they are committed to achieving those outputs, but teams should not be taking on unrealistic amounts of work. It can often (inevitably perhaps) be the case that urgent, short-term requests (maybe from senior stakeholders) are asked of the team in addition to the work that they have committed to. The principle should be that wherever possible those requests should go into the next work sprint or planning process and if they absolutely have to be worked on immediately that something else is deprioritized.

This brings us to reprioritization. There are a number of prioritization methodologies that are all helpful in their own way, but organizations should find one that works best for their own unique contexts. The principles behind the prioritization are, however, important to pay attention to. Tasks on the backlog should be prioritized using a balance of customer and business value. While individual teams may have their own quirks around the prioritization methods that they use, where there are multiple agile squads working alongside each other it can help to have common and transparent approaches. This ensures that across teams everyone understands why and how work has been prioritized as it has and helps to mitigate the politics that can occur from competing agendas. Looking closer at a couple of key prioritization frameworks is useful in understanding some of the key principles that should be universal in this process.

The MOSCOW framework, for example, sets out the fidelity of understanding that we need for sizing tasks on the backlog and the principle of deprioritizing low-value work.

- **Must have** (M): Work that is about to be worked on needs to be sized in detail in order to ensure an accurate picture of complexity and/or time and effort involved.

- **Should have** (S): This relates to work that is coming down the line, perhaps within the next month or two. The level of detail needed in sizing here is less than the work currently being done. It will need to be understood to a reasonable degree but it doesn't add value to work through sizing in detail at this stage since this may change as the work gets closer to the top of the backlog.

- **Could have** (C): An even lesser degree of detail is needed for work that is still some way off since it is again likely that this will change.

- **Won't have this time** (W): The key principle here is that low-value work is deprioritized in favour of higher-value work. The definition of value should be the balance between customer and business value that we discussed earlier, but this should be a continuous process. The team should always be looking to deprioritize low-value work, particularly when there is higher-value work that needs to be done. Deliberately asking the question '*what can we NOT do?*' helps to challenge assumptions around the value of work and create space and capacity.

Teams and businesses can typically be poor at both prioritization and deprioritization. The former can fall foul of internal politics and competing agendas between stakeholders or teams, which can slow progress. The latter is rarely considered since teams and individuals are often expected to continue with all of their previous responsibilities and work while also taking on additional projects and work. It's rare that teams deliberately look to identify work that they can actually stop doing in order to create space. The value of frameworks like MOSCOW are that they force teams to actively question the value of the work that they are doing and ensure that teams are always focused on doing the highest value work that they can with the capacity that they have.

FIGURE 7.2   WSJF

$$\text{WSJF} \; = \; \frac{\text{Cost of delay}}{\text{Job duration / size}}$$

Another common prioritization framework (which originated in the SAFe agile methodology) is 'Weighted Shortest Job First' (or WSJF). This incorporates some useful principles around taking account of the economic value of the work and the cost of not doing it. In WSJF, the cost of delay (defined as the user and business value combined with time criticality and how the work will either reduce risk or enable further opportunity) is divided by the job size and/or duration.

This enables tasks to be prioritized, with those that have a high cost of delay and low duration being the ones that should be done first and those tasks that have a low cost of delay and high duration being prioritized last. This technique enables a team to deliver maximum value in the shortest amount of time but as a broader principle agile marketing teams should *always* be asking how they can maximize high-value tasks over low-value work.

The value of feedback

The street finds its own use for things.

(William Gibson)[1]

It should go without saying that expertise is hugely important in marketing teams. Experts can be invaluable in designing, finding and recommending appropriate solutions. Yet as soon as marketing activity or a product or service goes out into the market and real users begin to interact with it, feedback becomes just as powerful. Feedback can often surprise us as users begin to interact with content or assets or propositions in ways that are different than predicted. It can take us in new directions. It can mean that we are much more informed as we go through a process. It can reveal insights that can enlighten and spark new ideas. It can enable us to adapt to changing contexts and behaviours. This means that we need to balance expert inputs with the learning that we are gaining through feedback. Both are powerful tools, but we ignore either at our peril.

Feedback in the team environment is also powerful. As I'll discuss later in the book, establishing the right communication norms in the team is critical to moving fast and collaborating well. Continuous, informal feedback is a useful way to constantly adjust and adapt behaviours and approaches to optimize how the team is working. Feedback opportunities are also opportunities to actively listen, learn, motivate and develop. Positive affirmation and honest feedback on areas to improve can help a good team become a truly high-performing team when handled well.

USING RITUAL DISSENT

Ritual dissent is a simple method for giving feedback in the team environment that was created by Dave Snowden of Cognitive Edge.[2] It's designed to enable teams to test and improve proposals, ideas or other content and builds from the understanding that receiving feedback isn't always easy, particularly when it is negative. The technique is focused on enabling all types of feedback to be delivered for an idea in ways that don't damage team relationships and enable a psychologically safe environment. The process involves a presenter talking through their ideas to a group who remain silent while the presenter is speaking. The presenter then turns their chair around so that they have their back to the group and listens in silence as the group feedback ritualized dissent (or challenges) or assent (positive alternatives) to the idea. The process depersonalizes the feedback, ensures people really listen and helps to make it more supportive while also being challenging in ways that can improve the idea. This helps avoid decision-making that is overly consensus-based and helps plans to become more resilient.

FIGURE 7.3   Feedback loops

Fast feedback loops

Feedback loops should be the key drivers in continuous improvement and adaptability when working in agile systems. During a feedback cycle, work is conducted and progress made, the work is tested or put live and metrics are used to assess the impact of the work with a view to identifying adjustments, improvements or pivots. A simple feedback loop might look like Figure 7.3.

This loop may look similar to existing strategy or optimization cycles, but the key difference here is frequency. In agile marketing, teams cycle through these loops continuously and at a faster cadence at an executional level. While strategy is closely linked to execution each of these will operate at a different tempo. Writer and technology visionary Stewart Brand originated the concept of 'pace layering' in his book *The Clock of the Long Now*[3] as a way of demonstrating the different cadence to which elements of

FIGURE 7.4   Feedback loop pace layering

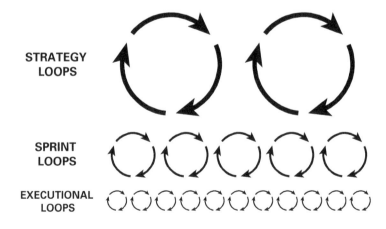

society (fashion, commerce, infrastructure, governance, culture) operate. In a similar way, teams may be getting continuous feedback via executional loops, which means that these run faster than sprint loops (if teams are using sprints) and strategy loops.

Strategy loops are informed by sprint loops, which are in turn informed by executional loops. There should be a continuous flow of inputs that are enabling executional optimization, sprint reprioritization and adaptive strategy.

The key to good feedback loops is to ensure that teams are truly empowered to make smarter decisions through the inputs that they are getting and then to adapt. It's important for teams to consider several different facets in order to optimize this opportunity:

- **Set up:** The team will need to have easy and timely access to relevant data, inputs or measures. It will create unworkable dependencies if a team is reliant on seeing feedback that it takes a long time to secure or if they don't have the relevant tools. Dashboarding or self-serve can help improve access to key data and can really help a team to move and iterate fast. Having analytics roles embedded in small, multidisciplinary teams or agreed point-people and SLAs within centralized analytics teams can also help.

- **Frequency of feedback:** If a team is working in sprints, the sprint planning process and retrospective process create their own kind of feedback loop and an opportunity to take a step back, look at the latest known contexts and adjust accordingly. Even when not working in sprints and when a team is in the mode of continuous delivery feedback loops can help to regularly assess performance and situational context with a view to identifying options to improve. The key thing to remember is that the feedback should be regular enough to enable timely optimization or adjustments based on robust patterns of data or inputs and not so infrequent that the team are missing out on opportunities to improve.

- **Audiences:** There are different types of feedback loop that can be directed towards different audiences and optimizing key objectives around customer interaction and engagement, team performance or stakeholder involvement. Customer feedback loops ensure that the team is getting timely inputs on the performance of marketing campaigns or assets via analytics. Team feedback loops help to gather frequent input on team working and performance. Stakeholder feedback loops keep the connection between strategy, the wider business and team execution, and they can help bring stakeholders on a journey. Inputs may range from campaign performance data, to team discussion and demo conversations with stakeholders.

Feedback loops should be used to take ongoing inputs and be the driving force behind a continual process of adaptation. Teams that are tracking metrics and other inputs properly should be able to identify changing dynamics and required adjustments, and wherever possible minimize big reveals or surprises at the end of a process or project.

One of the under-recognized benefits of feedback loops is that they connect team members through to the impact and difference that they are making with the work that they are doing. Being able to see customers responding to the work in a positive way through direct user feedback, customer interaction or even just a shift in the metrics is very motivating for the team. There is an important principle at work here, which has been emphasized by work done by author and academic Adam Grant. Grant once did a study using a group of telemarketing fundraisers who were raising money to provide student scholarships for underprivileged students. There was a huge turnover of staff at the call centre but Grant brought in a student who had been a beneficiary of a scholarship to talk to the fundraisers. The student talked about how the scholarship had changed their life and given them access to an education that they wouldn't have otherwise been able to access. The average amount of money that was being raised by the call centre staff rose by 142 per cent following that meeting and the average number of minutes that they spent on the phone went up by 171 per cent.[4] When people are connected to the impact of the work that they are doing, motivation goes up and so does productivity. Feedback loops are essential to making this happen.

The shift to regular adaptation based on feedback can involve a significant mindset shift from more traditional, linear and waterfall ways of laying out work. In the latter, visibility is likely to be high at the start of a project (when it is scoped out) and at the end (when the result of the work is revealed), but it can dip in the middle of a project or initiative as the team focuses on delivering against a relatively fixed plan. This tends to be the case even if conceptually we believe that we are connected to the progress being made throughout. Even if a linear initiative is populated with regular stage gates, the impact of the work that the team is doing will not become evident until the end of the initiative. The opportunity with agile ways of operating is that visibility can be maintained at a relatively consistent rate throughout the work. We can represent this difference in the chart shown in Figure 7.5.

If teams fail to acknowledge these mindset shifts they can become real barriers to a successful agile implementation.

FIGURE 7.5   Project/initiative visibility

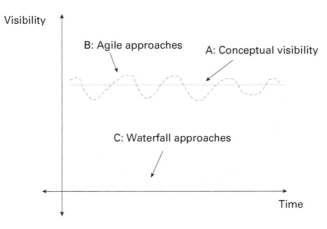

Transparency and velocity of work

A key principle in agile marketing is that the work should be as transparent as possible. Since everyone that matters has sight of the work, this transparency supports alignment, more efficient working and the building of trust among team members and stakeholders. In teams where trust and transparency are low, leaders frequently feel that they need to be in the detail of what the team is actually doing often in order to check that progress is being made in the right direction. This is not always helpful for teams that want to move quickly and valuable leadership and team time can be lost on unnecessary reporting, status updates and catch-ups. Having tools and processes that support greater transparency of work ensures that the team is accountable for the work it is doing but also facilitates trust and greater autonomy. Using a Kanban board (as discussed earlier) is a good example of a tool that supports greater transparency. One of the benefits of visualizing tasks on a Kanban board is that as tasks move from the left to the right the team can visibly see progress being made. The transparency of working keeps team members connected to not only what everyone else is doing but also the progress that is being made.

There is real value in this principle of motivation through progress. Teresa Amabile, Professor in the Entrepreneurial Management Unit at Harvard Business School, has conducted extensive workplace research based on thousands of work diaries and surveys to define what she calls the 'Progress Principle'.[5] Her work has shown that out of all the things that can boost workplace perception and motivation the single most important is making progress in meaningful work.[6] Alongside motivation, the progress principle is a key driver of creative and productive performance, above more visible and extrinsic rewards.

When teams are using estimation techniques to size the work that they are about to undertake it can be useful to also track the velocity or throughput of work that the team is achieving. Burndown charts are good ways to show the amount of work that has been completed so far in an epic, campaign or a sprint and can also be used to assess the amount of work still to do and forecast the likelihood of that work being completed in the time available. They require the work tasks to be sized and estimated (estimation was discussed earlier in the section on sprint planning) and so the team will need to be aligned on their estimation statistic or the measure by which they will size the work tasks (for example, time to complete, complexity or a points score based on both). Once the tasks in a sprint, campaign or epic are sized, the velocity by which the work is completed can then be tracked by looking on an ongoing basis at the total size of work completed and the total size of the work yet to be done. This can be compared against the sum total of all the tasks so that at any time a team can see the amount of work left to be done and take any necessary steps to mitigate challenges.

FIGURE 7.6   Example burndown chart

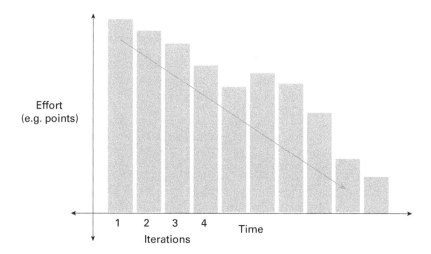

The burndown chart is unlikely to descend evenly since there will be unforeseen complexities that may mean that the work slows temporarily, or there may well be other occasions where the team are able to make much better progress than anticipated. The chart helps the team to track progress and to take steps to stay on track should they be needed and it can also be useful to see when scope creep is resulting in additional work, which may impact timescales. It can also be useful and motivating to keep track of work completed, not just work left to do on the chart (see Figure 7.7).

FIGURE 7.7   Burndown chart – work completed/work left to be done

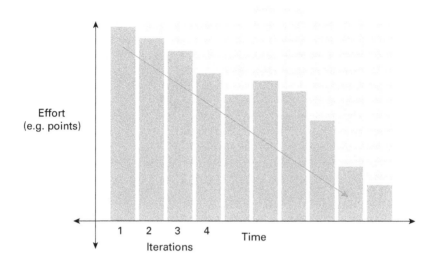

The burndown chart should be as realistic as possible and it will quickly become evident if a team is not committing to enough work in the sprint (since they will finish early) or are overloaded with work (they will fail to complete all the tasks). Charts can be applied to sprints or campaigns or even to epics.

The final tool that can be used to drive velocity and transparency of work is the daily stand-up. Regular stand-up meetings have become a very visible aspect of agile working but they play an essential part in ensuring that the team are staying on track, able to progress well and aware of what the rest of the team are doing. The meetings should always be short (perhaps no more than 15 minutes) and informal and focused on work in progress. The idea is to flag any blockers to progress that need to be dealt with (perhaps by the squad lead) and understand what everyone is working on and what progress has been made. Typical questions which are answered in a daily stand-up include:

- What did I accomplish yesterday?
- What will I do today?
- Are there any impediments to progress?

It's important to keep the meetings short and avoid lengthy discussions on work in progress or challenges. Any problems identified in the meeting can be dealt with afterwards but the meeting itself should be all about connecting with each other and with the work.

Trust, transparency and tracking of progress are all important elements of agile marketing. Using the tools that I've mentioned here enables teams to move fast, align and adapt well and feel motivated by the work that they're doing.

Defining good hypotheses

When a team wants to conduct a test, it needs to define the hypothesis that it will be testing. Experimentation and testing should be fully integrated to how an agile marketing team works and a continuous process where teams are always looking to optimize, improve and run tests that can try out new ideas and understand quickly if there is value in them progressing. Testing and experimentation is how a team learns fast. This is as much about mindset as it is about process.

Using hypotheses is an important part of the testing process. Any idea should really be treated as an assumption until it has been validated, wherever possible with real customers. Hypothesis-driven test and learn is also a good way to avoid confirmation bias (looking for the data that will support our pre-existing beliefs) since it is just as valid to disprove a hypothesis as it is to prove it. Both results are valid since they both enable us to learn and frame our next hypothesis for testing. Essentially, a hypothesis is a statement or proposed explanation for an observation, occurrence or idea. It can be informed by research (qualitative or quantitative), by customer observation and ethnographic inputs, by speaking to customers, by customer feedback or by data and analytics which tells us about behaviours and actions or even results from other tests. It's important, however, that a hypothesis is formed from valid inputs and that it is testable. This means that it needs to have a theory or supposition, the expected outcome and the measure which will identify success or failure. Author and technologist Barry O'Reilly has framed a useful way of setting this out in what he calls hypothesis-driven development:[7]

- We believe <this capability>.
- Will result in <this outcome>.
- We will have confidence to proceed when <we see a measurable signal>.

This structured approach to testing can enable a team to avoid baking-in assumptions to a process and facilitate learning through testing.

GOOD RULES FOR RAPID EXPERIMENTATION

Simi Agbaje from the *Financial Times* has outlined some useful principles for rapid experimentation using hypotheses.[8] Paraphrasing and building on these core principles, we can understand the techniques that can help teams to learn well:

1 Diverge and then converge. It can be useful to gather a wide variety of inputs and ideas that can inform a hypothesis. Ideas may come from the team or from stakeholders or even customers. Inputs can come from data or research. Then it's important to narrow down to define the actual hypothesis that you want to test and align the team on how best to conduct the experiment.

2 Plan for failure. It's critical that the team agree on the criteria or standards by which they would define success or failure. It's worth considering what will happen if the test fails. A good approach here is to use the learning that has been gained from the failed test to reframe your next hypothesis. A simple decision tree can help set out your options if a test fails (for example, it might be that more information is needed).

3 Get from the 'what' to the 'why'. This is about bringing quantitative and qualitative inputs together. Data and testing can help learning, but qualitative inputs can help a team understand why certain things are happening. An example of this might be using interaction data from site analytics and combining that with customer interviews to establish the 'why' behind the patterns of behaviour. This might then frame another hypothesis to test.

4 Analytics is your friend. Running a quick succession of A/B tests can enable a team to test multiple hypotheses rapidly, but that requires access to quick analytics feedback. This means that the team will need to draw on analytics expertise in a way that doesn't slow them down.

5 Size is important. A test with a very small number of users may show up patterns but may also lead to inconclusive results.

6 Use 'fake door' tests. These are tests where users are provided an option for something that has not yet been built (for example, an option to sign up for an upcoming feature or proposition). This can help reveal whether the proposition is serving a valid need without spending too much.

'Safe to fail' experimentation

Iterative, test and learn approaches can be used to gain knowledge and understanding fast and solve many different types of problems. They can be used to optimize existing processes, customer journeys and propositions and also to innovate and experiment with new ideas, concepts and territory. In complex adaptive environments there may well be an evolving or irregular relationship between cause and effect which means that outcomes are less predictable and teams may need to experiment more to create more emergent approaches to solving problems.

Creating 'safe to fail' environments is critical in enabling agile marketing teams to experiment and learn fast. Concerns or uncertainty over the level of risk involved in running tests or a company and team culture that does not support learning from failure as well as successes can dramatically dampen experimentation and a team's willingness and appetite to try new things out. The concept of 'safe to fail' can be applied to any testing regime that the team might be doing, but it is particularly valuable when the team is moving into relatively unknown or new territory.

Put simply, taking time to define tests or experiments that maximize learning but don't generate unnecessary risk is important in moving fast and building knowledge without putting the team or company reputation on the line. Teams need to learn from both successes and failures in order to learn well, and this means that an adept understanding of how to run tests and experiments that limit the 'blast radius' of impact can ensure a sensible approach is taken.

The objective should always be to learn and build knowledge into the system and so is definitely *not* about avoiding failure at all costs. Instead it can be useful to enhance, build on and amplify successes while also failing in small, contained and tolerable ways that enable a team to enhance their understanding. Breaking down large challenges, concepts and ideas into smaller chunks can facilitate a series of controlled experiments based around identifying relevant hypotheses, understanding what success and failure look like, and then conducting rapid tests and/or prototypes to learn fast. In complex challenge areas, 'safe to fail' experiments can allow a team to test hypotheses that come at a problem from a variety of angles so that they might observe emerging possibilities.

In the late nineteenth century and early twentieth century engineer Peter Palchinsky played an important role in introducing more scientific methodology to Russian industry. He believed that Russian engineers were poorly equipped in dealing with challenges in the competitive world because rather than take an adaptive scientific approach to generating solutions, they would view every problem as a technical one and assume that if a proposed solution utilized the latest science and technology it was automatically the best solution. He had observed a number of huge Soviet infrastructure projects go disastrously wrong (like the introduction of large irrigation systems, which contributed towards turning part of the Aral Sea into a desert). In response he introduced three simple rules for industrial design that would enable greater adaptability while mitigating risk:

1 **Variation:** Seek out ideas and try new things.

2 **Survivability:** Where trying something new, do it on a scale where failure is survivable.

3 **Selection:** Seek out feedback and learn from your mistake as you go along.

A good example of Palchinsky's thinking was his reaction to seeing the plans for a huge new hydroelectric dam on the Dnieper River. He recommended that instead of one large dam, a series of smaller dams and coal-fired power plants be built to solve the energy problem in the area. This would enable the engineers to learn from the dams built first and to adapt plant and dam designs to best serve the needs for electricity while also providing water and power control closer to the point of use and limiting the floodplain. The power needs and electrification requirements of the local area would survive abandoning a single small dam. His views were ignored and the huge dam was built near the southern city of Zaporizhzhya. As the project proceeded, it fell behind schedule and vastly exceeded projected costs. Thousands of farmers were forced to abandon their farmland with little or no compensation, and many were forced to work on the project in terrible conditions. In 1941, as Nazi German troops swept through Soviet-era Ukraine, Stalin's secret police blew up the Dnieper Dam, flooding many villages in the banks of the river and killing thousands of civilians.

Unfortunately, Palchinsky and his principles fell increasingly foul of Stalin's preference for huge projects that were controlled centrally from Moscow with little regard for local conditions and where safety was sacrificed at the altar of outputs. Stalin believed that all Soviet industrial and engineering projects should be great in size and perhaps even the biggest in the world (a philosophy that came to be known as 'gigantomania' by the Western observers). This approach led to high accident rates and often to poor-quality production.

Eventually, Palchinsky was arrested and sadly executed in 1929. Yet his principles live on as a reminder of the dangers of 'gigantomania'. Variation, survivability and selection. Always seek out and try new things. Always try new things on a scale where failure is survivable. Always seek feedback and learn from your failures as you go along.

Using review and retrospective

It's important to regularly take a step back from the flow of delivery and work to review progress and consider ways to improve. The review and retrospective are key to this process. In a sprint these will happen at the end of the sprint cycle, but even when teams are working in a continuous flow the principle of scheduling frequent opportunities to review and learn is a good one.

The purpose of a review session is to consider the outputs that the team has achieved in that time period and they can also be useful in updating and getting feedback from stakeholders. It's most productive to keep reviews relatively informal and to demo outputs (in other words, to show the work) rather than produce presentations and reports. Remember, the purpose of the meeting is to consider the outputs from the team and to get inputs from stakeholders, so slide decks and reports are actually not the best way to do this. Far better to actually demonstrate what the team has been working on. Outputs can be assessed against goals that have been set (for example, when working in sprints goals that have been set at the start of the sprint in the sprint planning meeting). The review may also consider any market or customer contexts that may have changed the expectation around the work that has just been completed or that will impact the next reprioritization. Review is also an opportunity to take an inclusive approach with stakeholders, bringing them on the journey and ensuring that there are no nasty surprises. It's important to enable everyone to input to the meeting and having those key stakeholder/s present in the review means that the team can elicit feedback that can inform the reprioritization of the tasks on the backlog.

If the review is primarily focused on the work, then the retrospective is primarily focused on how the team works. It can be tempting for teams to merge review and retrospective sessions in order to save time, but this can often be a mistake. Ensuring separation between the two means that dedicated time is allocated to both and the retrospective, for example, is not squeezed into non-existence or thought of as a luxury. Both the review and the retrospective are opportunities to embed regular alignment and learning into the fabric of how the team is working (as agile scales, so learning scales) and so they are essential elements in the process.

In a retrospective session, the team should reflect on how they have worked as a team, how they worked with other teams, how their process worked and how delivery and outputs can be improved. There are a number of common frameworks for retrospective that are useful, and teams should select one which works best for them. They can use real or virtual white-boards or dot voting to make them more interactive and have something tangible as the basis for discussion. Some of the most common frameworks include:

- Start, Stop, Continue
- Liked, Longed, Lacked, Learned
- Happy, Confused, Sad
- Keep, Add, More, Less

In each case it's helpful to avoid groupthink by allowing individuals to think and input on their own first, before discussing the aggregated feedback. Some retro methods use visuals to help. For example, a 'sailboat retrospec-tive' involves drawing a sailboat, island, wind, rocks and anchor on a whiteboard. Team members individually feed back on the goals (the island), the wind (team), the rocks (risks) and the anchor (constraints) before conducting a teamwide discussion on how to improve. A timeline retrospec-tive can be used to visualize a longer period of work, with team members indicating high points and low points through the project. The key here is for teams to explore different options for how to run their own retro but to land on a method that they feel gives them maximum learning. When running the retrospective it's important to set the right tone and atmosphere in order to encourage open feedback. This means plenty of active listening, taking inputs from everyone and focusing on improvement rather than blame.

The key with both review and with retrospective is to maximize align-ment and learning. The US military have a useful way of framing this as outputs that you should aim for. Their 'after action review'[9] (typically used in post-action debriefs) is focused on answering four key questions:

1 **What did we expect to happen?** Ensuring there is common understanding around objectives, goals and expectations.

2 **What actually happened?** A review of key work, team dynamics, actions, events or challenges conducted in a blameless way.

3 **Why was or wasn't there a difference?** What were the differences (if any) between desired and actual outcomes, and why did this difference occur?

4 **What can you do next time to improve or ensure these results?** What (if anything) are you going to do differently next time? What worked and what needs fixing? What should you do more of/the same/less of?

These questions can be used as a checklist to make sure that you're getting good outputs from the review and retrospective process, whichever framework you select to use. Ensuring alignment around these outputs helps to solidify learning and team understanding but also helps to bring stakeholders on the journey with the team. Many marketing teams are poor at taking time out of the flow of work to think about what they can learn and how they can improve. Embedding this practice into the fabric of how the teams work ensures that the learning and improvement are continuous.

Measures and KPIs

A classic approach to marketing measurement is to use a hierarchical approach that begins with the business objective at the top and sets out a small basket of critical KPIs underneath that can indicate progress towards that overarching goal. These KPIs can in turn be defined by a small number of metrics that ladder up to the broader performance indicator. Setting measures against critical objectives, understanding the relationship between metrics and KPIs and avoiding so-called vanity metrics (high-level metrics that may have significant numbers attached to them but are not real indicators of performance) are all essential here.

In agile marketing measurement and tracking should be embedded into the fabric of how a team works. Each team should have a small, focused number of metrics that align to the mission or objective that the team is aligned to. This ensures that the team is able to progress in a measurable and accountable manner towards their goal but also that they can optimize activity well and easily find what works and what doesn't and use that to inform the next iteration. It can also inform the tests and experiments that the team might undertake to try out new ideas and generate opportunities for delivering the goal in a more efficient or effective way. These metrics provide a guiding path for each team. Amazon used to call these the 'fitness function'. An example of the fitness function may be a small, multidisciplinary team working on customer product recommendations that was evaluated based on the number of customer interactions (clicks on recommended products or four- and five-star against these products) that were stimulated by the actions that the team were taking. Focusing on this, rather than just revenue generated, ensured that the measure applied to a broad set of customers and wasn't skewed by a small number of users.[10] The principle is that each small team is focused on a small basket of focused metrics that are customer focused (wherever possible) but lead to positive business outcomes and aligned with the overarching strategy. Metrics should, of course, reflect the missions and outcomes that the team has been set (for example, a team that is focused on acquisition may track several measures of customer behaviour that all contribute towards that goal).

As a team will need to continually track and optimize against these metrics it's important to provide them with the means to access analytics in real time (via a dashboard for example) so that the team is not held back by dependencies. A slow turnaround time on analytics requests can be one of the key blockers to learning fast so enabling access in real time is critical. Using a small number of metrics rather than a singular measure is more helpful in giving a team a broader perspective on what is working and what's not working, meaning that they can be more informed as they move through the process. A watch out for using singular metrics is Goodhart's Law, which may be expressed as: 'When a measure becomes a target, it ceases to be a good measure'. This is the tendency for people to optimize for that target regardless of the consequences. An overly narrow focus on measures can ironically lead to teams missing opportunities for insight and understanding that will actually help optimize their activity in the best way possible.

Alongside classic marketing and customer-focused measures, it can be useful for agile marketing teams to track several other key metrics that focus more on how the team is working. These include:

- **Velocity of work and throughput:** As discussed earlier in the book, using burndown charts can be a useful way of tracking progress and the speed at which the team is working.

- **Testing frequency:** Looking at the number and regularity of tests and experiments that the team are doing is a good way of tracking whether they are optimizing well or whether there are any blockers to regular testing (for example, technical, time, knowledge).

- **Planned-to-be-done ratio:** This measures the ratio between the number of items that were committed to in a sprint (in the sprint planning process) and the number that were completed at the end. This will help reveal whether a team is overcommitting or has spare capacity.

- **Team engagement:** As I'll discuss later in the book, finding ways to measure the communication norms, staff engagement and happiness in the team is a useful way of optimizing team culture and working.

Using OKRs

It's no mistake that OKRs (or objectives and key results) have become a popular way of connecting team and individual goals among agile teams. Originating in the 1970s, OKRs were later introduced to Google by Intel executive and Google board member John Doerr as a way to help them align organizational objectives with team and individual goals and measurable results as the company scaled. Google still uses OKRs to this day but their application has since broadened across a wider range of technology and digital businesses (including LinkedIn, Twitter and Oracle) and beyond into many other sectors.

Implementing OKRs involves setting a small number of specific, measurable objectives at a company, team and individual level (typically three to five) and then aligning a small basket of quantifiable measures against those objectives. These are usually revised on a quarterly basis to ensure that they are in line with changing needs and are often shared to help both alignment but also empathy and understanding. Being aware of the OKRs of others makes it easier for teams and individuals to find common ground and better understand the priorities of other people in the organization.

There are clear benefits to using OKRs in agile marketing. As mentioned, they support alignment at every level through the organization and the marketing team and provide clear expectations and focus for staff. Revising them every quarter allows a marketing team to be more adaptive to shifting contexts but also to align staff objectives with strategies and plans that may have been derived from QBRs (quarterly business reviews). Strategy therefore links through to execution.

OKRs also drive accountability. Each objective should be stretching but achievable and have perhaps three or four measurable results through which performance can be assessed. Grading may be scored 0–100 or 0–1.0 and

FIGURE 7.8   Cascading OKRs

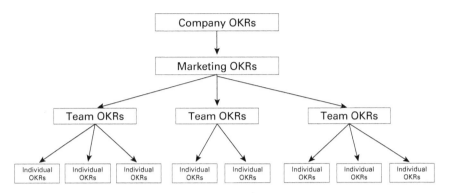

can be updated through the quarter. Scoring should demonstrate that the objectives set were challenging but attainable so a score of 100 per cent might indicate that they were too easy, but a score of 75 per cent may be considered successful. OKRs can be focused on supporting shorter-term objectives or progress towards longer-term goals. Each time they are reviewed the context of the latest known business and marketing strategy and contexts should combine with the development needs of the team or individual.

Endnotes

1 W Gibson (2017) *Burning Chrome*, Gateway, Washington.
2 Cynefin.io. Ritual dissent, November 2021. cynefin.io/wiki/Ritual_dissent (archived at https://perma.cc/VT4F-E4ML)
3 S Brand (March 2000) *Clock Of The Long Now: Time and Responsibility – The Ideas Behind the World's Slowest Computer*, Basic Books, New York.
4 Knowledge at Wharton. Putting a face to a name: The art of motivating employees, 17 February 2010. knowledge.wharton.upenn.edu/article/putting-a-face-to-a-name-the-art-of-motivating-employees/ (archived at https://perma.cc/XK6R-T74E)
5 T Amabile (2011) *The Progress Principle*, Harvard Business Review Press, Boston. progressprinciple.com/books/single/the_progress_principle (archived at https://perma.cc/NXP8-SU74)
6 T Amabile (2011) *The Power of Small Wins*, Harvard Business Review Press, Boston. hbr.org/2011/05/the-power-of-small-wins (archived at https://perma.cc/9H4J-WBVJ)

7 B O'Reilly. How to implement hypothesis-driven development, October 2013. barryoreilly.com/explore/blog/how-to-implement-hypothesis-driven-development/ (archived at https://perma.cc/HZ4Z-R6LU)

8 S Agbaje. 6 lessons from rapid experimentation at the Financial Times, FT Product and Tech, 30 June 2021. medium.com/ft-product-technology/6-lessons-from-rapid-experimentation-at-the-financial-times-19524ea36040 (archived at https://perma.cc/BSC4-QEGC)

9 G Cronin and S Andrews. After action reviews: A new model for learning: Gerard Cronin and Steven Andrews explain why after action reviews are an ideal model for healthcare professionals to analyse and learn from events, *Emergency Nurse*, June 2009, 17, 32–35.

10 J Xavier. How does the team performance metric, or 'fitness function', which translates the business value of the team into a single number & needs to be approved by Jeff Bezos, work at Amazon? Is it still being used? How do teams come up with their functions?, Quora, 2013. www.quora.com/How-does-the-team-performance-metric-or-%E2%80%9Cfitness-function-%E2%80%9D-which-translates-the-business-value-of-the-team-into-a-single-number-needs-to-be-approved-by-Jeff-Bezos-work-at-Amazon-Is-it-still-being-used-How-do-teams-come-up-with-their-functions (archived at https://perma.cc/95QM-3AHK)

PART FOUR

Scaling agile marketing

08

Agile marketing structures

Small, multidisciplinary teams

One of the key tenets of agile marketing is breaking down team and functional silos to capitalize on the many benefits of cross-functional, concurrent working. Driving operational and process efficiencies is often a key motivator here. Many marketing teams are slowed down by multiple hand-offs from discipline to discipline that create cumbersome, linear processes and reduce the ability for adaptability and responding with speed. Bringing functions together to work on problems or objectives simultaneously can not only improve efficiency, but it can also support greater learning and collaboration, improved cognitive diversity, heightened responsiveness and ultimately better outcomes. Research by Alison Reynolds of Ashridge Business School and David Lewis of London Business School has demonstrated the correlation between higher cognitive diversity in teams and team performance and problem-solving ability.[1] The researchers point out the cultural barriers that can arise as people gravitate towards other people who seem to think and express themselves in similar ways. This can easily mean that organizations end up with like-minded teams and that performance suffers. Such functional bias can be a particular problem for teams when they face complex or uncertain situations since a lack of cognitive diversity limits the team's ability to see new possibilities and engage with the problem in different ways.

Richard Hackman, a Professor of Social and Organizational Psychology at Harvard University, has shown in his research that team homogeneity can impact team performance. While it may be tempting to put people together that get along well and have similar views, the research actually shows that creativity and problem-solving is improved by having a diverse mix of people (and even people that have real differences of opinion in how work should be organized and executed). As Hackman says: 'It is task-related conflict, not interpersonal harmony, that spurs team excellence.'[2]

Allied to this principle around cross-functional collaboration is the idea of keeping teams small. This is critical in driving agility and important for a particular reason. Richard Hackman has demonstrated through his research the challenges of trying to move at pace when the team becomes large. As the number of team members increases the communication overhead within the team rises exponentially.[3] A small team of 6 people has 15 links between team members but a team of 12 people has no fewer than 66, and a team of 50 actually has 1,225 links between people to manage.

FIGURE 8.1   The exponential rise in the lines of communication in teams

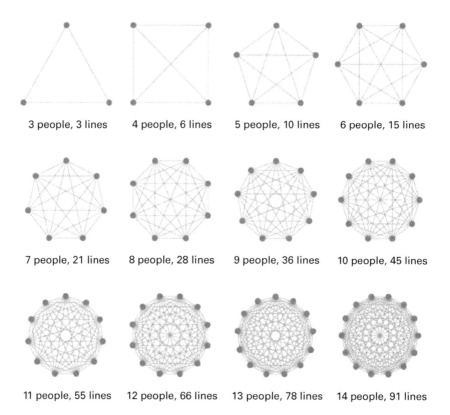

3 people, 3 lines   4 people, 6 lines   5 people, 10 lines   6 people, 15 lines

7 people, 21 lines   8 people, 28 lines   9 people, 36 lines   10 people, 45 lines

11 people, 55 lines   12 people, 66 lines   13 people, 78 lines   14 people, 91 lines

More lines of communication means more emails and status updates that are sent, need to be read and actioned. More emails sent mean more replies sent. As the number of team members grows, people start to lose track of what other people in the team are doing, which results in more status meetings and more catch-ups. More team members means more work to align everyone, more discussion and a high likelihood of slower decision-making. As Hackman says, research shows that 'the number of performance problems a team encounters increases exponentially as team size increases'.[4]

That's not all. Research by James Evans of the University of Chicago and Dashun Wang, Associate Professor at the Kellogg School of Management, has shown how good small teams are at originating new ideas.[5] The research, based on an analysis of millions of science and technology papers, projects and patents, revealed that while large teams more often develop and consolidate existing knowledge, small teams are far more likely to come up with new and breakthrough ideas. Says Evans:

> Big teams are almost always more conservative. The work they produce is like blockbuster sequels; very reactive and low-risk.[6]

Amazon's 'two-pizza teams' concept famously expresses how teams in the company should get no larger than the number of people it takes to feed with two large pizzas (six to eight people). Many teams have ownership over an end-to-end customer experience, are equipped with the resources they need to develop, test and iterate without significant dependencies, thereby pushing ownership and decision-making down to the team level. The teams are accountable for a clear set of customer-focused KPIs and are able to develop solutions without the need to solve problems across multiple lines of business.

It becomes habitual in many large organizations for project teams to grow beyond the number of people that can reasonably work and collaborate at speed. It can be tempting to include people or functions because they may be needed at some point or to fulfil an internal political need. Yet every additional person in the team has the potential to slow it down and make it less manoeuvrable, so it's wise to keep teams to less than 10 people and to think carefully about who is in the team and who is not. Small, cross-functional teams, empowered by technology, can achieve great things. They are the engine behind agile marketing.

Squad roles and responsibilities

A key part of scaling agile marketing is to establish a common approach to defining roles within the small, multidisciplinary squads. This will likely be informed by the context of your organization, the strategy and jobs that the squads need to achieve in order to deliver against customer and business needs. There are, however, some key principles to follow here that are relevant for most contexts and some common key team roles that are essential to agile working.

Squad lead

It's important to have someone in the team that is taking the lead on the work that is being delivered. This role is akin to the product owner role that is often seen in agile product teams and teams that are operating using Scrum methodologies. The *Scrum Guide*, by Jeff Sutherland and Ken Schwaber, defines a product owner as 'accountable for maximizing the value of the product resulting from the work of the Scrum Team'.[7] This involves developing and articulating the product goal, generating, prioritizing and communicating the product backlog items and ensuring that the backlog is visible to both key stakeholders and the team. In agile marketing, the squad lead is a pivotal member of the team and plays a critical role in team success, taking responsibility for some key areas.

FIGURE 8.2   Accountabilities of the squad lead

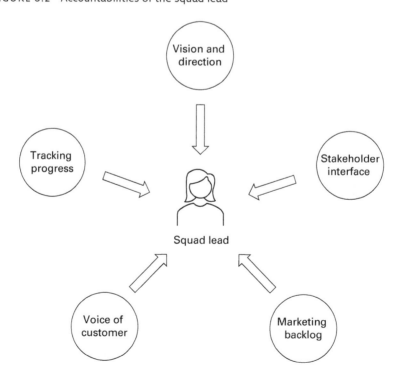

Key responsibilities of this role are:

- **Setting the direction:** A key part of this role is developing and communicating the goals and vision that the team is working towards. Ultimately, the squad lead is accountable for translating wider marketing goals and strategies, and business requirements into specific tasks that might be placed on the backlog.

- **Liaising with marketing and business stakeholders:** The squad lead will be the key route for stakeholder input to the team. While stakeholders may need to speak to individual members of the delivery team, the squad lead brings a degree of protection for the team, shielding them from short-term stakeholder demands and ensuring that inputs are prioritized in the right way. This can be helpful in giving the delivery team the space and focus that they need to progress with the tasks that they have taken responsibility for delivering. They will also be the key conduit through which stakeholders can understand what the team is working on and what outputs and value they are creating. The squad lead may need to work with other squad leads (and key stakeholders) to mitigate dependencies and share learning about customer inputs and optimal ways of working.

- **Overseeing and prioritizing the marketing backlog:** The importance of the backlog means that this is a key accountability for this role. The squad lead should be responsible for ensuring that the backlog is regularly reprioritized and that necessary inputs that can support effective prioritization balancing customer and business needs are accommodated. In addition to this, the squad lead will likely play a key role in juggling the scope of tasks being undertaken with resourcing and budget considerations. They will also need to balance these with time to ensure that the team are delivering outputs in a timely manner.

- **Understanding and articulating the needs of customers:** While the wider marketing strategy might be born of the opportunity to serve business and customer objectives better, the squad lead is responsible for bringing customer understanding into the work that the team is undertaking and the prioritization of tasks on the backlog. This doesn't mean that the squad lead should be directly responsible for drawing in inputs from data and analytics (an agile marketing team will often have an analyst or data specialist as part of the delivery team that can do this), but they should be using all inputs to understand customer needs, bringing that understanding into the team conversation and reflecting those needs in the work that the team does.

- **Evaluating progress:** The squad lead should also be tracking the progress of the work that is being done and ensuring that the team is on course to deliver the outputs that they have been tasked with achieving. This may mean working with the scrum master to remove impediments to progress, but it will also likely mean using tools such as burn-down charts to monitor pace of work and outputs.

The squad lead requires a broad set of skills including strategic competencies, good market understanding and analysis, strong project management capabilities, great communication skills and the ability to appreciate and articulate customer needs. They are a real lynchpin in the team since they bring together business and marketing strategy with customer needs and insights and take accountability for the work that the team is doing.

Scrum master

Just as it is essential to have one team member taking overall responsibility for the work that is being delivered, it is just as important to have one person in the team that is focused on how the team themselves are working.

FIGURE 8.3   Accountabilities of the scrum master

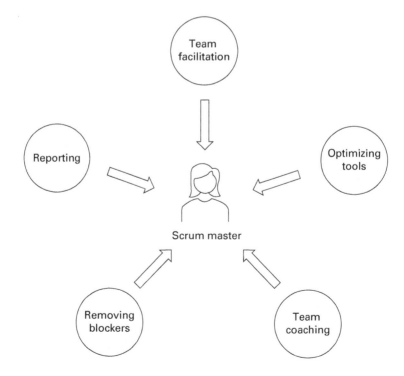

The *Scrum Guide* defines this role as being accountable for the team's effectiveness and ensuring that the team can continuously improve their working practices.[8] This might involve coaching the team to make sure that they are working in optimal ways and retaining and optimizing agile tools and methods. It may also mean helping the team to remove blockers to progress, to ensure that they are working on high value tasks and helping to run team ceremonies and events to support productive outputs.

The key responsibilities of this role in agile marketing are therefore:

- **Meeting and team facilitation:** This person plays a key role in hosting ceremonies such as daily stand ups to ensure that the outputs are as productive as possible. They should also work to support optimal communication among the team.

- **Tool maintenance:** Making sure that the tools that the team are using (including agile project management tools) are optimized for the requirements that they have and that the team are using the tools in the optimal way.

- **Coaching team members:** This is important at a one-on-one level and also at a wider team and organization level. The scrum masters are agile specialists and can act as advocates for the methodology, but they can also make sure that the team is not drifting away from core agile principles and back into linear thinking. They can also play a role teaching agile.

- **Removing roadblocks:** Alongside the squad lead the scrum master can play a role in removing impediments to progress that the team face. Part of this may include protecting the team from outside interference (for example, making sure stakeholder feedback is channelled through the appropriate roles).

- **Reporting:** Creating burn-down charts and ways of tracking work velocity. While the squad lead is ultimately responsible for monitoring the work, the scrum master may support this process by providing the data and reporting that shows the outputs.

The scrum master draws a lot on people focused skills including facilitation and coaching but is also a strong communicator and proficient in agile techniques and principles. They can play a key role acting as an agile champion and advocate within the wider marketing team and business.

The delivery team

One of the key decision areas in setting up agile marketing teams is team composition. It's important that the business defines a common approach to deciding which roles will be core across all teams and where a degree of flexibility may be needed. Roles such as squad lead and scrum master will likely be a key part of every team. Similarly, there may be other key roles such as delivery managers or data and analytics inputs that might be common. The key strategy here is to define team composition based on the job-to-be-done for each team. Each squad should have within it the critical skills and roles that are needed to achieve the outcomes required. Yet it is also important to keep the core team small, which means making smart decisions about who is in the core team and who is set up in a supporting role.

FIGURE 8.4   Example team composition

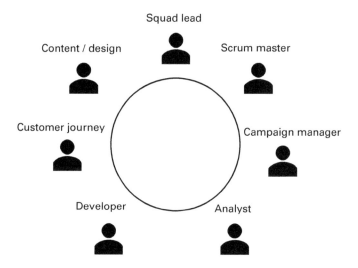

Key roles that might be included within agile marketing teams include:

- **Delivery or campaign manager:** While the squad lead is responsible for the work that the team is doing and for liaising with key stakeholders, agile marketing teams may require additional resources focused on campaign or executional delivery. This role may be dedicated to ensuring that the work that the team is producing is delivered in the optimal way and that campaign and marketing activity is tracked, optimized and reported on. It's likely that this role would work closely with the squad lead, scrum master and analytics resource.

- **Conversion rate optimization specialist:** Where conversion is the key goal or where teams are aligned around customer journeys that have conversion as an essential component a specialist may be required.
- **Data and analytics:** The team will likely need analytics inputs. Where these are required frequently it may be sensible to have analysts as core members of the squad.
- **Customer journey:** Where teams are aligned to customer need states or journeys it can be useful to have one person focused on optimizing the customer journey.
- **Content marketing:** Depending on the requirements for content, it may be useful to have a dedicated content role within the team. This can help the team create, deliver, adapt and post content assets rapidly as required. A common alternative to this however, is to enable the team to draw on content expertise via a content centre of excellence.
- **Developers:** Where squads require frequent changes to be made to sites or apps it can help to have technical expertise embedded.
- **Compliance:** Where this needs to be an integrated part of the process (for example, in highly regulated industries) having compliance as an embedded part of the core team can be useful.

Having functional expertise embedded within the squads can minimize dependencies and ensure that teams can deliver rapidly. Having functional expertise brought together into a team 'centre of excellence' that squads can draw on as and when required can make it easier to drive functional quality, shared best practice and discipline learning. This is a balance that will be dependent on the unique contexts of the business and marketing team and the work that needs to be done. The key is to resource and structure teams in ways that can support continuous delivery while maximizing quality and learning, and mitigating barriers to moving fast.

Establishing 'centres of excellence'

In a scaled application of agile marketing multiple squads may be aligned to customer need states or journeys or other business-focused domains. Many of these squads may need to draw on expertise that is not required frequently enough for that expertise to be embedded permanently within the team. At the same time, cross-team channel coordination may be required when multiple teams are deploying activity continuously. An example of this might be where a number of teams are utilizing the CRM system to send out emails or other communications. There is a cross-team need to coordinate the communications that are going out to ensure that individual prospects or customers are not being over-communicated to or that there are multiple messages that might overlap.

In this case, establishing 'centres of excellence' can support good cross-team coordination while also enabling the level of autonomy that teams need to move fast. Centres of excellence can take different forms. It may be that a single functional specialist can play a cross-team role in coordinating channel activity. In my CRM example above this might mean that a single 'Head of CRM' can act as a discipline centre of excellence. Their role would be to coordinate activity from teams at the channel level, act as champion for the channel and a source of functional expertise and advice. It would drive cross-team excellence in execution, ensuring that the teams are getting the most out of the tools and driving continuous improvement in functional capability. They might also be required to make recommendations around how channel effectiveness and efficiency can be improved. It's important that when setting up a centre of excellence in this way, a team is not creating bottlenecks in process or dependencies that will slow execution. Workflow mapping (discussed later in this section) can help here, but there should be a conscious effort to set up coordination and excellence roles like this in ways that don't slow teams down.

The other type of 'centre of excellence' brings together functional expertise and capability into a team that provides capability and services that multiple squads can draw on. An example of this might be an in-house content team or other key areas of capability such as data and analytics, technical, design, SEO, PPC and social media. Creating a scaled centre of excellence in this way can support functional excellence and efficiencies. If, for example, the marketing team requires a significant volume of content or design inputs delivered in a timely manner, it can make more sense to bring together content marketers, producers and designers into a single team, which can then act as a service centre for delivering to the requirements of multiple squads. The important consideration here is again how the team and working processes can be set up in ways that don't create bottlenecks or dependencies that will slow the squad's progress.

Both individual and team centres of excellence are ways of ensuring a good balance between squad delivery and execution, and horizontal expertise, coordination and capability.

Endnotes

1 A Reynolds and D Lewis. Teams solve problems better when they're more cognitively diverse, *Harvard Business Review*, 30 March 2017. hbr.org/2017/03/teams-solve-problems-faster-when-theyre-more-cognitively-diverse (archived at https://perma.cc/Q6B8-Y4PV)

2 Harvard Business School. Working knowledge, leading teams: Setting the stage for great performances – the five keys to successful teams, July 2002. hbswk.hbs.edu/archive/leading-teams-setting-the-stage-for-great-performances-the-five-keys-to-successful-teams (archived at https://perma.cc/EBF8-KASK)

3 D M Messick and R M Kramer (2004) *The Psychology of Leadership: New Perspectives and Research*, Psychology Press, New York.

4 Harvard Business School. Working knowledge, leading teams: Setting the stage for great performances – the five keys to successful teams, July 2002. hbswk.hbs.edu/archive/leading-teams-setting-the-stage-for-great-performances-the-five-keys-to-successful-teams (archived at https://perma.cc/EBF8-KASK)

5 D Wang and J A Evans, Research: When small teams are better than big ones, *Harvard Business Review*, 21 February 2019. hbr.org/2019/02/research-when-small-teams-are-better-than-big-ones (archived at https://perma.cc/PJP4-CMJR)

6 D Wang and J A Evans. Research: When small teams are better than big ones, *Harvard Business Review*, 21 February 2019. hbr.org/2019/02/research-when-small-teams-are-better-than-big-ones (archived at https://perma.cc/PJP4-CMJR)

7 J Sutherland and K n Schwaber, Scrum guide, 2020. scrumguides.org/ (archived at https://perma.cc/8BCB-949H)

8 J Sutherland and K Schwaber, The 2020 scrum guide, 2020. scrumguides.org/scrum-guide.html#scrum-master (archived at https://perma.cc/HTJ2-M85D)

09

Agile marketing at scale

Aligned autonomy – governance, oversight and empowerment

Harvard professor J Richard Hackman has studied teams across multiple industries and contexts to define the critical characteristics of effective groups and what separates a real team from a 'co-acting' group of people. His 'five factor' model, based on his research, sets out a number of attributes that demonstrate the twin needs for both a clear direction and a healthy sense of autonomy:[1]

> Setting good direction for a team means being authoritative and insistent about desired end-states, but being equally insistent about not specifying how the team should go about achieving those end-states.[2]

1 **Being a real team:** Hackman mentions several criteria here including the team having a shared task, clear boundaries on who is in the team and who is not and the stability of the membership. The last point is the hardest for leaders to directly control, but in project-based teams this would relate to stability over the course of that project.

2 **Compelling direction:** The team need to have clarity on direction and goals that are challenging and meaningful (SMART – specific, measurable, achievable, relevant, time-bound).

3 **Enabling structure:** How a team is organized has a clear impact on effectiveness. This means keeping the team to a manageable size (small teams, not in double digits in terms of size, are most effective), making sure that key members have good social skills and can support good team behavioural norms and enable everyone to contribute.

4 **Supportive context:** As smaller groups are brought together across the wider team it's important to link reward to team performance and

cooperation, to enable individual development and learning, empower autonomy to work within established boundaries and to facilitate ease of access to necessary materials and data to develop and apply skills.

5 **Expert coaching:** This may happen through day-to-day interaction or more formalized intervention.

I'll discuss many of these characteristics in more detail later in the book when I consider how to empower high-performing agile marketing teams, but there are some clear themes emerging from Hackman's work, notably around the need to balance clear direction and alignment with supportive contexts and autonomy. Both of these attributes are essential in scaling agile ways of working.

Greater autonomy brings empowered decision-making into the team environment, which enables a team to move fast and be responsive and nimble to latest inputs and changing contexts. An overly hierarchical approach where leaders feel the need to approve every move or to make

FIGURE 9.1   Aligned autonomy

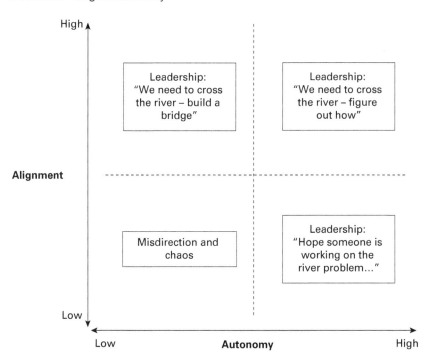

Adapted from Spotify's 'aligned autonomy', Spotify Engineering Culture Part 1, March 2014. labs.spotify.com/2014/03/27/spotify-engineering-culture-part-1/

decisions on behalf of the team will inevitably slow everything down. Taking an approach that distributes authority more widely, while also ensuring clear direction, boundaries, an inspiring vision combined with good cross-team alignment creates a truly effective balance.

Spotify's concept of 'aligned autonomy' (shown in Figure 9.1) articulates this balance well. For agile marketing this means a number of important strategies for leaders:

- **Autonomy:** Set clear boundaries for the territory and domains that teams will take ownership of, encourage ownership of the decisions within this territory and equip the team with the tools, inputs and permissions necessary to move fast.

- **Alignment:** Ensure that the marketing strategy (and wider business strategy) is well understood and that teams are all aligned around a clear focus that ties into this strategy in meaningful ways. Mitigate dependencies wherever possible. Bake quality assurance, governance and clear metrics into agile processes to empower accountability.

Too much autonomy and not enough vision and guidance will lead to teams going in different directions and missed opportunities. Too much alignment and not enough empowerment leads to top-down, overly hierarchical, slow decision-making. Getting the balance right is critical for agile marketing practice.

Scaling squads

When agile marketing teams deploy a scaled application of small, multidisciplinary squads it's important to consider how the team can be structured in ways that enable autonomy for individual squads but also coordination of work and alignment across the whole team. Agile marketing leaders should appreciate that there is no single approach to structuring that is right. As with methodology, every team has its unique contexts, which means that no two agile marketing structures will look exactly the same and it's important for teams to find the approach that works best for them. There are, however, a number of key principles that are useful and pragmatic to apply.

The 'squads, chapters and tribes' model that originated from Spotify has become a popular approach and is based on grouping squads together into defined 'tribes', horizontal functional 'chapters' and looser, more informal 'guilds':[3]

- **Squads:** These are the basic unit of delivery and are small, multidisciplinary teams of no more than 10 people. Squads are aligned around focused

KPIs (often customer-related metrics), work iteratively in sprints to deliver continuous value and comprise the key competencies needed to deliver the outcomes set. In the Spotify model product owners play a key role in representing customer and business needs and focusing on the work that the team are delivering, but in an agile marketing environment this function may be fulfilled by a squad lead.

- **Tribes:** Squads are grouped together into tribes, which might be related to specific business or product areas. There should be a maximum of 150 people in a tribe to ensure ease of communication and coordination. The tribe leader plays a key role in that coordination of work across the squads and with other tribes. They manage resourcing across the squads, help unblock barriers to progress, mitigate dependencies and ensure alignment to deliver the wider objectives, priorities and strategy.

- **Chapters and guilds:** These help squads to form horizontal links to facilitate functional best practice and enable wider inter-team knowledge sharing. Chapters bring together functional experts in the squads who work in similar areas within the tribes. The chapter lead is likely to be the line manager for other functional experts in that tribe but is also a squad member themselves. They take responsibility for people development and performance reviews, and facilitate functional gatherings that can share learning and best practice. The guilds are looser and broader communities of practice or interest. These can go across the wider team or even broader across the whole organization as a way of bringing together communities and groups that can share knowledge and learning.

FIGURE 9.2   Squads, chapters and tribes

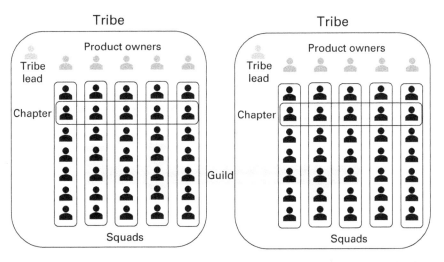

Inspired by: Henrik Kniberg and Anders Ivarsson, October 2012, Scaling Agile @ Spotify, with Tribes, Squads, Chapters and Guilds. blog.crisp.se/wp-content/uploads/2012/11/SpotifyScaling.pdf

ING'S AGILE TRANSFORMATION

ING Bank is one example of a broad, scaled application of this model. They have embarked on a multi-year journey involving the reorganization of 3,500 staff in their group headquarters in the Netherlands away from functional silos into around 350 nine-person squads and 13 tribes.[4] The squads have clear end-to-end responsibility for particular areas of focus and operate with relative autonomy within clearly aligned missions and boundaries. Chapters run across squads and bring together functional expertise. Tribe leads oversee coordination of work, budgets and group priorities as well as interfacing with other tribe leads.

Sensibly, there was a staged approach to the reorganization and ING have continued to iterate their model over the years to ensure that it is optimized for customer and business value. They focused on enabling factors for the teams including more frequent release cycles and an agile performance management model, which aligns rewards more towards outputs and knowledge rather than just quantity of resource. While the restructure was a scaled approach, some areas of the business (including functions such as HR, finance and call centres) remained structured in more traditional ways but adopted agile mindsets to support change.

Time and energy were spent on building the knowledge, culture and mindset (including customer-centricity, empathy and ownership) to enable the shift. An example of this was how, as part of the onboarding process, every staff member moves around teams to build informal networks and knowledge but also spends a week in the customer call centre. Squad meetings are informal, and each squad has a clear, written mission to guide the work and the autonomy to prioritize daily activities. Quarterly business reviews (QBRs) are where each tribe shares their achievements, biggest learning objectives for the next quarter and what's required from other tribes.

This new structure has dramatically improved the bank's speed-to-market and rate of innovation and positioned them well as the primary mobile bank in the Netherlands.

The squads, chapters, tribes model provides a scaled approach to agile that is weighted towards delivery and customer value, but it is not a one-size-fits all solution. Marketers should avoid simply copying and pasting this approach to their own teams, but there are some essential principles at the heart of it that are useful to apply in scaled structures:

- **Small, multidisciplinary squads are the unit of delivery:** Don't be tempted to expand teams beyond 10 people. Customer-back approaches should be baked in to how the teams work and deliver value. This ensures genuinely customer-centric mindsets and working. The squad lead plays an essential role in overseeing the work and outputs of the team, providing a connection to other squads, groups and the rest of the business.

- **Squads should be grouped together into logical areas:** Grouping squads enables better coordination of work, avoids duplication and helps mitigate dependencies. Examples of group alignment may be customer need state, discrete audiences, stages in the customer journey or business and product area. These squad groups may comprise only a few teams, but no group should get larger than 150 people. Evolutionary anthropologist Robin Dunbar has posited that cognitive limitations mean that this is the maximum number of people with whom we can maintain stable, meaningful social relationships.[5]

- **Fix and flex:** It's useful to have persistent teams that are consistently focused on generating value in one area of focus but also to balance this (wherever possible given the size of the team and resourcing constraints) with the ability to spin up project teams as required to 'swarm' a particular challenge. This requires a higher degree of resourcing flexibility than is typical in marketing teams, which in turn requires careful oversight and coordination, and mindset change and support for staff. Over time it may also be helpful to swap individuals in and out of teams as required to refocus expertise as requirements and challenges evolve and also to enable staff development and shared learning.

- **Catalyse functional learning:** The scaled application of squads is all about breaking down functional silos and enabling disciplines to work together more concurrently to deliver regular value. The primary orientation of people working within a squad (whether that squad is aligned to customer or business needs) should be the squad itself. Yet there is still benefit in bringing together functional expertise in ways that can support learning, help coordinate cross-team activity (for example, around a particular channel) and improve functional best practice and shared learning. It's sensible therefore to establish mechanisms that can support this as agile structures scale. In teams where a large number of squads are grouped together, a 'chapters' approach can bring together functional experts within a group. In a smaller marketing team where there are fewer squads grouped together it is likely better to enable this horizontal functional connection across multiple squad groups. This might be through a 'communities of practice' approach that I discuss later in the book where specialists in one discipline can come together regularly in formal and informal ways to share learning and best practice. Establishing centres of excellence (which may comprise a single person or a small team) focused around channels or specific areas of expertise can also support good coordination.

• **Oversight and coordination:** In a scaled approach ensuring alignment, reducing cross-team and group duplication, and mitigating dependencies are essential to success. I'll discuss specific strategies to support this later in this chapter but the group lead and establishing good oversight at a senior level (for example via the 'mission control' approach that is described later) play a key role in enabling this. Leaders need to consider how their approach can take account of this essential need.

• **Link to the rest of the business:** As well as establishing good horizontal links between squads (via functional chapters, communities of practice or centres of excellence) and good oversight from marketing leadership, it's likely that teams will benefit from establishing productive relationships with key functions or areas of the business that sit outside of marketing. A group lead may play a key role in establishing those links (particularly more formal ones that are essential to team outputs) and acting as a channel to unblock barriers or source inputs that teams within the group need. It may also be necessary though for individual squad leads to establish relationships with key business functions to facilitate team working. An example of this may be product expertise. With the blurring of the lines between product and marketing, squads may have product marketers as permanent members of the team that provide a clear link between marketing and product. It's likely though that to do their job well, product marketers will need to work closely with product managers or relevant business stakeholders that are outside of the marketing team. The primary orientation of the squad is to their own goals that align to the marketing strategy, but establishing good relationships with key business partners helps everyone to win.

AGILE MARKETING STRUCTURES

As previously mentioned, there is no single blueprint. However, an example agile marketing team structure may look something like Figure 9.3.

This example structure features a number of key defining attributes:

- **Squads:** Multiple squads are grouped together around common areas of alignment (customer need state, customer journey stage, product or business focus). Each squad has its defined mission and associated KPIs, and a squad lead.

- **Squad groups:** Groups are overseen by a group lead whose job it is to coordinate activity within the group and with other groups.

- **Project teams:** Several project teams have been spun up to work on specific challenges (for example, innovation, a specific competitive challenge, a strategic need or a major campaign). These projects are overseen by a project lead.

- **Functional expertise:** This is brought together horizontally in chapters or communities of practice, which may well work with centres of excellence.

- **Centres of excellence:** These may be teams. An example here could be analytics experts that are embedded in squads working as part of a community of practice with a data and analytics functional support team. Or it might be an insight team that is providing a service across multiple teams. Equally, a CoE might be individuals. An example here may be squad members that are responsible for channel coordination across the team. For example, CRM squad members may work with a head of CRM who coordinates activity and capability across the channel for the wider team. There may be multiple coordinating CoE roles across different channels (for example, paid search, SEO, programmatic and content), but these individuals are embedded squad members.

- **Mission control:** The groups, projects and functional support teams are overseen by a mission control that comprises a small number of key senior marketing stakeholders.

This approach to agile marketing structures enables a squad approach to scale while still enabling effective coordination of activity and delivery of the strategy across the team. The squad structure ensures that customer-centricity is baked into resourcing and alignment as well as ways of working. It breaks down

FIGURE 9.3 Example agile marketing structure

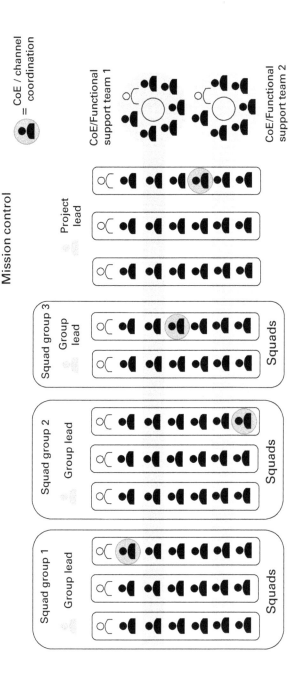

functional silos and enables much more concurrent, efficient working practices that avoid cumbersome hand-offs. Centres of excellence and functional support teams allow for effective channel and horizontal coordination as well as good shared learning and best practices.

In an agile marketing transformation it's likely that teams will not get their organizational design entirely correct at the first pass. It is important for marketing teams to appreciate the need to iterate, evolve and learn in their transformation process in order to continuously improve and find the optimal structure for their own contexts. In other words, agile marketing teams need to 'be agile' about how they implement agile. Teams should never stop evolving how they are structured to solve the challenges and objectives that they are tasked with.

Mitigating dependencies

As agile practice scales, different types of dependencies can become a real barrier to teams moving fast. In fact, if not dealt with, dependencies can potentially derail an entire implementation of agile ways of working, so it is essential to manage and mitigate them. Agile squads will inevitably require inputs from outside of the team at various stages of their work and so it's critical to set teams up in a way that enables them to get these inputs in a timely and usable way. Failure to do this can easily result in teams becoming blocked or stalled. These challenges can be amplified when agile squads face into areas of the business that are not agile. In this instance they can find that the other areas are working to a very different cadence or are using linear processes that require sign-offs or other inputs that take time to acquire.

So what are the strategies for mitigating dependencies? It's important that senior stakeholders consider upfront how they can set the teams up in ways that can minimize these challenges, and then accept that there will be a learning process involved with navigating through dependency challenges. There are several key strategies that leaders and teams can use.

Workflow mapping

Mapping workflows is an essential tool to use upfront in order to understand how the agile marketing process will actually work in practice or how a team can improve it. Mapping processes and the flow of work can create a visual representation of all the key tasks, decisions and actions that are undertaken in order to achieve particular outputs or outcomes. There are a number of key watch outs for doing process mapping well:

- Maps should be as comprehensive as possible, incorporating all the elements that are critical to getting the work done but without over-complicating with contexts that are infrequent or not related to the reality of what happens.

- It's helpful to focus on the system or process elements (such as the teams or inputs) rather than the people involved. The mapping should be done in a collaborative, open way and where possible with the people actually involved in the process.

- Defining the start and end point before you start helps to ensure clarity on the scope.

- Before you start, consider all the information that you'll need to inform the exercise and have that available.

- The use of commonly used symbols on the map can help avoid misunderstanding. For example, a process map is often shown as a flow diagram with ovals illustrating the start and end of a process, rectangles showing key actions or instructions, diamonds representing key decisions and arrows indicating the direction of progress.

FIGURE 9.4   A simple workflow map example

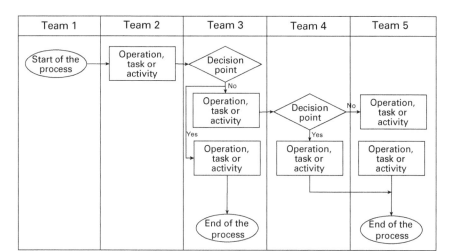

Workflow mapping enables teams to visualize processes and focus on areas of inefficiency. They can be used to help improve and bring greater agility to current processes as well as set agile marketing teams up for success. When introducing agile ways of working into marketing teams, it can be particularly useful to map existing workflows and then to map an ideal agile workflow in order to compare and identify potential blockers and challenges.

- **Mapping existing workflows:** Before an agile implementation begins, creating a process map for how campaigns and other relevant marketing activity gets done enables the team to understand and visualize the flow of work in its current state. This allows for a better awareness of inefficiencies, perhaps through multiple hand-offs or overburdensome authorizations.

- **Mapping agile workflows:** When setting agile teams up, mapping out an ideal workflow enables the opportunity to gain common understanding on how work will get executed and also the identification of process blockers. The opportunity here is to identify likely dependencies and to take steps to mitigate them before the team starts the work. When teams are already working agile, workflow mapping can similarly enable them to improve the flow and identify regular challenges that are arising and that are a potential barrier to moving fast in the course of daily operations. It can therefore be a useful tool for continuous improvement.

Dependency types

It's important for stakeholders and teams alike to understand the different types of dependency that might arise so that they can better determine how to deal with it. This may relate to something as simple as insight or data inputs that are needed from another team at a particular point or a sign-off that is required from a stakeholder, but delays in getting these inputs can stall progress for a team and even bring them to a complete halt. The most common types of dependency include:

- **Process or activity:** This may relate to specific activities that are required to be done outside of the team in order for progress to be made. Or it could well result from business processes in the wider organization that are moving at a different cadence. For example, if an agile team need rapid inputs from the finance or compliance team but the typical response cycles are too slow or the processes themselves are not aligned to agile ways of working.

- **Expertise or input:** In this instance, specific external inputs or expertise may be required at distinct points, or on a more ad-hoc basis, but the inability to get this acts as a brake on momentum. An example of this could be approvals that are needed or when domain expertise that sits external to the agile team is required to help the team make informed decisions.

- **Technical:** When an agile team requires technical inputs or changes in order to complete a task this can also create dependencies, particularly when they struggle to get these prioritized with other teams.

In short, anything that is beyond the direct control of the agile team is a potential dependency that can derail a team's progress so it is essential that when setting teams up senior leaders take steps to put in place working practices that can prevent them from becoming an existential barrier for the team. One of the considerations here could be to look at the frequency with which the dependencies are occurring. Those that are ongoing (happening consistently and often) or that are driven by particular processes or schedules are clearly a higher priority to avoid than those which might be a one-off. Considering the frequency of occurrence can also help to inform which strategies can be deployed for mitigation. These strategies include:

- **Establishing 'collaborators' or 'point people' within connected teams:** In the next section we'll look at a model for a scaled approach to agile resourcing, which involves setting up collaborators within teams that typically have a higher frequency of inputs than are required. For example, analytics inputs and expertise will likely be required at regular intervals during the team's work and if that capability or access is not sat within the agile team it can easily become a dependency. Having a point person within the analytics team that is allocated to pick up requests from the agile team and that is working to agreed response times or service level agreements (SLAs) helps to minimize the risk of the team becoming stalled.

- **Standardization or automation:** This can help establish common approaches to avoiding or compensating for potential blockers to progress. Automation can ensure that a team is able to access key inputs for example, without the need for human intervention.

- **Preparation:** Identifying in advance everything that the team will need in order to achieve the outcome that they are tasked with can help them plan for dependency risks. It's important here that the team is aware of any assumptions that have been made as these can hide potential risk. Tracking the flow of work can help identify when dependencies are slowing the team down. Making known dependencies or assumptions visible on the project management tool that the team is using ensures that they are identifiable.

- **Retrospective:** Doing regular retrospectives can help identify commonly occurring challenges and enable the team to discuss ideas for solving them. Doing less frequent but regular retrospective with other teams (for example, doing quarterly retros with high-contact teams which are required often for inputs) can help establish improved collaboration and better ways of working.

- **DIY:** While it may not always be possible or advisable, the team may find that they can take action themselves to complete the task required. The watch-out here is obviously around ensuring that the team are not stepping beyond the realms of their expertise and authority in ways that generate unnecessary risk. They may also find that with one-off dependencies they are able to defer taking a task into the current workflow until the dependency is resolved.

There is a clear role for senior leaders here in setting up teams in ways that enable them to move forwards at pace and in helping to compensate for dependencies that arise in the flow of work. There is also a clear role for the team in doing everything that they can to establish working relationships and practices that don't slow them down. Ultimately, the team needs to be able to move forwards with confidence that they can complete their tasks in the time that has been specified.

Setting up 'agile team onions'

Teams can easily be susceptible to a kind of 'planning fallacy' or tendency to overestimate team capability and underestimate task completion time. It's therefore important to test and learn, and adapt structures and team composition accordingly. Yet there are also some key principles that are important to remember when designing resourcing. Agile marketing teams need to be kept small. As I discussed earlier in this section, a maximum team size of six to eight people helps ensure that a team can always move fast. This maintains efficiency of working, alignment to outcomes, keeps teams connected with each other and the work, and reduces relational loss (the feeling that it is difficult to get support in large teams). Small, empowered teams can achieve great things when they have access to the right tools and right ways of working.

There are, however, inevitably going to be inputs that will be required from other specialists and functions as the team progresses. These inputs may be needed infrequently, episodically or at key times in the delivery process. Examples may include HR policies, finance information or legal and compliance contributions or advice. These can all create dependencies that can slow teams down. In this case it may not be necessary to have this expertise positioned as a key part of the core team, but instead to set it up in a way that enables inputs to be sourced in a timely manner if and when the team needs them.

Agile team onions, a model originated by Agile practitioner Emily Webber, is a way of understanding how resourcing can be organized to minimize dependencies and enable core teams to be kept small.[6]

The onion is classified into the core team, 'collaborators' and 'supporters':

- **Core team:** The small, multidisciplinary squad that is responsible for delivering to the agreed outcomes. This team will be working concurrently.

- **Collaborators:** Working in teams or functions that may be required to contribute inputs to squads on an ongoing but potentially infrequent or irregular basis. Here it is important to establish 'point people' within the relevant areas that can work with a squad (and potentially multiple squads) to provide timely inputs as required. SLAs of more informal

FIGURE 9.5   Agile team onions

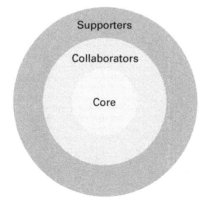

agreements about response times and the nature of requests can be help-ful to prevent input dependencies and bottlenecks. If collaborators are working more frequently with individual squads, they may attend agile meetings and even work alongside them for periods of time, but they are not part of the core team.

- **Supporters:** These are the key stakeholders that maintain alignment across multiple teams, help remove blockers to progress where necessary and feed business and marketing priorities and strategy into the squad lead. They may interface with the team during review or demo and ad hoc as and when needed, but the squad lead is the point of contact through which this input flows.

A marketing team may have multiple agile squads, supported by a cohort of collaborators from key functional areas and disciplines. Collaborators may be set up to work with a number of squads concurrently. A small group of supporters can be established to help ensure alignment across all squads and collaborators. This means that an agile marketing team may consist of over-lapping team onions.

Team onions are a key way to manage and mitigate dependencies across multiple squads. In this way, scale can be achieved while keeping agile teams small and nimble, maintaining momentum and preventing too many impediments to progress.

FIGURE 9.6   Scaling team onions

Creating a 'mission control'

The more that agile marketing squads are scaled, the more important alignment becomes. It's critical that there is a clear connection between senior stakeholders, marketing and business strategy, required high-level outcomes and the work that the teams are doing. This connection should go both ways. Senior stakeholders need to make sure that the squads are aligned to achieving goals. They need to be briefing them on key requirements and strategy. They need to have clear oversight over the work. This governance does not mean, however, that leaders need to be in the detail of decision-making on behalf of the team. It's therefore essential that stakeholders and leaders are kept informed about progress, blockers and bottlenecks, and the key activities of the squads. This may well happen via review and demonstration, where the teams are showing the work that they have done. Or it may be useful to establish regular forums that bring squad leads from multiple teams together with stakeholders to review and align on a regular basis.

The key connection point here is between the squad leads and what is often a small group of stakeholders that might be called a 'mission control'. If each squad has its own defined mission, the role of mission control is to support, align and enable. These bodies should be a small group of relevant stakeholders drawn from key areas of the business. An example mission control may be a small cohort of senior stakeholders from the marketing team (the CMO and a couple of other key roles) or may even comprise the CMO and key stakeholders from other aligned areas of the business (for example, the CTO and/or chief product officer). Mission control acts as a key link back to the strategic needs of the business, ensures good oversight to the work that the teams are doing, takes key strategic decisions about priorities and resourcing, and helps the teams to access what they need in order to optimize the achievement of outcomes.

Reducing duplication

One of the key roles of mission control is to reduce duplication of effort and activity. In a large, complex marketing team or organization this can be a common source of inefficiency as teams start to lose touch with what other teams are doing and initiatives start to overlap and look similar. As well as being wasteful of people's time, effort and creative inputs, duplication can generate unnecessary team politics and misunderstandings. It can occur when there is a lack of organizational alignment, communication or sharing. The job of mission control or the senior marketing leadership is to enable better alignment and in doing so mitigate duplication through clear parameters and communication. There are several key strategies that can help with this:

1 **Clear territories:** Creating clearly differentiated but aligned team objectives and a clear 'job-to-be-done' or mission for each team, which mitigates the challenges that come from blurred boundaries. It's inevitable that there will be a degree of cross-over between teams but defining as clear a territory and mission as possible helps a team to understand where its territorial borders lie. This also enables greater autonomy within those boundaries. When a team is about to step over the border there should be some way of flagging or notifying the relevant teams.

2 **'Scrum-of-scrums':** Where multiple small, multidisciplinary squads are working alongside each other, this is a time-boxed session that brings together a representative from each of the teams to share high-level updates on the work they are doing and to discuss progress and impediments. Think of this as a kind of 'meta-scrum'. It helps create a platform for better cross-team collaboration, reducing duplication, sharing and tackling dependencies, and to address points of conflict. As an example, the technology team of the US Government's General Services Administration suggests running these in a similar (but more extended) format to a daily stand-up, where the team representatives answer four questions:[7]

   a. What has your team done since we last met?

   b. What will your team do before we meet again?

   c. Is anything slowing your team down or getting in their way?

   d. Are you about to put something in another team's way?

   These 'scrum-of-scrums' sessions should be run with the same principles as apply to an agile team – in other words, no more than 5 to 10 people. They are invaluable in coordinating work across multiple teams and reducing duplication of effort.

3 **Ownership and assumptions:** I'll discuss the importance of creating a culture of ownership in more detail later in the book but this behavioural attribute is important in making sure that teams are delivering against their defined goals and territories in proactive rather than reactive ways. It's easy to make assumptions that another team understands what our team is doing or that someone else will take responsibility for taking

action on something. Never assume. As author and American political scientist Eugene Lewis is credited with saying, 'assumption is the mother of all mistakes'.[8]

Endnotes

1 J R Hackman (2002) *Leading Teams: Setting the Stage for Great Performances*, Harvard Business Review Press, Boston.

2 Harvard Business School. Working knowledge, leading teams: Setting the stage for great performances – the five keys to successful teams, July 2002. hbswk. hbs.edu/archive/leading-teams-setting-the-stage-for-great-performances-the-five-keys-to-successful-teams (archived at https://perma.cc/D9S2-HECM)

3 H Kniberg and A Ivarsson. Scaling agile @ Spotify, with tribes, squads, chapters and guilds, October 2012, dl.dropboxusercontent.com/u/1018963/Articles/ SpotifyScaling.pdf (archived at https://perma.cc/54UK-72Q6)

4 McKinsey. ING's agile transformation, January 2017. www.mckinsey.com/ industries/financial-services/our-insights/ings-agile-transformation (archived at https://perma.cc/Z8LM-TM6N)

5 BBC. Dunbar's number: Why we can only maintain 150 relationships, BBC, 2019. www.bbc.com/future/article/20191001-dunbars-number-why-we-can-only-maintain-150-relationships (archived at https://perma.cc/GY2F-TUW6)

6 Emily Webber, August 2016, The Team Onion, https://emilywebber.co.uk/ agile-team-onion-short-free-ebook/

7 US General Services Administration. Conducting a scrum of scrums, GSA Tech Guides, 2021. tech.gsa.gov/guides/conducting_scrum_of_scrums/ (archived at https://perma.cc/88X4-ZXWS)

8 L Pasqualis. Assumption is the evil mother of all mistakes, CoderHood, May 2017. www.coderhood.com/assumption-evil-mother-mistakes/ (archived at https://perma.cc/2MW9-Q2EM)

10

Agile resourcing

Using the Hollywood model

For much of the so-called 'Golden Age of Hollywood' from the 1920s to 1960s, making films in Hollywood was dominated by the studio model. This saw a small number of powerful movie studios dominate the production and distribution of films. These films were produced on the studio's own film-making lots, with actors, actresses, directors and other members of the crew all signed on long-term contracts to work exclusively with one studio. They were all effectively studio employees. This system also saw studio control over distribution and exhibition of their films, which resulted in manipulation to boost additional sales through techniques like block booking.

In 1948 this studio system was challenged in the Supreme Court who ruled to separate production from distribution and exhibition, thereby accelerating the end of this model of filmmaking. By 1954 it was over. The Hollywood model that emerged to replace the studio system was characterized by the optimal team needed to work on specific films being assembled and only working on that project for as long as it took for the film to be produced. The team then disbands.

The Hollywood model has good parallels with an increasingly common approach to flexible resource management being adopted by an ever-larger number of businesses. As the *New York Times* describes it:

> This short-term, project-based business structure is an alternative to the
> corporate model, in which capital is spent up front to build a business, which
> then hires workers for long-term open-ended jobs that can last for years, even
> a lifetime.[1]

The model has benefits for businesses and for employees. For companies it brings a level of flexibility that can enable greater agility and flexibility.

Teams can scale up and scale down more easily in response to changing contexts and important calendar events or times of the year when there may be bottlenecks or teams may be less busy. It can allow businesses to bring in required specialist expertise as and when it is required without increasing FTE headcount (you don't need all of the people all of the time). It can help a business orient faster around areas of opportunity or boost resourcing in critical areas as required. It can help them to manage an altogether more efficient variable cost model. For staff it allows a high degree of flexibility as well and the ability to work in different environments, to learn more, to work on interesting projects and have more control over their time and commitments. It's an altogether more adaptable model.

In agile marketing, there is an opportunity to use the Hollywood model to create a more on-demand, flexible workforce that has the ability to scale as and when required. The pool of freelance and specialist resources that marketing teams can draw on has never been larger, which gives organizations a real opportunity to bring in specific domain expertise as and when required.

Project and persistent teams

While the Hollywood model and on-demand staffing can really empower greater agility in the marketing team, one of the watch-outs is that it can potentially negate the benefit that can come from teams working together over extended periods of time and the accumulation of experience, learning and more proficient ways of working that can come from this. Marketing leaders therefore need to appreciate the optimal balance between agile teams that are brought together on a project basis and those that are more persistent in nature, working on one area of defined focus for a lengthy amount of time.

Project teams can be really useful in empowering greater resource flexibility across the team and in enabling focus to be brought rapidly to areas of opportunity, short-term strategic needs or innovation activities. They can also be energizing for staff who get to work on different areas of challenge within the team. The risk with a scaled application of project-based teams is that it is harder to accommodate long-term learning and to apply the judgement and expertise that can come from extended experience in one area of focus.

Persistent teams can benefit from embedded learning over time, which can mean that they solve problems faster and also from the efficiencies and improved productivity that can come from a team that has worked together for a long time and really understands how to get the most out of individual team members. The risk with only having persistent teams is a lack of flexibility in resourcing and the inability to 'swarm' problems and to rapidly place additional resourcing on solving short-term challenges or capitalizing on short-term opportunity.

It can often work well to have a combination of persistent and project teams. The former can work well where teams are aligned around customer need states, journeys or particular areas of strategic focus and products since these are domains where improved learning over time can really help to optimize outputs and continuous, incremental improvements. The latter can work well for innovation projects or where a team needs to be spun up to tackle a short-term challenge or strategic opportunity.

PROJECT-BASED AND DURABLE TEAMS AT THE FT

Anna Shipman, Technical Director at the *Financial Times*, has written about how and why her Customer Product group at the FT (which builds the FT.com website and apps) moved from project-based to more durable teams. It's a good example of the benefits and challenges that can come from each approach. Anna describes how the objective of the group is to deliver as much value as possible, which requires a tricky balance between keeping the technology estate operational and reliable while also focusing on delivering value to customers and to the business.

The group of 11 multidisciplinary squads were initially formed around projects that often had a product focus (for example, a conversion team charged with turning casual readers into subscribers). New teams were formed around new initiatives. This transitioned to a new structure comprising nine durable teams, each focused on a specific product area and the associated technology estate that goes with it (for example, a team focused on content discovery, another on content innovation, one on apps, another on data journalism and so on).

The key advantage in the initial project-based structure was that it enabled a clear focus on one product goal for a team, which meant it was easier to see the value delivered. There was also greater flexibility, which meant the team could 'swarm' on problems as they arose, and it was easier to budget for. The main disadvantage was that teams would often disband before they had the opportunity to form into truly high-performing units. Bruce Tuckman's well-known model for team development follows four critical stages:[2]

1 **Forming:** When a new team first comes together it can take a time for team members to become clear about the team's purpose, and way in which they work as a team and with other teams.

2 **Storming:** As the team becomes more established, friction between team members or with other teams can occur as team members start to challenge boundaries or ways of doing things.

3 **Norming:** At this stage, team members start to respect each other's differences and strengths and also the authority of the leader of the team as they begin to understand each other better. Working through challenges together can help this.

4 **Performing:** Here the team will reach its full potential, with faster and more efficient working, and progress towards well-understood objectives. The team is optimized in ways of working, and individual team members take greater ownership, going above and beyond to take on additional responsibilities. Roles can become more fluid as the team works more cohesively towards outcomes.

The risk with project teams, as Anna points out, is that teams never reach the performing stage where they are fully optimized and fulfilling their true potential. It can take teams a good while to get up to full speed, which can mean that they become inefficient. Managing a flexible approach to spinning teams up and disbanding them again can create resource management challenges. If a team is spun up to tackle a particular problem or objective, they can potentially feel a lack of ownership of the problem domain if the objective has already been set. A project-based approach can also mean that relevant domain knowledge that has been acquired in the process of solving specific challenges can be lost as teams disband and reform. This can mean that other teams need to relearn what has already been learnt elsewhere.

The benefits of moving to a more durable team approach for the FT came in the ability to map team responsibilities in ways that ensured there were no gaps, to minimize wastage from stopping and starting teams and to build organizational memory and fine-tune ways of working. The ability to see real progress over the long term was motivating for durable teams, and it brought greater clarity over capacity across the whole team. It also made it easier for other teams across the FT to understand who they needed to talk to about specific needs or domains.

It's clear that there are both upsides and downsides to both project-based and durable, persistent teams. Agile marketing leaders should be aware of both when designing teams that are able to balance continuous learning with greater resourcing flexibility.

Insourcing and outsourcing for agility

The question of what capabilities to have in-house and what to outsource for marketing teams has been subject to a number of shifting dynamics over the past few years as client-side teams look to balance different needs around efficiency, cost-effectiveness, agility, scalability and expert inputs. Decisions around what to do in-house and what to outsource are nuanced and context-specific. Each marketing team has its own dynamics to consider and what works for one may well not work for another. There are, however, some useful high-level considerations that can help marketers to make decisions that can support greater agility.

Broadly speaking, more capability in some notable areas including content, data and analytics have been brought inside organizations driven primarily by a desire for efficiency in cost and speed. The evolution of marketing technology platforms and the MarTech stack has enabled far more capability to come in-house and far less reliance on external providers for production and execution. The increasing focus on first-party data, direct-to-consumer or service-driven propositions and owned media assets has catalysed the need for marketing teams to keep data capability close in order to support agility in feedback and decision-making. This has combined with greater pressures around media proficiency, accountability, attribution and ROI to give a heightened importance to in-house analytics. The development of more competency around data in customer experience, rapid testing and optimization has compounded this effect.

Programmatic is another area that has seen shifting dynamics around insourcing and outsourcing. Overall, programmatic approaches to advertising have grown dramatically in prevalence, accounting for 68 per cent of digital ad spend worldwide (and over 80 per cent in the United States and Europe) according to research conducted by the Internet Advertising Bureau.[3] That same survey found that a desire for brands to have more control over their programmatic advertising has led to a trend towards increasingly bringing some or all of this capability in-house (48 per cent of businesses in the survey had partially moved programmatic in-house in a hybrid approach, and

21 per cent or businesses had moved it completely inside). This trend has been driven not only by a desire for control but also a need for greater transparency, which, when combined with first-party data capabilities, enables greater efficiency, reach and effectiveness. Control over campaign strategy, setting KPIs, data management, ownership of contracts, publisher data relationships and campaign analysis and reporting are all seen as good reasons to consider an in-house approach.

In addition, the growth in content marketing and social has resulted in the need for a more continual flow of content production and distribution, and teams increasingly need both quality and quantity of content alongside a requirement to respond quickly to short-term needs as they arise. A team looking to optimize a proposition or campaign can easily find that they need to rapidly adapt existing assets or generate new ones based on analytics and feedback. A lengthy workflow and sign-off process using an external agency can prevent the team from moving quickly. While there is still broad recognition of the value that creatively driven external partners can bring to the marketing team in terms of big brand insights, external thinking and perspectives and creative ideas, there is also recognition that teams need to be more efficient and agile in how they are able to access, create and deliver content assets, which has resulted in more creative capability coming in-house.

This has been a not insignificant shift and it is one that has accelerated over recent years. Research conducted in September 2020 by the World Federation of Advertisers (WFA) and The Observatory International found that 74 per cent of in-house creative studios and agencies had been established in the last five years.[4] According to that research, the COVID-19 pandemic had also dramatically accelerated the move to bring creative operations in-house with creative in-housing being practised at 57 per cent of multinational companies. It's notable however, that this is often not an all or nothing approach. For example, 95 per cent of the companies in the WFA research had continued to work with external agencies in some way.

There are some key benefits and disadvantages that marketers can consider when making choices around whether to bring capability in-house. For creative, agencies can benefit from working across multiple clients and sectors and can bring fresh perspectives, ideas and creative thinking into the marketing team. This can work particularly well for challenging a marketing team to think about their market and consumers in a different way and in the origination of big brand ideas and platforms. This model can become more challenging however, when lengthy processes characterized by multiple hand-offs can reduce the flexibility and agility that a team needs to move fast. In a world where a brand's annual marketing calendar might be dominated by two large campaigns and spikes of activity, an outsourced model that involves lengthy briefing and asset production processes may work fine. Yet in a world that is characterized by the need for always-on communication, a continual flow of assets, and the need to adapt and respond quickly this model becomes challenged. This means that marketing teams need to consider how they might combine in-house and outsourced approaches or even bring creative entirely inside the organization.

DYNAMICS AROUND IN-HOUSING

The key dynamics to consider around in-housing and outsourcing can be summarized as follows:

- **Agility and speed:** Defining where you need to move fast and where you don't is helpful in understanding when capability needs to be kept close to the team. Areas that require rapid feedback, optimization, continuous learning and greater adaptability need to be set up in ways that enable easy access and fast response times.

- **Efficiency:** This dynamic can relate to efficiency in process and/or efficiency in cost. For example, bringing content creation in-house in areas that require volume, repeatability or a high-frequency of change and adaptation can generate significant benefit.

- **Control:** In some areas of marketing (for example, the use of data or in managing end-to-end customer experience) it has become increasingly important to maintain control and have clear governance, oversight and supervision. This may mean the need to keep this inside the team.

- **Competency, knowledge and learning:** Marketers should identify where they need to maintain competency in-house and also where they need to build and accumulate knowledge and learning over time and draw on it regularly from within the business. External partners can also enable access to specialist expertise that may not exist within the team.

- **Perspective, ideas and inputs:** External partners can bring independent, fresh thinking into a team that can challenge existing ways of looking at a challenge or seeing customer segments, needs and behaviours. An injection of creative thinking can bring huge benefits to a team.

- **Talent:** Related to the value of external perspectives, knowledge and ideas are the benefits that ready access to talent can bring to a marketing team.

- **Scalability and flexibility:** A key dynamic that may be impacted by decisions around in-housing and outsourcing is the ability to scale up and down on demand. External partners can be particularly useful in enabling short-term scalability and resourcing.

A report by the AAR Group into evolving client and agency models (also written by the author) sets out a useful fundamental framework for understanding the dynamics of in-housing around creative and media.[5]

FIGURE 10.1 In-housing dynamics

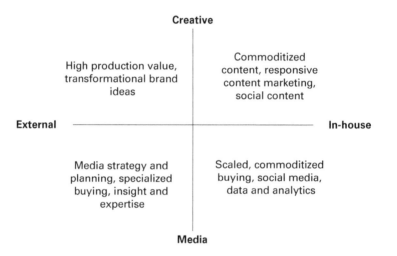

Making smart decisions around which capabilities exist in-house and where there is greater benefit on relying on external partners is of increasing importance in supporting greater agility for marketing teams.

Endnotes

1 A Davidson. What Hollywood can teach us about the future of work, *New York Times Magazine*, 5 May 2015. www.nytimes.com/2015/05/10/magazine/what-hollywood-can-teach-us-about-the-future-of-work.html (archived at https://perma.cc/7EZR-JY6A)

2 J Stein. Using the Stages of Team Development, MIT Human Resources, 2021. hr.mit.edu/learning-topics/teams/articles/stages-development (archived at https://perma.cc/U7TA-N6B7)

3 IAB. IAB international report on programmatic in-housing, September 2020. www.iab.com/wp-content/uploads/2020/07/IAB_2020ProgrammaticInHousing_International_2020-08.pdf (archived at https://perma.cc/RB2C-9WHU)

4 WFA. Creative in-housing hits 57% among multinationals, WFA report, September 2020. wfanet.org/knowledge/item/2020/09/04/Creative-in-housing-hits-57-among-multinationals-WFA-report (archived at https://perma.cc/HV2Q-X7PY)

5 AAR Group. AAR reports, 2021. aargroup.co.uk/insights/reports/ (archived at https://perma.cc/FQ5D-V95K)

PART FIVE

Agility from data

11

Why data is the foundation of agile

Putting data at the centre of agility

Data can inform decision-making right through the marketing organization. It can help marketers to define strategy, identify opportunities for growth, understand audiences, optimize activity, test, learn and experiment. The breadth of this application means that in agile marketing teams, data is threaded right through decision-making, process and execution. This is about the fabric of how teams work but also the ways in which they think, solve problems and create value. Evidence-based decision-making is as much about mindset as it is about process.

Data strategy building blocks

A good data strategy is aligned to marketing and wider business objectives, sets out a clear approach for how the marketing team will derive benefit from data and has an appreciation of what types of data will be most valuable and how teams can effectively access that value. It's key that the strategy reflects the fact that not all data is created equal and that the dynamics between different types of data are evolving. I'll cover this latter point later in this section but for now let's be clear at the most basic level about the key types of data to consider:

- **First-party data (1P):** Data and information that is collected directly from customers and owned, stored and utilized by the marketing team. CRM data, website analytics or customer interaction data from other owned media assets or touchpoints can all be examples of 1P data. This type of data is potentially very valuable to agile marketing teams since it is easily accessible, comes directly from customers and can reveal granular insights into customer behaviour and preferences. 1P data can be used for personalization but also to predict customer behaviour and trends, and to empower more sophisticated targeting. So-called 'zero-party data' (a term originated by Forrester[1]) is a form of 1P data whereby customers actively choose to share their preferences with an organization, for example in return for more personalized experiences. Since the data comes directly from customers themselves, it is potentially very accurate and valuable, yet also challenging to acquire in quantity and depth without propositions that are specifically designed to do this (for example, subscription services that have preferences built in to the onboarding process).

- **Second-party data (2P):** If 1P data is collected by an organization from its own customers, then 2P data relates to when a client team makes use of someone else's 1P data. This might involve using a partner's acquired customer data to empower targeting or communication or to augment understanding of particular audiences. It can give valuable additional insights into audience segments beyond those which a company has via its own 1P data. An example of this might be utilizing lookalike audiences on Google or Facebook, where prospects that look or behave similarly to existing client segments can be targeted on those platforms. It's important for the team to work with reputable partner organizations to ensure quality of data.

- **Third-party data (3P):** This type of data is typically sourced from data aggregators and vendors that will not have been directly involved with transactions or have direct links to customers. These aggregators will draw from a wide range of data sources to pull together large data sets that are then categorized and sold on. A common use of 3P data is to augment targeting in programmatic advertising and it can be used more generally to add to the understanding that teams have of particular audiences, especially when combined with 1P and 2P data. It brings scale but can lack granularity and is not as transparent as 1P or 2P data. As well as augmenting audience understanding, 3P data can be used for enabling a broad approach to targeting, which may build from the understanding developed from 1P data and use 3P to drive scale. It can help in enabling broad initial approaches to targeting, which can then be narrowed using optimization to more tightly specified targeting.

The adept combination of 1P, 2P and 3P data can help agile marketing teams to use and improve customer understanding to improve targeting, reach, personalization and customer experience as well as marketing and business outcomes.

PEPSICO'S USE OF FIRST-PARTY DATA AND AI

As a consumer packaged goods business, PepsiCo has always relied on mass marketing and promotions, and large-scale distribution through retailers and outlets. This approach ultimately meant that they were mediated by third parties, potentially reducing the degree of customer visibility they have in a rapidly changing environment. The company decided to place first-party data at the centre of a strategy to better leverage consumer data and understanding and also to respond to changing dynamics around data privacy. There were four key strands to this strategy:[2]

1   Prioritizing customer relationships. The company built a media and consumer data team, which brought together data scientists, insights specialists and product owners to take a more data-driven approach to activation. First-party data acquisition became a key strategic priority in marketing, and they also launched two direct-to-consumer propositions (snacks.com and pantryshop.com) to deepen relationships. As an example, the head of PepsiCo's demand accelerator (DX) initiative has described how the company has built a number of large internal data sets, one of which has data on around 106 million US households, half of which include data at the individual level. Another store data set holds records on 500,000 US retail outlets. This enables the company to customize offers in highly personalized ways and link through to the retailer.[3]

2   Driving loyalty through the right value exchange. The full range of touchpoints, from campaign assets, to customer-engagement platforms like apps and even packaging was used to prompt customers to join a loyalty and rewards programme so that the business might develop an ongoing customer dialogue and deepen insights. This enabled greater personalization and the depth of understanding that can inform a more tailored approach to value exchange, which results in greater engagement, which means more data, which results in more value for the customer and the business.

3 Using integrated first-party data to drive business results. The depth of data that PepsiCo was able to secure helped it to personalize offers and promotions, as well as messaging and communication to more effectively support customers at different stages of the journey. For some campaigns this resulted in being able to improve ROI by a factor of three.

4 Taking the value beyond marketing. The investment in 1P data has enabled PepsiCo to benefit across multiple areas of its business. It has enabled them to create customer feedback loops through which they can test new flavours and conduct sampling exercises. It has given them useful data to predict consumer trends and launch new products. Beyond first-party data, the business has created an in-house tech platform called Ada, which combines human insight with AI algorithms to create actionable activities. The research and development teams for example, use AI to gather intelligence from multiple sources (including food consumption data and social media conversation) on trends in consumer behaviours and preferences and make predictions that can inform product development.

Beyond understanding the role of different types of data, it's important for teams to build a solid foundation for how data is used in the team. The relationship between data, information, knowledge and wisdom is a cornerstone way of understanding the fundamentals of deriving value from data.

FIGURE 11.1   DIKW

SOURCE Image: By Longlivetheux – own work, CC BY-SA 4.0

Representing these attributes as a pyramid can enable marketers to define specific strategies and questions at each level that can link a data strategy together. Data is the raw material and sits at the bottom of the pyramid since it has little value until we do something with it. In order to create value, we need to structure and organize data to create information that is more valuable to the business than just raw numbers. Then we need to apply meaning to that structured data to identify and interpret patterns. This creates knowledge that is more valuable still. Ultimately, we need to be effective in our application of knowledge to achieve our goals and realise the true value that data can bring.

Let's look at these levels one-by-one to define the essential questions that need answering.

Data

Raw data is the basis of decision-making and the foundation for success. Just as a poorly built foundation in a building undermines its structure, so poor strategies and execution here can result in the inability of teams to use data effectively to support decision-making right through the process and the team. A solid data foundation requires a good quantity and quality of data, which means strategies that are focused around data acquisition, data cleansing and governance:

- **Data collection:** Decisions around what types of data to collect and how should be directed by the marketing goals and the data strategy that has been defined. The shifting dynamics around data will be covered later in this section, but in many organizations the importance of first-party data acquisition has been amplified by the need for better customer understanding, targeting and personalization at scale. This then means that teams need to implement proactive strategies for data acquisition that take account of the value exchange needed to acquire first-party data and the partnerships and technologies needed to augment that with second- and third-party data.

- **Data aggregation and storage:** This relates to bringing data together in ways that enable access and organization. Smart decisions around technology and systems can establish the right foundation. For example, how a team might utilize databases (which are often good for aggregating related data in ways that enable key functional operations) or data lakes and data warehouses (which aggregate data from a wider range of sources and add in a layer of analysis, make it easily retrievable and often link up to multiple other systems).

- **Data cleansing:** Good decision-making using data requires good-quality data to make decisions with. That means regularly cleansing and preparing data sets for analysis by removing duplicate, incomplete or irrelevant data that can lead to poor conclusions. Teams should be able to rely on data that is up-to-date and as complete as possible, but if they're aware of where gaps exist they can take steps to mitigate this. Validating the quality of data inputs is good practice to get good outputs.

- **Data governance:** Good governance around data mean creating and maintaining clear roles, responsibilities and rules that can ensure compliance with regulation, that risks for the business are minimized and there is good communication and accountability around how data is collected, stored and used. Having auditable processes, clear standards and a culture of transparency around data can all help.

The important questions to ask at this foundational level include the type and quantity of data required, how well the team is set up to acquire and store this data, whether the data is subject to good governance and oversight and how they can validate the quality of data inputs.

Information

The next level in the DIKW pyramid of value is information. This relates to how data is structured and organized in ways that enable the team to then identify patterns and create knowledge. There are technology and process elements to this.

To structure data well, teams need to be empowered by the right systems and technology infrastructure. This might relate to how a team is able to use a CRM or marketing automation systems to make use of the data in segmenting customer profiles and empowering targeting communications at scale. Or it might relate to how a data management platform (DMP) can bring together different data inputs in ways that enable more sophisticated targeting through programmatic. Increasingly, the ability to bring together disparate data sources into customer-focused systems that can analyse and make sense of that data, and then enable many other systems to draw value from it, has led to the rise in popularity of customer data platforms (or CDPs). These platforms can augment customer understanding by bringing together different data sets and analysing, clustering and organizing them in ways that can provide better answers for the questions that the team may have. An example of this is the ability to create a single customer view where interaction, preferences and behavioural data can be attributed to a single customer profile.

In this way CDPs can enable much more sophisticated customer understanding and the delivery of truly omnichannel experiences and ultimately competitive advantage (as an example, the Salesforce 2021 State of Marketing report found that 78 per cent of high-performing businesses in their survey said that they used a CDP, compared to only 57 per cent of underperforming businesses).

The other related aspect to structuring data well is the practice and process of how teams define customer segments. Increasingly, data is enabling a much more sophisticated approach to segmentation that brings in multiple customer attributes and goes far beyond simple demographic segments. There are some fundamental approaches to segmentation which can be augmented through data:

- **Geographic segmentation:** Location data can be used here to define broad or narrow customer groups based on where they live or where they are and proximity. The balance in targeting here is between reach and performance. Put simply, more tightly targeted definitions (for example, shoppers near to a particular shop) may lack scale, but too broad a segmentation can miss opportunity to drive performance. Data inputs here may go beyond simple location, to specify attributes like weather and temperature that may change how prospects are communicated to.

- **Demographic segmentation:** Fundamental attributes such as age, gender, income, life stage and family status can give a basic level of understanding but will likely need to be augmented with other forms of data inputs to generate more sophisticated segments.

- **Psychographic segmentation:** These more subtle cues may bring in data that can reveal attitudes, interests, beliefs and even personality traits. An example of this is targeting groups of customers that are particularly focused on ethical or sustainable brands.

- **Behavioural segmentation:** This can encompass a broad set of customer attributes including online activity, purchase behaviour and preferences, product use and the stage in the customer journey that the customer is at. All of this understanding comes from the ability to define key behaviours and signals that can bring together groups of customers in useful ways.

- **Needs-based segmentation:** Data can also reveal the functional needs (what a customer wants to do) and emotional needs (how a customer wants a problem to be solved) that people have, and these can be grouped together into useful segments. This might also relate to specific problem areas that customers have (for example, a segment of customers looking for gluten-free alternatives in their diet).

- **Transactional segmentation:** Related to segmenting customers based on behaviours, the use of customer spending patterns can identify useful groups. As an example, RFM modelling is based on recency (how recently a customer purchased), frequency (how often they buy from you) and monetary (how much they spend) and can be used to identify a company's most valuable customers or appropriate messaging based on purchase history and behaviour.

It's important in agile marketing that teams are empowered to deliver segmentation in multiple ways and have the ability to test and learn around how different approaches to clustering can enhance performance or outcomes. That means a good foundation of data which is structured and organised easily. As mentioned in the previous section, different types of 1P, 2P and 3P data can be brought together to create a more sophisticated level of understanding around these different forms of segmentation. The sophistication here comes in how teams can blend together different criteria and different sources of data, and the agility comes from how easy it is for them to do this in ways that enable them to learn fast and optimize outcomes.

Knowledge

The knowledge level in the DIKW pyramid relates to how well patterns of data can be interpreted and translated into understanding. This is about generating the insights which can inform strategy, enable better execution and drive competitive advantage. These insights may well come from data analysts or scientists that are adept at evaluating patterns in data sets, but these patterns may just as likely be derived from machine learning algorithms which are applied to identify patterns in unstructured data (for example, to form new customer segments) or structured data (for example, by identifying common patterns in grouped data sets or by training a machine learning algorithm to identify specific attributes). Where information is more about answering questions like who, when and where, this is really about answering the 'how' and even the 'why' question.

An example of this knowledge level is how we choose to define customer personas. If the information stage is about structuring data in useful ways to drive sophisticated segmentation, then we need to represent those segments with an equally sophisticated approach to persona generation. Just as we do with segmentation, this requires the application of data to develop a more three-dimensional view of our customers that takes it beyond simple demographics and into a more nuanced approach that brings to life key emotional needs, motivations and frustrations that can all lead to improved insights, communication (for example through tone of voice) and opportunities to find and engage with them in more meaningful ways.

Another example of developing knowledge through pattern recognition is using data through the customer journey to identify opportunities to engage customers in ways that fulfil their needs, answer their questions and help them move to the next stage. Google's 'moments that matter' is a useful framework for bringing this to life and is based on the idea that there will be specific 'lean-in' moments through a customer journey where decisions are being made and preferences being determined. Customer data can help an agile marketing team to identify what these moments are and how the brand might engage in the most useful way to create a good customer experience or draw a customer further towards purchase or another action of some kind. Customer's behaviour and online interaction can reveal signals that can enable a brand to identify context (who the customer is, where they are, what type of customer they are, what needs they have) and intent (what they are trying to achieve, what questions they are trying to answer). Google define four key type of moments that matter:

- **I want-to-watch moments:** If a customer is looking for specific video-based content, it can often be a clear signal that they have a specific need or question to answer (for example someone looking for a 'how to...' video).

- **I want-to-do moments:** The need to complete a specific task can be signalled in whole variety of different ways that can reveal intent or a specific challenge that the customer has.

- **I need-to-find moments:** The way in which customers search can reveal clear insights into both context and intent, and can also give a location-based understanding. For example, comparing prices or looking for store locations can indicate that a customer is close to purchase.

- **I need-to-buy moments:** These are clearly strong signals of intent that may be shown through search behaviour or how a customer is navigating a site.

The opportunity at this level is to develop the kinds of insights that can truly inform action. This, of course, has no value unless this knowledge is applied in execution, and this brings us to wisdom.

Wisdom

Sitting at the top of the DIKW pyramid, wisdom is about the process that the team has for actioning insight. It's no good developing a lot of insights into customer behaviour if there is no follow-up response that enables the customer and team to benefit from that insight. Fast customer feedback loops are a great example of generating knowledge that can be turned into action and execution. Taking the example of using customer signals from online interaction, a marketing team needs to not only identify and define the 'moments that matter' through the journey, they also need to take that understanding back into the content, journeys and experiences that they are creating for customers. If knowledge is about understanding 'how' and 'why', the question at this stage is 'so what?' Adept understanding of customer data that is then translated into actions creates seamless journeys that feel intuitive and easy to navigate, but it also enables a team to optimize well against goals.

This is also about being data-driven, but combining this with being data-informed. The former is perhaps a more automatic, mechanical or rules-based way of making decisions. We interpret what the data is telling us, and we decide what to do next based on that data. To be data informed however, we need to bring in a more forward-looking human capability to extrapolate, project and even imagine future outcomes or possibilities. In other words, we might use the patterns we have identified in data to inspire new thinking, set a new course or create a new goal. This may often require ingenuity, empathy and creativity to be combined with data inputs. The agile marketing team is both data driven and data informed.

Data maturity

Descriptive, diagnostic, predictive and prescriptive analytics is a useful way of understanding maturity in analytics that comes originally from Davenport and Harris, adapted by Gartner.[4] The model sets out a four-stage continuum:

- **Descriptive analytics:** This level is about identifying patterns (in answer to 'what happened?'). This pulls in simple reporting around performance.

- **Diagnostic analytics:** Taking this a step further, this stage interprets patterns (in answer to the question 'why did it happen?'). This might include interpreting patterns of customer behaviour or marketing performance but like descriptive analytics is still facing back into past patterns and data.

- **Predictive analytics:** Looking forwards now, this stage is about interpreting and using patterns to identify what is likely to happen. Examples might include using predictive models to identify when something is likely to happen (like customer churn) or to forecast outcomes and trends or run simulations (in answer to the question 'what will happen?'). So-called 'next best action' models are another example of using predictive patterns to identify what customers are most likely to need next in a journey based on the behaviour of similar groups of customers.

- **Prescriptive analytics:** This involves taking predictive to a new level by applying machine learning to identify actions that can be taken to ensure a particular outcome (in answer to the question 'how can we make this happen?'). This can help inform a more sophisticated approach to automation since it enables understanding of both patterns and required actions.

This model provides a simple way of framing the maturity of analytics capability for an agile marketing team but it's important to understand that these levels do not operate in isolation. It's likely that a team will be using multiple aspects of analysis and automation along this spectrum and may well be applying machine learning across all of these stages to inform improved execution.

Shifting data dynamics

It's important to acknowledge that there are a number of evolving dynamics around data that agile marketing teams need to account for. There is, for example, growing complexity in the range and type of data sources that a marketing team has access to. A global survey of over 8,000 marketers by Salesforce found that the average number of data sources used by teams in 2021 is 10, but that this was projected to rise to 14 in 2022.[5] A total of 78 per cent of respondents reported that they were focusing on new or reprioritized metrics as a result of the upheaval driven by the COVID-19 pandemic. A ranking of the most popular customer data sources demonstrated the increasing value of zero and first-party data, and the need for data sources that can more directly attribute value and actions. Sources including known digital identities (such as a customer profile), transactional data and declared interests and preferences (zero-party data) appeared at the top of the list. Second-party data, inferred interests and preferences, anonymised digital identities and third-party data came further down the list.

The Salesforce survey highlights a significant strategic shift towards value from first-party data, personally identifiable information (PII) and data that is more directly attributable rather than inferred. The increasing focus on privacy that has gained momentum over recent years is another critical factor in driving this shift. With growing regulation (GDPR and CCPA, for example) and moves by technology players including Apple and Google away from supporting third-party cookies, this direction of travel is set to continue.

The erosion in the value and use of third-party cookies potentially impacts the visibility that marketers have of the funnel, some forms of optimization and the addressability of advertising. Yet it's also an opportunity for marketers to shift to more privacy-aware options and propositions and rebuild trust with consumers that has been eroded, for example through poor execution of programmatic advertising. One of the key strategies that has emerged in response to these changes is an increasing focus on first-party data acquisition to augment understanding of customers. The growth in customer data platforms mentioned earlier in this chapter is a sign of the marketer's intent to build more sizable and robust data pools that are within their control and then to utilize this data to drive better experiences and communications for customers. Many of these systems 'bake in' privacy awareness to how the systems store and use data, making it easier for teams to comply with regulation, but it is also important to integrate this awareness into the processes the team uses.

VALUE EXCHANGE AND DATA ACQUISITION

The growing focus on acquiring more first-party data requires teams to adopt specific strategies that can maximize a good range of opportunities. An increasing proportion of physical products have developed digital services that are based on known customer identities (for example, direct-to-consumer subscription services or the fact that our cars are now computers on wheels). These can offer an opportunity to develop richer and deeper customer understanding over time both through analysing individual customer behaviour and preferences and through identifying patterns of customer behaviour across larger groups of people. The more a customer uses a service, and the more customers that use that service, the richer the information a marketing team will have.

Beyond this it's key for a team to use as many opportunities as are at their disposal to drive 1P data collection. This might include being smart about campaign assets or how different touchpoints can be used. Marketers also need to play close attention to the value exchange that they are creating. This means generating a compelling reason for customers to submit their data, an appreciation that can only really come from a good understanding and empathy with customer needs. It's important to recognize that the objective here shouldn't always be to acquire as much first-party data as possible, but instead to understand which types of data and which types of customer it is most useful to have data on. This will typically be not only the data that will deliver good value to the business but also that which will enable customer experience or value to be enhanced.

Applying machine learning in agile marketing

Machine learning (ML) is driving fundamental change in the practice and execution of marketing. The tools for ML are becoming increasingly democratized as large technology platforms and marketing systems bake in capability and make it more easily accessible than ever, meaning that almost every team has access to relatively sophisticated tools to optimize and enhance marketing activity. ML can be used in a wide variety of marketing use cases including empowering more sophisticated ad targeting, defining new and more detailed customer segments, predicting trends and customer behaviour, enhancing customer journeys and experience.

Machine learning is a subset of artificial intelligence, which can broadly be defined as computer systems able to perform tasks that typically require human intelligence. It is pattern recognition from data at scale. IBM for example have defined machine learning as: 'a branch of artificial intelligence (AI) and computer science which focuses on the use of data and algorithms to imitate the way that humans learn, gradually improving its accuracy'.[6] In turn, deep learning is a subset of machine learning. Where machine learning is best for smaller and more simplified data sets, deep learning can be used to get a better understanding of larger and more complex types of data set. In order to understand how teams can apply machine learning, it's useful to consider it in its different forms.

- **Unsupervised learning:** This involves an algorithm drawing out previously unidentified patterns from unstructured data. It can be useful in understanding the relationship between data points that are not pre-labelled and clustering and organizing data. It has the potential to uncover patterns and trends that teams had not previously noticed and group data together in useful ways. A team using this technique needs to determine whether the patterns surfaced by the algorithm have value for the business or not. An example of using unsupervised learning might be in customer segmentation, where common behaviours may be identified and customers grouped together into useful segments. These segments can be used to look at correlations with other attributes like demographics in order to build understanding around customer types or to define new segments for targeting.

- **Supervised learning:** This involves training an algorithm with pre-labelled data and can therefore be used when there is a specific outcome that a team is going after and a right and wrong answer involved. The training might involve giving lots of pre-labelled examples to an algorithm to analyse, classifying each example and creating a feedback loop so that the model can learn if it has made the right choice or not. An example of this might be creating a model that can predict the likelihood of customer churn by training an algorithm on data from customers that have already churned. Or it might be used to identify the factors involved in a particular customer behaviour.

- **Reinforcement learning:** This type of learning differs from supervised and unsupervised in that the algorithm learns through interacting with an environment and gaining reward signals for positive progress. It is a more expansive approach than supervised learning in that it has a broader feedback loop and can identify the optimal sequence of actions that need to be taken to arrive at an outcome. Examples of the application of reinforcement learning might be evaluating the response to various messages and using the outputs to determine the optimal frequency of communication, the best sequence of messaging or adapting bids and messaging in a programmatic environment by predicting customer responses.

In agile marketing the application of ML has a number of key benefits including faster access to higher-quality data analysis and learning (the ability to analyse more data in less time), to quickly organize data sets and identify useful new patterns, to automate some marketing processes and save on resource and time and to enable improved content personalization, recommendation systems (for example, based on product combinations – people who bought this, also bought that) and next best action (customers like you typically went on to take this action next). It's also increasingly at the heart of advertising targeting where it can be applied to improve segment targeting, trigger targeting (showing ads to users that have taken a certain action) and even predictive targeting (showing ads to users because of their likelihood to be interested in the message or product). ML can also deliver improved analysis around measures and effectiveness (for example, return on ad spend or ROAS) and can drive better forecasting (for example of customer lifetime value or churn rate).

Essentially, ML supercharges agile marketing data capabilities. It can enable them to be far more empowered in using data across a whole variety of use cases, to optimize efficiencies in working and campaign delivery and to become more proactive in planning and execution (through its use in segmentation and automation, for example). In order to realize the full potential of ML it's useful for the marketing team to understand the fundamental principles at play and its potential applications and then to be supported with data competencies that can help design algorithms and use statistical modelling in the right way to give the team what they really need. Realizing value from ML in agile marketing is founded on good-quality data and the ability for the team to learn fast and improve outcomes.

Balancing risk and complexity

When making decisions around the application of automation, ML and AI in agile marketing it's useful to consider both the level of complexity in the decisions that are being made and also the level of risk involved if something goes wrong. Marketing technologist Scott Brinker has created a useful high-level decision framework that can enable teams to differentiate between how they might apply ML and AI across a range of contexts.[7]

FIGURE 11.2   Complexity and risk in AI decision-making

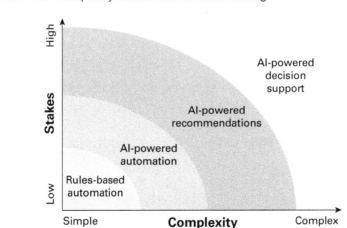

SOURCE Scott Brinker[8]

For simple decision-making where the stakes are low (for example, the colour of a call-to-action button on a page) simple rules-based automation can be helpful in driving scaled efficiency. For more complex and higher-risk contexts AI-powered automation can enable a more sophisticated approach and as complexity and the decisioning stakes grow, AI-powered recommendations and decision support can bring in an element of human oversight to ensure optimal outcomes while still enabling higher-quality and more efficient decisions.

Data resourcing

Since data is a critical competency for the modern, agile marketing team it is important to invest well in this area and to keep data capabilities close to the rest of the team in order to empower access and agility. Skills in this area are in high demand. A survey by LinkedIn in early 2021 revealed a steep rise in demand for digital skills in marketers. It showed that marketing roles that were significantly data-driven including paid social, ad serving and analytics were among the most in demand.[9]

Given the importance of all levels in the DIKW pyramid, it's key to understand the resourcing needed to ensure that maximum value can be derived from data. Key to this is understanding the need for and difference between, data science, analysis and engineering.

- **Data science:** This typically uses mathematical and statistical models, scientific processes and methods to extract actionable insights from large, noisy data sets that might be both structured and unstructured. IBM have described how data science is a multidisciplinary approach that 'encompasses preparing data for analysis and processing, performing advanced data analysis and presenting the results to reveal patterns and enable stakeholders to draw informed conclusions'.[10] Data scientists may well use tools such as algorithm design, machine learning and programming.

- **Data analysis:** Related to data science, data analysis is the process of systematically applying logical techniques to describe, evaluate, illustrate and report on data. The difference between data analysis and data science is that the former typically works with data that has already been structured into more user-friendly formats, where the latter may well work with raw data.

- **Data engineering:** This involves creating the right infrastructure and backend foundation to enable analysis and value creation from data. An example of this might be maintaining a data warehouse and designing data sets that can be utilized by the team.

The agile marketing team needs to have data-driven decision-making running through daily activity and this means having the resourcing to support true advantage from data. The flow of information between marketing and data resources should be continuous and free flowing. Data specialists will need to work alongside marketers on an ongoing basis and be kept close at hand in order to minimize unnecessary dependencies.

A DATA MATURITY MODEL FOR AGILE MARKETING

Taking account of the different elements that we've covered in this chapter, it's possible to create a simple data maturity model based on four levels of sophistication:

- **Elementary:** This is the earliest stage of the journey where data exists within the organization but is not being used effectively by teams to support decision-making, strategy and execution

- **Enlightened:** The business now understands what it needs to do to derive true value from data and has started on the journey, but while advances are being made in some key areas there is still a largely fragmented approach

- **Enabled:** At this stage the business has made good progress and is applying more advanced analytics techniques to support greater efficiency and effectiveness

- **Empowered:** Data is truly at the heart of business and marketing value, is used in fluid, highly efficient ways to empower high quality decision-making and exceptional customer experience and to deliver highly optimized outcomes, new thinking and innovation

TABLE 11.1   Data in agile marketing

Elementary	Data is siloed and not joined up. Processes around data are slow and not agile. Execution is largely reactive. Use of data in channels is basic, e.g. simple CRM or owned media analytics, limited use of customer data and fragmented customer profiles, infrequent optimization, no test and learn, descriptive and diagnostic analytics.
Enlightened	Data is starting to be joined up and a more integrated approach to data acquisition taken. More customer data is collected and utilized to inform strategy and execution, but metrics are still isolated and channel-focused. Limited use of automation. Some channel-specific personalization, limited use of predictive analytics.

(continued)

TABLE 11.1 (Continued)

Enabled	Much greater use of 1P data, and more advanced customer profiling around a single customer view. More sophisticated customer segmentation and integration of different data sources to empower personalization, targeting and prediction. Use of ML and AI to enhance capability in key use cases. Wider and faster access to data insights but still lacking in responsiveness in some areas.
Empowered	Highly automated execution with sophisticated application of AI, efficient real-time data-driven decisioning combined with real-time analytics, insights, measures, optimization. Data-empowered experimentation and continuous test and learn. Highly joined-up omnichannel customer experience, advanced customer profiling and personalization.

Endnotes

1 S Liu. Straight from the source: Collecting zero-party data from customers, Forrester, 30 July 2020. www.forrester.com/blogs/straight-from-the-source-collecting-zero-party-data-from-customers/ (archived at https://perma.cc/WJ55-AJHA)

2 ThinkWithGoogle. How PepsiCo uses first-party data to build direct relationships with consumers, October 2021. www.thinkwithgoogle.com/intl/en-gb/future-of-marketing/privacy-and-trust/consumer-data-relationship-pepsico/ (archived at https://perma.cc/GHK9-F475)

3 VentureBeat. How Pepsico uses AI to create products consumers don't know they want, June 2021. venturebeat.com/2021/06/28/how-pepsico-uses-ai-to-create-products-consumers-dont-know-they-want/ (archived at https://perma.cc/C6BS-3A7J)

4 K Król and D Zdonek. Analytics maturity models: An overview, March 2020. www.researchgate.net/publication/339672162_Analytics_Maturity_Models_An_Overview (archived at https://perma.cc/APH9-3EDL)

5 Salesforce. State of Marketing in 2021: 78% Report New or Reprioritized Metrics, August 2021. www.salesforce.com/news/stories/state-of-marketing-in-2021/ (archived at https://perma.cc/W8PK-9CYD)

6 IBM. Machine learning, July 2020. www.ibm.com/uk-en/cloud/learn/machine-learning (archived at https://perma.cc/XVS9-SYGD)

7 S Brinker. Applying automation and AI, LinkedIn, 2020. www.linkedin.com/posts/sjbrinker_martech-activity-6710908160690982912-XVA0/ (archived at https://perma.cc/A3X9-5683)

8 S Brinker. Applying automation and AI, LinkedIn, 2020. www.linkedin.com/posts/sjbrinker_martech-activity-6710908160690982912-XVA0/ (archived at https://perma.cc/A3X9-5683)

9 L Teserras. Steep rise in demand for marketers with digital skills, Marketing Week, 5 February 2021. www.marketingweek.com/steep-rise-demand-marketers-digital/ (archived at https://perma.cc/Q4KP-BV49)

10 IBM, Data Science Introduction, May 2020. www.ibm.com/cloud/learn/data-science-introduction (archived at https://perma.cc/MM7H-UYRA)

12

Learning well with data

In agile marketing moving fast is not an excuse for making mistakes. We need to move with speed but also to make high-quality decisions. And yet with so much data available to marketers it has potentially never been easier to make missteps and oversights without realizing it. Our judgements and decisions can be prone to systematic bias and heuristics that can so easily lead to poor decision-making. It's really important therefore for marketers to be aware of common biases and to take steps to ensure that they are avoiding needless mistakes.

In his renowned book *Thinking, Fast and Slow*,[1] psychologist and behavioural economist Daniel Kahneman famously described two subsystems for our thinking. System 1 thinking is more intuitive, fast, emotional and unconscious. Many everyday activities that we conduct may well make heavy use of this type of thinking. System 2, however, is more calculating, logical and effortful and so may be slower, more conscious and more infrequent. Thinking carefully about particular problems will make use of this system. Kahneman describes how system 1 thinking often involves associating new information with patterns or thoughts that already exist whereas system 2 is more likely to involve the creation of new patterns. For this reason system 1 can be particularly susceptible to cognitive bias. Misdirection can more easily happen when decision-making is more associative and automatic (system 1) rather than deliberate and logical (system 2). Bearing this in mind, how can marketers avoid bias and misjudgement when being agile and potentially moving quickly?

Avoiding simple errors

A good starting point for avoiding poor decision-making is to ensure that you are not falling foul of the kind of basic errors that might be considered to be easily avoidable but which are actually surprisingly common. Simple errors can often lead to significant consequences, particularly when they are mistakenly designed into services and systems that we might be using. As an example, in 2007 the US Air Force were flying six of their brand-new Lockheed Martin F-22 Raptor aircraft from Hawaii to Japan for their first overseas deployment. Halfway over the ocean the aircraft navigation and fuel systems crashed simultaneously in all the planes forcing them to make an emergency about turn and fly back to Hawaii.[2] When the problem was looked into, it was discovered that flying over the international dateline had triggered a glitch in the software that had knocked out many of the plane's systems. Software glitches can result in hidden trip wires that can lead to poor outputs without us even realizing. As teams become ever more reliant on software systems, having robust testing procedures in place to highlight any problems before the software is put live is an obvious watch-out, and it's important for teams to consider a wide range of scenarios for how the system will be used. Moving fast and using agile approaches is not an excuse for poor quality. Quality assurance (QA) and testing can be embedded into agile processes in order to ensure high-quality outputs.

Avoiding errors when using software doesn't stop with having a robust testing regime to account for unforeseen software glitches. We also need to use the right software in the first place. Common mistakes here include trying to utilize systems for jobs that they were never intended to do, using software that hasn't been updated properly and thereby creating risk and evolving software over time through bolt-on solutions and ending up with 'spaghetti systems' with large proportions of technology spend going on maintenance of core, outdated systems and hundreds of workarounds and bolt-ons creating a highly complex house of cards. For many years this was the challenge faced by the big banks, who relied on legacy mainframe systems and needed to spend up to 80 per cent of their not insignificant IT budgets to undertake expensive system updates rather than investing in new, more agile technology solutions. These short-term fixes acted as a brake on innovation, giving a head start to new and nimble fintech banks like Monzo, Revolut and Starling. As HSBC's chief technology architect once said, these spaghetti systems can generate their own technology dependencies: 'Everything is connected to everything else, pull on one thread and every-thing comes with it.'[3]

Earlier in the book I looked at the role of technology in supporting agile marketing but even at the individual team level it is important for teams to make smart choices about using appropriate tools in order to avoid unnecessary errors and risk. In the autumn of 2020, at the height of the COVID-19 pandemic, almost 16,000 COVID cases went unreported due to a poorly thought-through use of Microsoft Excel.[4] Public Health England (PHE) had set up an automatic process to pull data from commercial companies that were paid to analyse swab tests of the public into Excel templates. The data in these Excel files was then uploaded and made available to the NHS Test and Trace team and government COVID dashboards. Unfortunately, the PHE developers had selected an old XLS file format to do this, which meant that each template was limited to handling only 65,000 rows of data rather than the one million rows that Excel is actually capable of dealing with. As each test result created several rows of data, this meant that each template had an upper limit of around 1400 cases that it could record and any additional cases that came in after that were simply not recorded. The mistake of using outdated software meant that there were eight days of incomplete data and thousands of cases that were not reported or passed on, with potentially very serious consequences. As the BBC noted at the time, Excel's XLS file format goes back to 1987 and was superseded by XLSX in 2007, which would have been able to handle 16 times the number of cases had it been used.[5] The lesson here is not to skimp on investment in the tools that support better working practices for agile marketing teams, but it is also the responsibility of the teams themselves to ensure that they are using appropriate tools and to highlight where there are gaps in capability that might open up the potential for risk.

Simple errors with potentially significant consequences not only occur through using the wrong software but also through the use of the tools themselves. In his book *Humble Pi: A Comedy of Maths Errors*[6] Matt Parker notes how spreadsheets are the perfect environment for mistakes to compound and grow unchecked. He notes how The European Spreadsheet Risks Interest Group,[7] an organization set up to look at this problem, estimates that 90 per cent of all spreadsheets contain errors. The 'horror stories' page of their website contains a whole series of spreadsheet challenges and errors.[8] These include the scientific body that is in charge of standardizing the names of genes (the HUGO Gene Nomenclature Committee) needing to provide guidelines to scientists for originating names for newly identified genes to avoid problems created by Excel auto formatting (for example, Excel changing a gene's alphanumeric symbol of MARCH1 into the date 1-Mar).[9] Then there's the spreadsheet mistake that delayed the opening of a new £150 million Scottish hospital and led to £16 million of remedial work needing to be done to make the critical care rooms fit for use.[10] Or how about the spreadsheet input error that lost a state fund set up in Ireland to support jobs a total of 750,000 euros because a number was wrongly input as euros rather than dollars.[11] Or the errors on a couple of spreadsheets from a County Sheriff's Office in the United States that cost that particular county almost half a million dollars. The County Sheriff is quoted as saying at the time that 'the spreadsheets were emailed back and forth… Because of some cutting and pasting, not all the formulas were pasted correctly. It was an unintended error'.[12] The list goes on. The key point from these examples is how easy it is to make basic mistakes on even the most common of tools. As I've said before, moving fast and being agile is not an excuse for lack of oversight or attention to detail in the right places. Simple checks would likely have avoided all of these unintended mistakes.

And there's more. Basic errors can not only come from using the wrong software or using the right tools in the wrong ways but also from just not thinking things through.

USING GOOD JUDGEMENT IN AGILE MARKETING

Matt Parker gives the example of a promotion that Pepsi ran in 1995, which almost cost them over $20 million.[13] The promotion involved customers being encouraged to collect Pepsi points that they could exchange for Pepsi merchandise like a T-shirt (75 points), sunglasses (175 points) and a leather jacket (1,450 points). As a memorable gimmick the TV ad that supported the promotion included a Harrier Jump Jet, which could apparently be yours for 7 million Pepsi points. Unfortunately no one at Pepsi or their advertising agency stopped to do the maths. Even more unfortunately for Pepsi, John Leonard did. He worked out that the US Marine Corps were at the time buying AV-8B Harrier II jets for around $20 million. One of the terms of the promotion was that customers could buy additional Pepsi points for 10 cents each, which effectively meant that John Leonard could spend $700,000 on Pepsi points and get himself a new Harrier Jump Jet worth $20 million. Leonard made sure he followed all of the rules of the promotion, collected a minimal amount of Pepsi points and submitted a cheque for $700,000 to claim his jet. Pepsi refused his request and so Leonard got lawyers involved and the dispute eventually ended up in court. Somehow, Pepsi got away with it and Leonard never got his Harrier jet, but the case is a salutary lesson for all marketers on the need to do the math.

Matt Parker notes that humans are not naturally good at judging the size of very large numbers and are not born with the intuition to be able to handle them well. We know a million, a billion and a trillion but often fail to appreciate the huge differences between these large numbers. A million seconds from now is just short of 11 days and 14 hours, which doesn't feel too long. But a billion seconds is over 31 years and a trillion seconds from now would take us past the year 33,700 CE. As Parker says:

> As a species, we have learned to explore and exploit mathematics to do things beyond what our brains can process naturally... When we are operating beyond intuition, we can do the most interesting things, but this is also where we are at our most vulnerable.[14]

In the era of so-called 'big data', the use of statistical and mathematical models allows us to step beyond what our internal hardware was designed to do and achieve great things but we have to learn how to apply models well. Along the way we may well make mistakes. The key is not to allow the mistake to be worth $20 million.

Smarter interpretation of data

Answer this question:

> A bat and ball cost $1.10.
>
> The bat costs one dollar more than the ball.
>
> How much does the ball cost?

If you answered 10 cents, you're likely aligned with what the majority of people would say. Yet the correct answer is, of course, five cents. This simple challenge, cited by researchers Manel Baucells and Rakesh K Sarin in their 2013 paper on guided decisions processes,[15] is a straightforward example of how a snap decision can often lead us astray. While this example is harmless, simple misjudgements of this kind can lead to poor decision-making in problem areas where the cost of error may be much higher.

Conjunction fallacy, for example, is a bias that leads us to believe that two events happening in conjunction is more probable than just one of those events happening alone. The fallacy is sometimes called the 'Linda problem' in reference to an example originated by Amos Tversky and Daniel Kahneman:[16]

> Linda is 31 years old, single, outspoken and very bright. She majored in philosophy. As a student, she was deeply concerned with issues of discrimination and social justice and also participated in anti-nuclear demonstrations. Which is more probable?

Linda is a bank teller.

Linda is a bank teller and is active in the feminist movement.

The majority of those asked chose option two, and yet the probability of two events occurring in conjunction is always equal to or less than the probability of either one occurring alone. In other words, option two is mathematically less likely. Tversky and Kahneman argue that most people choose this option because the answer seems more 'representative' of Linda based on the description given of her.

Conjunction fallacy is closely related to so-called 'gambler's fallacy' because of the way in which gamblers can mistakenly believe that a particular random event is more or less likely to happen based on the outcome of previous events. An example of this would be when we believe that a red number will be more likely to be next to appear on a roulette wheel after a series of black numbers appearing. The more black numbers appear in sequence the more likely we are to believe that the next number will be red. Yet we forget that the probability between red or black appearing resets to 50:50 every spin of the wheel. This heuristic is sometimes called the 'Monte Carlo' fallacy after a famous example of the phenomenon that happened in the Monte Carlo casino in 1913.[17] In one game of roulette that happened in August of that year, the ball fell in black 26 times in a row. The probability of one colour appearing 26 times in a row is extremely low (around 1 in 67 million), but gamblers lost millions of francs on that day betting against black because they mistakenly believed that as the sequence played out the probability of a red appearing was increasing. They were wrongly associating past events with the probability of something occurring in the present, forgetting that every time the wheel was spun the probability of red or black appearing was reset.

A similar misplaced enthusiasm once infected an entire nation. In 2005 the number 53 had not appeared in the Italian national lottery for almost two years. Italians began placing increasingly large bets on the elusive number in the mistaken belief that it was more likely to appear as time went on.[18] Over 50 lottery players succumbed to the belief so badly that they ran up debts, lost their homes and even became bankrupt. There were even four deaths attributed to the mania including a woman who drowned herself in the sea off Tuscany after losing her family's savings betting on the number. It is believed that an average of 227 euros for every family in Italy, or a total of 3.5 billion euros, was spent on number 53.

As we can see from these examples, it's so easy to mistakenly believe that because certain outcomes have happened in the past, it is increasing the probability of other events happening in the future. Well thought through use of past data however, can clearly enable us to make better decisions. Sticking with gambling, one example of this is the practice of card counting in blackjack games. At its simplest level, a card counter would allocate a positive score when a low-value card appears and a negative score when a high-value card appears. In blackjack high cards benefit the player (it's easier to get close to 21) and low cards benefit the dealer. Since there are a finite number of high and low cards in a deck, keeping track of the score as the cards are played enables the player to play according to probability. A succession of low cards would increase the count indicating that there is a higher probability of high cards remaining in the deck. The Hollywood film _21_[19] recounts the story of the MIT blackjack team who famously used more sophisticated card counting techniques to win millions of dollars at multiple casinos.[20]

The lesson from these examples is how easy it is for us to make poor decisions when looking at data. And when data is becoming so central to marketing operations it becomes ever more important for marketers to be cognizant of the risks associated with simple cognitive bias and to be aware of some of the most common misinterpretation errors. Daniel Kahneman's concept of representative bias for example, can easily lead marketers to make wrong assumptions about audiences through our tendency to ignore base rates (or the naturally occurring frequency of a phenomenon through a population). Kahneman gives an example of representative bias in the example of seeing a person reading _The New York Times_ on the New York subway. When considering whether it would be more likely for the reader to either have a PhD or to not have a college degree at all our natural bias would lead us to assume that the PhD would be a higher probability. Yet in choosing that option we are potentially ignoring the fact that many more non-graduates than PhDs ride the subway and while a larger proportion of PhDs may read _The New York Times_, the total number of _Times_ readers without a college degree is likely to be much larger.

Ignoring base rates can have significant consequences. In 1988, at the height of the AIDS epidemic, the US state of Illinois passed a law that mandated that all couples that applied for a marriage licence had to undertake an HIV test. The base rate of HIV among engaged heterosexual couples was so low that very few cases of the virus were found, false positives dominated true positives and public outcry ensued.[21] The law caused unintended consequences including tens of thousands of people fleeing the state to get married and many more putting off getting married altogether. One analysis of marriage licences found that the number of marriages performed in the state had dropped by 14 per cent during the period when the law was in force.[22] After little more than a year, legislatures were forced to repeal a law that had caused economic damage and psychological distress.

Representative bias and conjunction fallacy are related. In the former we may subconsciously ignore the base rate probability of something happening. In the latter, through representative bias we may allocate a higher level of probability to an event occurring when it has higher specificity. As writer Shane Parrish describes, these biases exist because we 'make the mental shortcut from our perceived plausibility of a scenario to its probability'.[23] Put simply, the most coherent stories may be plausible but they are not necessarily the most probable. This can become particularly problematic in the realms of expert opinion and also forecasting where we may well be more likely to find scenarios that are more detailed and illustrative to be more persuasive.

Kahneman found in his studies that even when students were aware of the biases, they were still susceptible to them, meaning that it is not enough to simply know that these heuristics exist. We need to take positive action to mitigate them. As Shane Parrish points out, critical thinking, along with a good grasp of probability in action, can help tame our intuition where it needs to be tamed.[24] Remembering simple rules such as the fact that all probability adds up to 100 per cent. Remembering to anchor our judgement of the probability of an outcome on a plausible base rate. And remembering the importance of diagnosticity or the degree to which a source of data that we might be using can actually discriminate between a particular hypothesis and its alternatives. Heuristics can play a key role in our judgement and lead to illogical conclusions and poor interpretation of data. Actively embedding deliberate questions into decision-making processes (particularly those based on data) and taking a step back to purposefully check for bias and misdirection may not take much time but will improve the quality of those decisions.

Avoiding noise and groupthink

Daniel Kahneman has described organizations as factories of decision-making and judgement, saying that: 'judgment is much less stable and much noisier than most people think'.[25] The amount of noise around a decision can create an 'invisible problem', which can lead to poor decision-making.

Kahneman collaborator Olivier Sibony has described noise as 'the unwanted variability in professional judgments'.[26] Bias might be thought of as the average error in judgements but the effect of bias is not always predictable, and this can lead to high variability in inputs. For example, in a project scenario you might expect that as a result of bias a group of stakeholders may underestimate the amount of time it will take to complete the project (so-called 'planning fallacy'). Noise however, is the variability (and variability of error) of those forecasts. Noise can lead to inconsistencies such as different people making different judgements and recommending different actions based on the same scenario.

Sibony gives the example of performance reviews whereby a rating may be subject to noise based on the idiosyncratic response of the rater to the ratee, 'level noise' where some raters are on average more generous than others or 'occasion noise', which may be more dependent on how the rater feels that day.[27] Some people, says Sibony, may simply be better at judgement than others but there are mitigating techniques that can help reduce noise. Using algorithms and rules-based decision-making can help reduce noise but algorithms will not be suitable for all decisions, of course. Conducting a 'noise audit', which involves giving the same problem to many different people in the organization and measuring the differences in their responses, can help determine how much noise that people in the team are subject to. In situations where a group of people need to reach a decision together it can help reduce noise if each person writes down their answer before the discussion takes place. The effect of this is to maintain the independence of people's individual judgements before they are then brought together and avoid a situation where the person who is speaking first or who is framing the challenge to solve has too much influence.

Similar techniques can help avoid groupthink, which may be characterized by a group coming to a consensus without using proper critical thinking as a result of their desire for conformity and harmony. The practice of group brainstorming has become an entrenched method for teams to originate new ideas or solutions, and yet it simply serves to compartmentalize ideation into a small window of time and can easily be led by groupthink as people are led by the ideas of others in the group. Having a group of people consider a challenge or a question for an amount of time before pooling the ideas can help both the quantity and quality of outputs. As psychologists Michael Diehl and Wolfgang Stroebe noted in 1991:[28]

> Brainstorming groups produce more ideas than an individual but fewer and poorer quality ideas than from individuals working separately. In other words, brainstorms dilute the sum of individual efforts.

Keith Sawyer, a psychologist at Washington University, has also pointed out how many studies over several decades have concluded that brainstorming groups think of far fewer ideas than the same number of people who work alone and then later bring their ideas together.[29]

Using simple techniques such as these can help reduce noise and improve the quality of ideas and decisions. When running retrospectives or ideas sessions or any kind of meeting where input from the team is needed, consider allowing everyone the opportunity to individually consider their own answers and ideas first before sharing them with the group and using the collective thinking as the basis for discussion.

Asking better questions

Theoretical physicist Stephen Hawking once argued that 'philosophy is dead' and that instead 'scientists have become the bearers of the torch of discovery in our quest for knowledge'.[30] Scientific method has clearly contributed hugely to the canon of human knowledge and our understanding of the world and it continues to do so, increasingly providing answers to some of the most fundamental questions that we face. Yet if we ignore or misunderstand the contribution of philosophy we might never really find the answers to the really big questions. This is because the strength of philosophy comes not from providing answers but from asking better questions. The kinds of questions that cannot only create knowledge but identify where it is lacking. As science, philosophy and physics content creator Jack Lawrence memorably puts it, philosophy:

> undermines what we consider to be obvious. It creates space. It tests our
> foundations such that we can build them back better. Science is the other side of
> that coin. It does the answering, and fills that space.[31]

Lawrence points out the origins of the word 'philosophy' is the Greek philosophia or 'love of wisdom'. Wisdom differs from the pursuit of knowledge in that much of wisdom is rooted in identifying and recognizing our own ignorance such that we can address it.

So it is with agile marketing. I've discussed at length in this book about the value that can come from taking a more data-driven and scientific approach to testing, learning and generating value through marketing activity. Yet this should always be balanced with a desire to also ask the questions that can challenge our fundamental assumptions, that can lead us into exploring new territories, that can help us understand where the gaps in our knowledge are. Earlier in the book I explained how the DIKW pyramid is a way of understanding the fundamentals of value creation through data. The top two layers of value in that pyramid are knowledge and wisdom. We can turn knowledge into wisdom through the application of actionable insight and process. But as well as asking how we can apply our new knowledge in the best way possible, we also need to ask 'what don't we know that might be useful'? Asking the right questions at the lowest 'data' level of the DIKW pyramid can help us to create the right foundation for success and enable us to organise data effectively to create information. Asking the right questions at the 'information' level of DIKW can help us to understand how we can interpret and translate patterns in data to generate knowledge. Asking the right questions at the 'knowledge' level of DIKW enables us to understand how we can apply it to generate maximum value, but we also need to define what knowledge we are lacking that might enable us to generate wisdom in a different way, and what data we are lacking that might inform that knowledge.

Another way of thinking about this draws on what strategy can learn from the world of art. As Pablo Picasso is once credited with saying: 'Computers are useless. They can only give you answers.' It is in the asking of questions that we are able to imagine new possibilities. Artist Grayson Perry once wrote that 'my job is to notice things that other people don't notice'[32] and noticing things means asking interesting questions. In her writing about this topic strategist Harriet Kindleysides defines three key themes around how art seeks to ask questions that can be usefully applied to strategy as well:[33]

1 Question what you see. Artists are good at challenging themselves and their audience to break open assumptions and reframing and reimagining how something is seen.

2 Question how you see. It's easy for us to view things in a one-dimensional way without questioning the context of what we're seeing. This can be related to how we interpret data and feedback, but also the communication of ideas. As Harriet says: 'The format, time and surroundings through which an idea is delivered can completely shift its meaning, impact and relevance.'

3 Question what isn't being seen. The ability to unlock new perspectives around not only what is in plain view but also what isn't being seen is also a great strength of art. This means asking the questions that can take us beyond the obvious and into that which might be hidden from view.

There is great value in being interested in the problem domain and the work that is being done to solve it, and there is also great value in asking questions that stretch, that ask what we don't know and enable us to see a situation in a different way.

NASA has given us a good example of how partial knowledge and a lack of asking the right questions can lead us astray. A renowned business school exercise (originated by Jack Brittain and Sim Sitkin[34]) asks students to imagine that they are John Carter, the leader of a racing car team that is about to take part in a very important race. Winning the race could mean big prize money, winning a new sponsorship deal and great publicity. Yet in 7 out of the last 24 races the engine in the Carter race car has broken and failed. If the engine blows out on live TV it could put the driver's life and all the potential sponsorship and prize money in jeopardy. One of the team's mechanics has a hunch that the engine is failing in cooler weather. A graph plotting the weather conditions in the races where the engine failed shows a relatively broad spectrum of temperatures (between 55 and 75 degrees Fahrenheit) and is inconclusive. The forecasted temperature for the race is under 40 degrees, leaving the team principal with a quandary – should he race or not? Many business students opt for going ahead and racing as the data given is inconclusive, but almost none of them ask to see the missing data from the races where the engine did not fail. Including this data on the graph shows clearly that every race where the car finished were run on days that were above 65 degrees and every race run at below this temperature ended in a blown engine. The mechanic was right, but we might never have learned that lesson had we not asked to see the full data.

As mathematician Hannah Fry notes, this scenario is actually a representation of a real situation, which resulted in the disastrous launch of the space shuttle challenger in January 1986.[35] This disaster was found to be the result of failing 'O-ring' pressure seals on the rocket motors. The launchpad temperature on the day of launch was forecast to be particularly cold at 36 degrees. A hurriedly assembled data table showing the temperatures at which the seals had previously failed was faxed to the Kennedy Space Centre and discussed at an emergency teleconference before launch. While some engineers used this to argue that the launch should be delayed, the data presented was inconclusive and most of the experts were not convinced. When the launch went ahead, the O-rings leaked, the solid rocket boosters failed and the shuttle broke apart, resulting in the tragic death of the seven astronauts on board. As Hannah Fry says:

> The chart implicitly defined the scope of relevance—and nobody seems to have asked for additional data points, the ones they couldn't see. This is why the managers made the tragic decision to go ahead despite the weather.[36]

It's a salutary lesson about what can happen when we don't challenge what we are seeing and are presented with and why it's so important to ask good questions like 'What are we not seeing here'? There is always a balance to be struck between moving fast and maintaining simplicity in processes and opening yourself up to unnecessary risk through poor decision-making. Being agile should not mean that we are generating unnecessary risk for the business. Creating 'safe to fail' boundaries and asking the right questions can enable us to be more informed in our decision-making while also creating new possibilities.

GREAT QUESTIONS THAT AGILE MARKETING LEADERS CAN ASK TO OPEN UP NEW THINKING

Questions that define: Why? What's the real problem we need to solve? Why not? What's stopping us from doing this? What are our biggest assumptions? What's our biggest learning? How can we turn this setback into a win? What do we need to know before we start work?

Questions that change thinking: What if...? How would it be different if...? What are we missing? What don't we know? What new opportunities have emerged? How might this change the way that we think? What's the cost of not doing this?

Questions that extend thinking: What will customer needs look like in the future and how can we design around those? How can we not only meet customer needs but surprise and delight? What other way could we..? What would change if..?

Questions that focus: What makes us unique and hard to copy? What is the biggest frustration that the team has and how can we overcome it? What's the most valuable thing that the team could be working on now?

Our quest for knowledge in agile marketing is important. Teams should focus on continuous learning and the accumulation of understanding. However, regularly asking more challenging questions that break open our assumptions, reframe a challenge and question what we are *not* seeing can open up new possibilities for a team. It can be the difference between optimizing to get to good outputs and innovating to get to exceptional outputs. More than this, it can be the difference between absolute success and complete failure.

High-velocity decision-making

Day 2 companies make high-quality decisions, but they make high-quality decisions slowly.

(Jeff Bezos)[37]

In his 2016 letter to shareholders Jeff Bezos talks about the difference between a 'Day 1' and a 'Day 2' company.[38] Day 1 at Amazon is characterized by bold innovation, keeping a long-term focus and an operating model and company culture that is customer-obsessed.[39] Day 2 is described as stasis, growing irrelevance and painful decline, which may happen in extreme slow motion but still ultimately results in corporate death. That's why, says Bezos, it's always Day 1 at Amazon and this idea is so important to him that he named the Amazon building where he works Day 1 and when he moved buildings, he took the name with him. In the letter Bezos names four key attributes that keep Amazon as a Day 1 business including embracing external trends (and executing against them), resisting managing by proxy (for example, being open to challenge processes in order to get to a better customer outcome) and true customer obsession.

The fourth attribute is high-velocity decision-making. Bezos describes how important it is to make high-quality decisions but to make them at speed and how decision-making can slow down in large companies as they become characterized by a one-size-fits-all approach. When decisions are irreversible or have significant repercussions, it's important to make them carefully, to take time and to be methodical in your approach.[40] The reality is however, that many decisions are 'two-way doors' or reversible, and these can be made in a more lightweight way by small groups or 'high-judgement' individuals. Most decisions, he says, can be made with 70 per cent of the information that you wish that you had and if you wait until you have 90 per cent of the information in most cases you are probably being slow. As organizations become larger they can easily be dominated by more heavyweight decision-making, which slows them down, and can mean that they become unnecessarily risk averse and fail to experiment enough.

The key here is to be more selective in your approach. To understand the difference between 70 per cent and 90 per cent decisions. Recognize when you are facing a decision that is higher risk or difficult to change, and make sure that you have the time and inputs to make the right choice. But also recognize when it's possible to take a more lightweight approach and move faster with 70 per cent of the information you need, and then course correct if you need to. Either way, he says, it's important to be good at quickly recognizing bad decisions: 'If you're good at course correcting, being wrong may be less costly than you think, whereas being slow is going to be expensive for sure.'[41]

A culture of overly consensus-driven decision-making, where all stakeholders need to be in agreement before headway can be made, can also act as a brake on team progress. Amazon have a useful approach here too, using the phrase 'disagree and commit' as a way to acknowledge disagreement without holding back the project. As an example of this management principle, Bezos describes an Amazon Studios investment proposal that was presented to him, which he thought was complicated but not interesting enough. However, the Studios team were all aligned that they believed this to be a good idea and so he wrote back to them to say: 'I disagree and commit and hope it becomes the most watched thing we've ever made.' It takes time to gain universal approval, so while it's important to acknowledge everyone's point of view, this principle enables Amazon to move faster.

Teams can become choked by decision-making processes that are perhaps a legacy from a different era. Using these techniques can enable marketing teams to make high-quality decisions but to make them at pace.

When to pivot, when to persevere

In *The Lean Startup*[42] Eric Ries describes a pivot as 'a change in strategy without a change in vision'. In agile marketing a pivot may be thought of as a shift in strategy that goes beyond optimization of existing tactics. As with Eric Ries's definition, the overall goal may not necessarily be any different, but how the team achieves that goal may change. A change in strategy may be required when measures start to fall dependably short of what is required to reach the goal. In this situation it's important to ensure that enough time has elapsed to demonstrate a consistent pattern of metrics, but not so long that end results are impacted. Pivots may also be required following a significant change in contexts:

- **Competitive context:** Notable competitive activity that has resulted in revised market dynamics.
- **Customer context:** Notable shifts in customer responses as a result of an event, announcement or development of some kind.
- **Company context:** Notable changes in business needs or inputs that require new approaches.

FIGURE 12.1 Local and global maximums

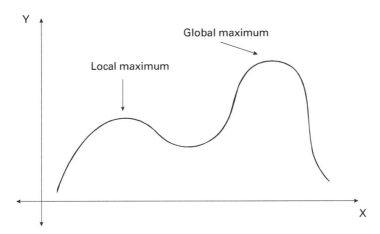

It's important to consider the limits of optimization in this context. There is clearly huge value that can be derived from continuous incremental improvements, but we may well find that gains begin to diminish and that we need to make a bigger change of some kind in order to take another leap forward. Andrew Chen, a partner at venture capital firm Andreessen Horowitz, has described how metrics can enable optimization around existing strategies to get to 'local maximums'.[43] These are the points at which a team may have reached the limits of the current plan, set-up or activity. In order to reach a new level or a 'global maximum', a change in strategy, thinking or applied resources is needed. It's therefore critical for teams to track metrics and continually optimize towards local maximums, but then also to recognize when new thinking or a pivot in strategy is needed in order to open up the potential for a new level and a global maximum.

When considering a pivot it can be helpful for a team to look outside of the existing metrics that they may be optimizing around in order to identify new patterns through different data points that can open up new thinking and new possibilities. Just as data can support incremental improvement and continuous optimization, so it can also reframe contexts and challenge existing thinking.

Keystone moments

Physicist Murray Gell-Man believed that 'the history that is actually seen is co-determined by the simple fundamental laws, and by an inconceivably long sequence of accidents or chance events'.[44] In other words, while there are fundamental laws that govern the world, it has also been shaped by random accidents and unforeseen occurrences that have created the opportunity for new possibilities but that might easily have resulted in a very different world had they gone another way. Writer Shane Parrish has described how these accidents become 'frozen in time', having a potentially significant impact on subsequent events.[45] Parrish references a couple of stories that are featured in Eric Beinhocker's book *The Origin of Wealth*,[46] demonstrating how impactful such frozen accidents can be. Beinhocker describes how sharpshooter Annie Oakley was one of the most popular acts within Buffalo Bill's Wild West Show, which successfully toured the United States in the late nineteenth century. Annie would demonstrate her skills using tricks that included shooting the flames off candles and her grand finale, which involved shooting the end off a lit cigarette held in the mouth of a brave volunteer from the audience. Since no one from the audience would ever come forwards Annie would plant her husband Frank in the audience who would then volunteer, allowing Annie to demonstrate her renowned skill. When the show was touring Europe in 1880 the young crown prince Wilhelm (who would later become Kaiser Wilhelm of Germany) happened to be in the audience for one of the shows and, much to Annie's surprise, volunteered for her grand finale trick:

> The future German Kaiser strode into the ring, placed the cigarette in his mouth, and stood ready. Annie, who had been up late the night before in the local beer garden, was unnerved by this unexpected development. She lined the cigarette up in her sights, squeezed… and hit it right on the target.

Many people have speculated how a slight tremor in Annie's hand in that moment might have changed the entire course of twentieth century world history. If Wilhelm had not survived perhaps World War I would never have happened, thereby saving millions of lives. Perhaps then the Communists might never have been able to overthrow the Russian government. Perhaps years later the Nazis would not have come to power following the German defeat in the first World War. While this is all based on a speculative example, it demonstrates how such moments can make it so difficult to predict future events and how moments that seem relatively insignificant at the time can potentially have such significantly disproportionate effects.

Beinhocker also gives the more recent example of how Bill Gates and Microsoft created their first operating system (OS). IBM first approached Gates and his co-founder Paul Allen in 1980, asking them to create a programming language for their new PC. They asked Gates to recommend an OS that the machine could run on and Gates suggested the Digital Research OS, which had become popular in the hobbyist microcomputers of the time. The founder of Digital Research, Gary Kildall, wasn't keen and so IBM asked Gates if he'd be interested in the OS project. Gates had never written an OS but said yes, and he promptly licensed Q-DOS (Quick and Dirty Operating System) from Seattle Computer Products for $50,000, wrote a few modifications and then relicensed it to IBM as PC-DOS. Then, as they were in final negotiations on the contract, Gates asked for one small change – to retain the rights to sell his DOS on non-IBM machines as a version called MS-DOS. Since IBM was primarily a hardware business at the time and they were getting a good price for the software, they agreed. The contract was signed in 1981 and the implications of that decision would echo through the next four decades. At the time of writing Microsoft has a market capitalization of $2.165 trillion and is the second most valuable company in the world by that measure.

Such moments in time are what we might describe as 'keystone moments'. A point of inflection from which events cascade into creating huge consequences. In masonry and architecture a keystone is the wedge-shaped stone at the top of the arch. This is often the final piece put in during construction and it locks all the stones in the arch into position. A good keystone enables the arch to bear significant weight. A bad one can result in the arch collapsing. But both of these results bear significant consequences. Keystone moments and cascading consequences show how hard it is to predict the future with a high degree of confidence. They demonstrate the false certainty of predictions and rigid forecasts and the need for emergent and adaptive approaches. As Shane Parrish says, we must learn that 'predicting is inferior to building systems that don't require prediction'.[47] It's important that leaders recognize the need to move quickly in adaptation in order to avoid negative cascades but also to move swiftly in identifying and capitalizing on positive cascades that build momentum based on rapid learning and feedback loops. In the next section we'll look at an example of creating positive cascades through 'flywheel' approaches.

One final thought on keystones. In his book *The Power of Habit*,[48] Charles Duhigg wrote about just how powerful habits are in driving and shaping our behaviour. One Duke University study for example, estimated that habits rather than conscious decision-making shape up to 45 per cent of the choices that we make every day.[49] Habits, says Duhigg, comprise the trigger or cues that start the habit, the action we take in response and the benefit that we get from doing it. The best way to change habits is to remake them, which entails being aware of the contexts in which the triggers occur, the responses that we typically make to those cues and understanding the reward and the need that the habit is serving. Once we understand this we can deliberately design different actions and different rewards in order to remake a new habit (he suggests writing a plan for change: 'When [*insert cue*], I will [*insert new routine*], because it provides me with [*insert reward*]').

Team leaders can use this technique to shape team behaviour and build positive habits. In agile marketing for example, we might want to make evidence-based decisioning more of a habit on the team. So we might design a plan that creates intrinsic motivation and reward for team members who have placed data-driven decision-making at the heart of their work. Even simple fixes (like the questions that leaders ask of the team and what they choose to recognize and amplify) can help remake habits if done in the right way over time.

Charles Duhigg also talked about 'keystone habits', describing them as 'small changes or habits that people introduce into their routines that unintentionally carry over into other aspects of their lives'.[50] Just as I described with keystone moments, these keystone habits are the kinds of behaviours that cascade into other behaviours and have the potential to generate significant consequences. In agile marketing, evidence-based or data-driven decisioning is one such keystone habit. It's a positive one since it directly influences an individual's and team's ability to optimize, amplify and identify potentially detrimental shifts early. At a personal level, saying 'yes' to every meeting invite might be an example of a negative keystone habit since it might result in a number of other consequences including a lack of time to get work done, stress, an inability to prioritize time to reflect and so on. Understanding both positive and negative keystone habits can really help build momentum behind the kinds of behaviours that can embed true agility into a team.

Going slowly to go quickly

The secret is to win going as slowly as possible.

(Nikki Lauda)[51]

Agile practices are often conflated with teams doing more with less and working faster to achieve outcomes, and it's true that in many cases the introduction of agile principles can result in higher productivity, greater efficiency and improved speed to insight and to market. However it's also important to recognize that moving fast and having a higher cadence of decision-making does not necessarily mean that it's OK to make poor-quality decisions.

Nikki Lauda, quoted above, knew that in Formula One the cars are delicate, have very little redundancy and need to be driven fast but also with precision and care. Drivers have to protect the engine and their tyres as they drive the race in order to ensure that the car lasts the distance. A driver that does not finish races is not a driver that will win the World Championship. Many of the drivers that have won multiple championships were famed for their ability to look after the car during the race while also driving astoundingly fast.

The skill of a good agile marketing team comes from moving fast while still making high-quality decisions. As I mentioned earlier in this chapter, this means understanding the context of the decision that needs to be made and whether it is a reversible '70 per cent' decision or one that is a higher-risk '90 per cent' choice that requires more information. Understanding this can be key to teams making good decisions over extended periods and really achieving and exceeding objectives and outcomes. Sometimes a team needs to move slowly so that they can then move quickly. If a team appreciates when they need to take time to make sure that they are making the right decision, and they are given the space and resources to do that, they will ultimately be more successful. Being agile is not only about moving fast. It's about moving fast with care and precision.

Creating 'flywheels' – positive reinforcing loops

The concept of 'flywheels' is a useful way of describing how positive feedback loops can build momentum. These compounding reinforcing loops can help business propositions to scale through data and create momentum within campaigns that can build impact. Originated by Scottish inventor James Watt, the flywheel is an energy-efficient wheel that develops a momentum of its own once it starts spinning which makes it easier to accelerate it to an even faster speed. The concept has wide application in the context of agile marketing.

The 'flywheel effect' can positively impact business growth. In his book *The Everything Store: Jeff Bezos and the Age of Amazon*, Brad Stone describes how Amazon built their business using this idea:

> Lower prices led to more customer visits. More customers increased the volume of sales and attracted more commission-paying third-party sellers to the site.

That allowed Amazon to get more out of fixed costs like the fulfillment centers and the servers needed to run the website. This greater efficiency then enabled it to lower prices further.[52]

Amazon realized that if they fed any part of this wheel it could accelerate the entire loop.

A similar example comes from the early days of Airbnb. Network effects is the principle that every additional user or node on a network increases the value of the entire network. Since the value of the network is the square of the number of people on the network, the potential is to create disproportionate increases in value for marginal increases in cost. The idea of 'cross-side' network effects means that the more supply Airbnb has (interesting places to stay) the more this creates demand (people who want to stay in interesting places). The more demand Airbnb has, the more supply it can create as apartment owners realize it is the best place to list their property. Similarly, an example of 'same-side' network effects might be that users who have had a good experience with the platform will advocate to other people that may not have used Airbnb, or that landlords recommend the platform to other landlords due to the high occupancy rate that they are getting. These compounding loops can contribute to rapid growth in scale. Where marketers are focused on building network effects and rapidly growing the number of users on a platform, they need to focus on the strategies that can build network value and create positive feedback loops.

Similarly, the flywheel effect can help build momentum at a business level around important areas of organizational focus such as customer experience. Aligning all areas of the business around delivering truly exceptional customer experiences can create compounding benefits by using the momentum of customer delight and advocacy to drive acquisition, referrals and repeat sales. Using the analogy of a mechanical flywheel, marketing technology business HubSpot describes how the amount of energy or momentum in the flywheel depends on how fast the wheel is spinning, how much friction there is in the system and how big the wheel is.[53] Each of these elements present opportunities:

- **Flywheel speed:** Initiatives and strategies that focus on the areas of most significant impact for marketing and customer experience are the 'forces' that can increase flywheel momentum. These might include a customer referral programme, paid advertising or inbound marketing. Strategy needs to identify where and how to apply these forces to maximum effect.

- **Removing friction:** In order to go fast it's also essential to remove friction from your strategy. This means eliminating the kind of executional resistance that can slow you down, including friction from inefficient processes, poor collaboration or communication, or lack of understanding and alignment around goals.

- **Flywheel size:** We might think of this in terms of the size of budget or resource that is behind the implementation of the strategy, but it is also about how a team can build momentum by continually building on success and impact through a focus on metrics, continual optimization and pivoting strategy at the right time.

Positive, reinforcing feedback loops can also be useful in building momentum towards specific marketing goals. Customer acquisition and engagement loops are simple examples of this tactic. The former happens when new users of a service help to recruit other new users through advocacy or the sharing of content. For example, TikTok rapidly built awareness by creating exceptional mobile-native video production tools within the platform and then making it as easy as possible for content creators to share videos on other platforms, each one of them watermarked with a TikTok logo. A positive customer engagement loop means that as more users engage and use a service it generates more engagement and use from other users. Facebook for example, are ruthlessly focused on driving the levels of engagement from their users and undertake thousands of tests involving small changes to the news feed in order to improve those metrics. They understand that greater engagement from users results in a more interesting news feed, which then leads to greater engagement from others. This loop then compounds, creating even more engagement and so on. Another example of a positive reinforcing loop could be the relationship between paid search (pay-per-click – PPC) and organic search on retail sites like Amazon. Organic ranking in search results driven by the search algorithms is often influenced strongly by sales velocity. In other words, the higher the rate of sales the higher the product is likely to rank in organic search results on the site. Using paid search activity to boost sales at the right time (for example, at the launch of a new product on-site) can drive sales velocity, which can drive organic search ranking, which can in turn drive even more sales.

Flywheels can support rapid innovation as well. As teams build new capabilities, the ability to rapidly share learning and make those capabilities available to other teams helps those other teams to build on top of that innovation. As an example, a team that is experimenting with ML may build a successful model that can be applied to serve multiple team goals. Sharing that model and allowing other teams to experiment with it and build on it creates a forward momentum around machine learning capability.

Agile marketing teams can build reinforcing loops into their strategy in multiple ways but the objective is always about driving exceptional growth.

Marketing ops and workflow

Marketing operations roles have grown out of a need for marketing teams to optimize workflow as they shape a technology stack that is fully optimized for their needs. The role can play slightly different functions in different teams. Some marketing operations roles are more focused on ensuring that the team can get the most out of the technology stack and that it is set up in a way that supports what the team needs it to do. Ongoing management and optimization of the systems may be a key part of this. The function may also incorporate making workflows and data flows around the use of the systems as efficient as possible. In a scaled application of agile teams, for example, these people can play a key role in enabling workflows that facilitate access to data and systems as and when teams need it. Operations staff may also work with data specialists to build dashboards and remote access to key information that can inform progress. They may even work more closely with other team members focused on campaign planning and reporting.

These roles have emerged and become more critical as the need to optimize workflow has arisen due to the increasing complexity of what teams are doing and the integration of technology and data into the fabric of the marketing process.

Endnotes

1 D Kahneman (2012) *Thinking, Fast and Slow*, Penguin, London.

2 J Wastnage. Pictures: Navigational software glitch forces Lockheed Martin F-22 Raptors back to Hawaii, abandoning first foreign deployment to Japan, Flight Global, 14 February 2007. www.flightglobal.com/pictures-navigational-software-glitch-forces-lockheed-martin-f-22-raptors-back-to-hawaii-abandoning-first-foreign-deployment-to-japan/72004.article (archived at https://perma.cc/5T4R-58ME)

3 Y Bobeldijk. Banks face spiraling costs from 50-year-old IT, Financial News, 2 October 2017. www.fnlondon.com/articles/banks-face-spiraling-costs-from-archaic-it-20170912 (archived at https://perma.cc/E4S2-GUT6)

4 L Kelion. Excel: Why using Microsoft's tool caused Covid-19 results to be lost, BBC, 5 October 2020. www.bbc.co.uk/news/technology-54423988 (archived at https://perma.cc/J4LP-LEJ2)

5 L Kelion. Excel: Why using Microsoft's tool caused Covid-19 results to be lost, BBC, 5 October 2020. www.bbc.co.uk/news/technology-54423988 (archived at https://perma.cc/J4LP-LEJ2)

6 M Parker (2020) *Humble Pi: A Comedy of Maths Errors*, Penguin, London.

7 The European Spreadsheet Risks Interest Group. www.eusprig.org/ (archived at https://perma.cc/ZW7K-943X)

8 The European Spreadsheet Risks Interest Group. Horror stories, October 2020. www.eusprig.org/horror-stories.htm (archived at https://perma.cc/NW2D-KCZ2)

9 J Vincent. Scientists rename human genes to stop Microsoft Excel from misreading them as dates, The Verge, 6 August 2020. www.theverge.com/2020/8/6/21355674/human-genes-rename-microsoft-excel-misreading-dates (archived at https://perma.cc/7HUU-25HV)

10 A Picken. Spreadsheet error led to Edinburgh hospital opening delay, BBC News, 26 August 2020. www.bbc.co.uk/news/uk-scotland-edinburgh-east-fife-53893101 (archived at https://perma.cc/RWZ6-QZFN)

11 D Murphy. State fund for jobs loses €750k due to 'human error', RTE, 26 November 2019. www.rte.ie/news/business/2019/1126/1095303-human-error-cost-ntma-750-000-on-an-investment/ (archived at https://perma.cc/F7SZ-TZYS)

12 R Ollikainen. Spreadsheet errors cost Clallam $494,157, Peninsula Daily News, 17 February 2017. www.peninsuladailynews.com/news/spreadsheet-errors-cost-clallam-494157/ (archived at https://perma.cc/3QST-H7BD)

13 M Parker (2020) *Humble Pi: A Comedy of Maths Errors*, Penguin, London.

14 M Parker. Bad math, Pepsi points, and the greatest plane non-crash ever, Wired, 23 January 2020. www.wired.com/story/bad-math-pepsi-points-greatest-plane-non-crash-ever/ (archived at https://perma.cc/T3QP-T5CP)

15 M Baucells and R K Sarin. Guided decisions processes, May 2013. link.springer.com/article/10.1007/s40070-013-0003-8 (archived at https://perma.cc/FD45-4G8Z)

16 A Tversky and D Kahneman, Extensional versus intuitive reasoning: The conjunction fallacy in probability judgment, *Psychological Review*, October 1983. archive.is/20130223193247/http://content2.apa.org/journals/rev/90/4/293#selection-285.1-293.44

17 T Stafford. Why we gamble like monkeys, BBC, January 2015. www.bbc.com/future/article/20150127-why-we-gamble-like-monkeys (archived at https://perma.cc/H3C9-GBU8)

18 S Arie. No. 53 puts Italians out of their lottery agony, *The Guardian*, 11 February 2005. www.theguardian.com/world/2005/feb/11/italy.sophiearie (archived at https://perma.cc/JL7D-N78D)

19 *21*, IMDb. www.imdb.com/title/tt0478087/ (archived at https://perma.cc/4T37-UD2P)

20 J Ball. How a team of students beat the casinos, BBC, 26 May 2014. www.bbc.co.uk/news/magazine-27519748 (archived at https://perma.cc/LTV8-QLX7)

21 I Wilkerson. Illinois is urged to repeal law For AIDS tests, *New York Times*, 4 February 1989. www.nytimes.com/1989/02/04/us/illinois-is-urged-to-repeal-law-for-aids-tests.html (archived at https://perma.cc/P8TB-9ENC)

22 AIDS Test Rule Brings 14% Drop in Illinois Marriages, *LA Times*, 28 April 1991. www.latimes.com/archives/la-xpm-1991-04-28-mn-1459-story.html (archived at https://perma.cc/44FY-GT3A)

23 S Parrish. Mental model: Bias from conjunction fallacy, September 2016. fs.blog/2016/09/bias-conjunction-fallacy/ (archived at https://perma.cc/Y892-AHC5)

24 S Parrish. Mental model: Bias from conjunction fallacy, September 2016. fs.blog/2016/09/bias-conjunction-fallacy/ (archived at https://perma.cc/Y892-AHC5)

25 UBS. Daniel Kahneman Nobel 2002, what determines human decisions? UBS Nobel Perspectives, 2021. www.ubs.com/microsites/nobel-perspectives/en/laureates/daniel-kahneman.html (archived at https://perma.cc/ZSB9-V69T)

26 McKinsey. Sounding the alarm on noise, May 2021. www.mckinsey.com/business-functions/strategy-and-corporate-finance/our-insights/sounding-the-alarm-on-system-noise (archived at https://perma.cc/T7Z5-4Q7S)

27 McKinsey. Sounding the alarm on noise, May 2021. www.mckinsey.com/business-functions/strategy-and-corporate-finance/our-insights/sounding-the-alarm-on-system-noise (archived at https://perma.cc/T7Z5-4Q7S)

28 M Diehl and W Stroebe. Productivity loss in idea-generating groups: Tracking down the blocking effect, American Psychological Association, September 1991. https://psycnet.apa.org/record/1992-05054-001 (archived at https://perma.cc/FX8E-HG4Y)

29 J Lehrer. Brainstorming: An idea past its prime, *The Washington Post*, 19 April 2012. www.washingtonpost.com/opinions/brainstorming-an-idea-past-its-prime/2012/04/19/gIQAhKT5TT_story.html (archived at https://perma.cc/QUP4-9KHL)

30 M Warman. Stephen Hawking tells Google that philosophy is dead, *Daily Telegraph*, May 2011. www.telegraph.co.uk/technology/google/8520033/Stephen-Hawking-tells-Google-philosophy-is-dead.html (archived at https://perma.cc/KBS8-4HM2)

31 J Lawrence. Is philosophy Dead?, TikTok, 2021. www.tiktok.com/@jack.lawro/video/7015280363287137542 (archived at https://perma.cc/NY2S-GVK4)

32 G Perry (2016) *Playing to the Gallery*, Penguin, New York.

33 H Kindleysides. Questioning things, A Strategist's Guide to Art, November 2020. astrategistsguidetoart.substack.com/p/questioning-things (archived at https://perma.cc/628Z-R7RQ)

34 J Brittain and S Sitkin. Carter Racing, 2006. execed.poole.ncsu.edu/wp-content/uploads/2020/06/Carter-Racing-A_B_C.pdf (archived at https://perma.cc/L5WJ-XUG3)

35 H Fry. When graphs are a matter of life and death, *The New Yorker*, 14 June 2021. www.newyorker.com/magazine/2021/06/21/when-graphs-are-a-matter-of-life-and-death (archived at https://perma.cc/W697-R28A)

36 H Fry. When graphs are a matter of life and death, *The New Yorker*, 14 June 2021. www.newyorker.com/magazine/2021/06/21/when-graphs-are-a-matter-of-life-and-death (archived at https://perma.cc/W697-R28A)

37 J Bezos. 2016 letter to shareholders. www.sec.gov/Archives/edgar/data/1018724/000119312517120198/d373368dex991.htm (archived at https://perma.cc/9YNW-4F3V)

38 J Bezos. 2016 letter to shareholders. www.sec.gov/Archives/edgar/data/1018724/000119312517120198/d373368dex991.htm (archived at https://perma.cc/9YNW-4F3V)

39 D Slater. Elements of Amazon's Day 1 culture, AWS. aws.amazon.com/executive-insights/content/how-amazon-defines-and-operationalizes-a-day-1-culture/

40 J Bezos. 2015 letter to shareholders. www.sec.gov/Archives/edgar/data/1018724/000119312516530910/d168744dex991.htm (archived at https://perma.cc/UJ5Q-6S9G)

41 J Bezos. 2016 letter to shareholders. www.sec.gov/Archives/edgar/data/1018724/000119312517120198/d373368dex991.htm (archived at https://perma.cc/9YNW-4F3V)

42 E Ries (2011) *The Lean Startup*, Portfolio Penguin, London.

43 A Chen. Know the difference between data driven and data informed, 2021. andrewchen.co/know-the-difference-between-data-informed-and-versus-data-driven/ (archived at https://perma.cc/ZR9L-FE4D)

44 M Gell-Mann. Interview, The Nobel Prize, December 2001. www.nobelprize.org/prizes/physics/1969/gell-mann/interview/ (archived at https://perma.cc/3S9L-GANJ)

45 S Parrish. Frozen accidents: why the future is so unpredictable, Farnam Street, November 2016. fs.blog/2016/11/frozen-accidents/ (archived at https://perma.cc/J3KE-MNBK)

46 E Beinhocker (2007) *The Origin of Wealth*, Random House Business, London.

47 S Parrish. Frozen accidents: Why the future is so unpredictable, Farnam Street, November 2016. fs.blog/2016/11/frozen-accidents/ (archived at https://perma.cc/J3KE-MNBK)

48 C Duhigg (2014) *The Power of Habit: Why We Do What We Do in Life and Business*, Random House Trade Paperbacks, London.

49 D T Neal, Wendy Wood and Jeffrey M Quinn, Aug 2006, Habits – a repeat performance, Research Gate. www.researchgate.net/publication/252798940_HabitsA_Repeat_Performance (archived at https://perma.cc/YG8Q-XKLL)

50 C Duhigg (2014) *The Power of Habit: Why We Do What We Do in Life and Business*, Random House Trade Paperbacks, London.

51 C James. Nikki Lauda wins by going slowly, *The Monthly*, April 2006. www.clivejames.com/niki-lauda-wins-going-slowly.html (archived at https://perma.cc/TVQ6-6Z66)

52 B Stone (2014) *The Everything Store: Jeff Bezos and the Age of Amazon*, Corgi, London.

53 HubSpot. The flywheel model, 2021. www.hubspot.com/flywheel (archived at https://perma.cc/79XR-VHD4)

PART SIX

Agile marketing culture and leadership

13

What is agile culture in marketing?

The attributes of agile marketing culture

There are a number of behavioural and mindset attributes that clearly run alongside much of the process and ways of working that I've discussed in this book and we might think of these as essential enablers. For example, the ability to combine evidence-based decisioning through data with human empathy, particularly in the context of understanding customer needs. A mindset that is customer-obsessed. An attitude that is biased for action and always looking to combine customer value with business results. Beyond this however, there are a number of important cultural behaviours that truly enable an agile marketing team to learn fast, collaborate well and deliver exceptional outcomes. In this next part of the book I'm going to dive into some of the following themes, which capture critical agile marketing behaviours:

- **Curiosity and exploration:** The hunger to learn continuously, thinking differently, searching for answers, creating the space for exploration and experimentation.

- **Autonomy and empowerment:** Teams that can make the decisions in the areas that they're responsible for are well-motivated and can move fast.

- **Collaboration and cooperation:** The ability to work in cross-disciplinary ways, to work horizontally with other team members and other teams in the service of solving problems and executing well. Solving problems better through diversity in background, personality and cognition.

- **Psychological safety:** Combining an environment of trust and respect with the ability to speak up and say what we really mean.

- **Ownership:** Taking responsibility and not making assumptions about someone else filling the gaps.

- **Growth mindset:** Seeing failure and challenge as an opportunity to learn and grow.
- **Support:** establishing networks and communities to share knowledge and support learning, the value of coaching in helping teams to stay agile.

AGILE CULTURE AT VARIANCE

Customer growth platform variance has a clearly articulated vision and values that can enable and empower a true culture of agility in the company.[1] Their vision is to build a platform that enables everyone in an organization to drive growth. The values that support this are framed around some explicit but inclusive expectations around ways of working (paraphrased below):

- **Users > buyers:** As a SaaS business, success is based on product usage, which means everyone in the organization must 'obsess over our product, our customers' usage and how we can constantly improve it'.
- **Brain > role:** Everyone has a specific role in the company, but everyone is expected to be a smart and vocal team member, meaning they should say something when they see it.
- **Impact > efficiency:** While technology can drive great efficiencies, benefit comes from leverage as well. 'Efficiency can become a celebration of activity while impact is about ensuring that every person, minute, dollar, and tool is focused on the tasks that will drive the most outsized outcomes.'
- **Growth = compounding success:** The most tenured employees are the most valuable because they have compounded knowledge, which means a focus on retention and professional growth. 'We feel the same way about our customers.'

The business believes in writing as much down as possible since it forces you to organize your thoughts. In their 'laws of meetings' this means avoiding presentations wherever possible and instead writing things out, having a meeting start with reading when it makes sense or using whiteboarding to think through challenges.[2] Meetings, they say, are great when they work and terrible when they don't but are one of the most expensive things that happen at a company. So there are clear expectations set around making meetings as valuable and additive as possible including questioning whether a meeting is really necessary, clearly stating the purpose, ensuring that the right people needed to make a decision attend and no more, being prompt and staying focused on the task at hand whilst there.

Breaking and remaking habits

Before we look at the individual cultural attributes that characterize a high-performing agile marketing team, let's consider the power of habitual behaviour. As mentioned earlier in the book, a study by researchers David Neal, Wendy Wood and Jeffrey Quinn at Duke University[3] estimated that habits (rather than conscious decision-making) can shape up to 45 per cent of the decisions and behaviours that we make every day. Habits are powerful. In a marketing team habitual behaviour can shape how we approach tasks, solve problems and prioritize value.

In his book on *The Power of Habit*[4] Charles Duhigg describes how the best way of getting rid of a bad habit is to replace it with a new one. This involves being aware of three things: the cues that trigger the start of the habit; the action you take; the benefit you get from doing it. The 'habit loop' involves cues triggering an action that is then reinforced through a reward. Bearing this in mind can help us to focus on how we can change each of these elements. Being aware of the contexts that surround us when we feel the prompt to respond will help us to identify the cues that occur most frequently and the factors that cause them. Looking at the rewards helps us to understand the needs that we have that we are satisfying. Having identified the cue and the reward, we can then remake a habit by changing up the routine.

A good way of thinking about building new habits comes from B J Fogg. In his book *Tiny Habits: The Small Changes That Change Everything*[5] Fogg defines long-term behaviour change as being derived from an epiphany, a change of context and the cumulative effect of lots of tiny habits over time. This means that we need to frame a compelling need for change and a new direction, but it also means changing the context around decision-making and making it as easy as possible for people to exhibit the right behaviours every day. In an agile marketing context, when a team is shifting to agile ways of working, there is a need therefore to root the change in solid reasoning and an inspiring vision and then to support the cultural attributes that can enable people to genuinely work in a different way. Everyday behaviours are what supports long-term cultural change. Fogg goes on to describe how behaviour is a function of the trigger, motivation and ability. If one of these elements is missing the behaviour can't happen. This means that leaders need to ensure that both the motivation and the ability are present for people to action behaviour change. Encouraging people to use cues and triggers that happen on a daily basis and starting with small changes in behaviour can create lasting change.

Since habits are such a powerful driver of behaviour, it is important for leaders to consider what the behaviours are that they would like the team to change and then to create the enabling environment in which people can remake habits.

Endnotes

1 Variance. Culture, 2021. www.variance.com/culture (archived at https://perma.cc/QM8M-NVNA)

2 Variance. Laws of meetings, July 2021. www.variance.com/culture/laws-of-meetings (archived at https://perma.cc/QM8M-NVNA)

3 D T Neal, W Wood and J M Quinn. Habits – a repeat performance, Research Gate, August 2006. www.researchgate.net/publication/252798940_HabitsA_Repeat_Performance (archived at https://perma.cc/398L-3CMP)

4 C Duhigg (2014) *The Power of Habit: Why We Do What We Do in Life and Business*, Random House Trade Paperbacks, London.

5 B J Fogg (2020) *Tiny Habits: The Small Changes That Change Everything*, Virgin Books, London.

14

A culture of exploration

Empowering curiosity

Agile marketing can deliver greater efficiency in marketing operations and practice but it is far from being just about doing more with less or doing it faster. It is also about continuous exploration, experimentation, testing and learning. Organizations like certainty but as the Italian theoretical physicist and writer Carlo Ravelli wrote:

> I believe that one of the greatest mistakes made by human beings is to want certainties when trying to understand something. The search for knowledge is not nourished by certainty: it is nourished by a radical absence of certainty. Thanks to the acute awareness of our ignorance, we are open to doubt and can continue to learn and to learn better. This has always been the strength of scientific thinking—thinking born of curiosity, revolt, change.[1]

When contexts are changing fast a team needs to be responsive and adaptive, but they also need to be learning continuously and being creative about how they are solving challenges. Curiosity is a significant value creator in this context. Agile marketing teams should always be focused on delivering and building value, but there should also be a continuous focus on exploration and bringing in fresh perspectives that can challenge assumptions and generate leaps forward in problem-solving, ideas and capability.

Artist Chuck Close once said:

> Inspiration is for amateurs. The rest of us just show up and get to work. If you wait for the clouds to part and a bolt of lightning to strike you, you are not going to make much work. All the best ideas come out of the process; they come out of the work itself.[2]

The essence of this advice, intended for young artists ('and anybody who'll listen to me'), is not to wait around for inspiration but instead to understand that you have to work at it. Similarly in agile marketing, teams need to be aware that inspiration may come at any time, but that it will come from doing the work. Teams need to be ready to absorb and act on creatively driven ideas, but they also need to create the space to continuously explore.

The challenge with this, of course, is that many corporate environments place low value on curiosity and time spent in exploring new ideas. The continual drive for efficiency creates significant tension between the time dedicated to delivery and time spent learning. All too often learning and curiosity is sacrificed at the altar of productivity and efficiency. Harvard Business School Professor Francesca Gino has conducted extensive research into the value of curiosity in business. Her research (based on inputs from 3,000 employees from a range of sectors) shows that greater curiosity in business results in staff thinking more deeply about decisions and being less susceptible to the kinds of cognitive bias that I mentioned earlier in the book, which means fewer decision-making errors.[3] In total, 92 per cent of the participants in that research believed that curiosity was a catalyst for high performance, job satisfaction, motivation and innovation. In spite of this, her research also revealed that 70 per cent of survey respondents said that they face barriers to asking more questions at work and only 24 per cent reported feeling curious in their work on a regular basis.

It's clear that while leaders may talk a good game about celebrating curiosity in the workplace, this is not carried through into the environment in which many employees work. A large study (based on 23,000 employees) conducted by Survey Monkey, working with Spencer Harrison, Associate Professor of Organizational Behaviour at INSEAD, revealed that while 83 per cent of senior leaders said that curiosity is encouraged in their company 'a great deal' or 'a good amount', only 52 per cent of staff felt that this was the case.[4] Over three quarters (81 per cent) of lower-level employees in that survey felt that curiosity had no material impact on their compensation.

The benefits of curiosity in the workplace are clear. As well as catalysing learning, idea generation and innovation, it can empower greater empathy and connection with each other and reduce unproductive conflict and politics in the workplace. For the agile marketer, curiosity is an essential attribute that can catalyse exploration, different thinking and highly productive team environments. Later in this section I'll look at some specific techniques that agile marketing leaders and teams can use to stimulate this vital behaviour.

The art of noticing

While curiosity can empower team learning, it's also important for agile marketing teams to notice when feedback or inputs are different to what was expected and to be curious about exploring and finding out why. It can be tempting to dismiss these anomalies or surprising data or feedback when it doesn't fit with our current view of the world. Yet it can uncover unexpected insights that no -one else has considered, spark new ideas and enable different thinking that can take a team in a completely different direction.

Amazing innovations throughout history have come from someone noticing something unexpected and then having the curiosity to pursue an explanation and understand what just happened. In 1895 a German physics professor, Wilhelm Röntgen, was experimenting with the conduction of electricity through low-pressure gases. One autumn evening in his laboratory he was testing whether cathode rays could pass through glass. He covered his cathode tube in heavy black paper, but he noticed that there was still a faint green light that was projected onto a nearby fluorescent screen. Curious about what was causing the green glow, he conducted a number of experiments placing various objects between the path of the unknown rays and photographic plates and found that thicker and more solid objects blocked more rays than thinner objects. He then asked his wife to place her hand in the path of the rays and cast the first x-ray image onto the photographic plates showing the bones in her hand and her wedding ring. This, he realized, would have huge medical benefits. Sure enough, within a year of Röntgen's discovery X-rays were being used across Europe and the US in the treatment of bone fractures, kidney stones and even gun shots. Röntgen won the first Nobel prize for physics in 1901, but the story might have been very different if he hadn't been curious about the green glow that he saw on the fluorescent screen.[5]

As an engineer, Percy Spencer spent World War II working for Raytheon and the US military on magnetrons or tubes that generate electromagnetic waves that can be used in radar. In 1945, while dabbling with magnetrons he noticed that a peanut cluster candy bar in his pocket had melted. Since the peanut clusters would melt at a much higher temperature than a simple chocolate bar, Spencer knew that the magnetrons were responsible, and the microwave oven was born.[6]

Around the same time that Spencer was inventing the microwave oven, George de Mestral returned from a hunting trip with his dog and paused to look at all the burdock burrs that had attached themselves to his dog's coat.

Intrigued to know how they had fixed themselves to the fur so easily, de Mestral took out his microscope and looked at the burrs, discovering that they were covered in tiny little hooks. Inspired, he wondered if he could create a fabric that could mimic the characteristics and makeup of the burrs to create a new type of touch fastener that was easy to pull apart. De Mestral had to persevere to finesse his invention and then find a manufacturer, but Velcro went on to be used in clothing around the world and even by NASA on Apollo missions.[7]

In 1968 3M's Spencer Silver was working on a project to develop an ultra-strong adhesive that could be used for building aircraft. A mistake in the process led to Silver creating a new adhesive (called acrylate copolymer microspheres), which instead of being ultra-strong, was actually an adhesive that stuck lightly to surfaces without bonding tightly to them. These microspheres were able to keep their stickiness but also enable surfaces to be attached lightly to one another and peel apart easily. For many years, Silver struggled to find a use for the microspheres adhesive but he never gave up. Another 3M scientist, Art Fry, had attended one of Silver's seminars on his invention. Fry went to choir practice every Wednesday night at his local church and used scraps of paper to mark the hymns that they were planning on singing in the Sunday service, but by Sunday the scraps of paper had often fallen out of the hymnal. Fry was struck with inspiration. He worked with Silver to turn the invention into a product. They started writing notes to each other using the first versions of their new product. Fry said: 'I thought, what we have here isn't just a bookmark, it's a whole new way to communicate.'[8] Today, 3M sells more than 50 billion Post-it notes a year.

There are so many of these inspiring examples. Alexander Fleming discovered penicillin when he left out some cultures of Staphylococcus aureus in his lab for two weeks, and then noticed that the bacteria had not grown in areas where a mould, called Penicillium notatum, had. In the early nineteenth century, Tabitha Babbitt was living in a Shaker community and noticed people struggling to cut wood with long saws that needed two users and could only cut in one direction. Inspired, she attached a circular blade to her spinning wheel and invented the much more efficient circular saw. Ada Lovelace is credited with writing the first computer algorithm after adding her own notes while translating those of mathematics professor Charles Babbage. Matchsticks were invented by British chemist John Walker who became curious after accidentally scraping a stick coated in chemicals across his hearth and finding that it caught fire. Edward Benedictus invented safety glass after knocking over a flask in his lab and then noticing that the reason the glass hadn't shattered into a thousand pieces was because it was coated in cellulose nitrate. Inkjet printers originated after a Canon engineer accidentally left a hot iron on his ink pen. Hollywood actress Hedy Lamarr worked with George Antheil, whom she met at a dinner party to invent a revolutionary communication system that used the principle of 'frequency hopping' among radio waves. Originally developed to guide torpedoes to their target, the technology became the basis for the wireless communication via Wi-Fi and Bluetooth that are so ubiquitous today.

The point about all these examples is that without the inventor noticing something unusual, and without their curiosity and desire to explore further, none of these would have come to fruition. Where would we be today if Röntgen hadn't been curious to explore what the green glow was, if Spencer hadn't thought something was unusual about the peanut cluster bar melting in his pocket, if Art Fry hadn't had the sense to imagine a new application of Silver's idea or if Fleming had dismissed the effect of the mould as an anomaly? All these inventions might seem as though they happened as a result of happy accidents, but it was the curiosity of their individual inventors that made great things happen.

In agile marketing we might not be inventing penicillin or coming up with ideas for products that will end up being used by millions of people, but noticing, curiosity and a willingness to explore are just as important.

The tyranny of best practice

As companies scale they can easily become very inwards facing. Instead of always searching for new perspectives from a broad set of inputs and sources, teams often narrow their focus so that they become fixated on what is happening within their sector. Instead of looking at a wider set of businesses, ideas and practices and identifying ways to challenge their own norms, teams can easily focus on just what is in front of them. Instead of spending time exploring more unconventional examples and contexts and considering how these ideas might step-change their own capabilities, teams can end up spending their time obsessing about the competition.

Google co-founder Larry Page has spoken of the limitations around always focusing on the competition. If, as a team, you want to do truly amazing things then it's important to break out of sector-specific norms and assumptions:

> I worry that something has gone seriously wrong with the way we run companies… How exciting is it to come to work if the best you can do is trounce some other company that does roughly the same thing? That's why most companies decay slowly over time.[9]

There is significant value in incremental improvement but as was noted earlier in the book there is a limit to optimization. Always focusing on what was done before but with a few minor changes can result in missed opportunities to make a real leap forward in how outcomes can be achieved or what outcomes are even possible. Taking the most interesting or challenging concepts and learning from other sectors and asking 'what might be our version of this?' is a simple method for generating potentially game-changing ideas.

The tyranny of 'best practice' is that it posits that there is one singular method or process that is the optimal solution and teams only need to find and follow that practice to deliver the best possible results. Best practice can, of course, be useful in level setting and standardizing working methods to a high standard (for example, across markets where the level of maturity differs). Teams can develop their own best practices and use playbooks or methodologies to socialize and disseminate common approaches and standards. Yet the risk with best practice is inherent in precisely this uniformity of approach. Best practice can easily lack the nuance of specific context, which can become a challenge in rapidly evolving environments. It can easily become out of date. It can restrict productive adaptability. If every team in the sector is following the accepted best practice for example, where is the differentiation? Where is the advantage that can come from creative solutions that have been uniquely generated by a single team?

For this reason it is important to use best practice approaches judiciously to disseminate high-quality ways of working, but it is just as important to recognize the importance of fresh perspectives and new and creative approaches to methods and achieving results. The danger is that teams can get stuck in one approach and lose sight of the outcome that they are actually setting out to achieve. Jeff Bezos has written about how as companies become larger and more complex there is a tendency to manage to proxies and how process as a proxy is a common example of this.[10] A good process can support good execution, but if a business is not careful, he says, the process can become the proxy for the outcome that you actually want. Instead of focusing on how an outcome can be best achieved in the most effective and efficient way possible, a team can assume that by simply following the process that has commonly been used they will achieve the optimal outcome. As he puts it: 'The process is not the thing. It's always worth asking, do we own the process or does the process own us?'[11]

In a similar way, Bezos also describes how market research and customer surveys can become an oversimplified proxy for what customers really think and feel. Research and surveys are not inherently a bad thing, but a team may become overly reliant on this form of feedback, rather than spending time and energy on deeply understanding customers and developing the kind of intuition that can take them beyond the averages that are found in surveys. Testing and research can help a team discover their blind spots but a remarkable customer experience: 'starts with heart, intuition, curiosity, play, guts, taste. You won't find any of it in a survey'.

Thinking differently

He hung up the phone, finished breakfast, and left his apartment so he could spend Sunday digging a grave for John Fitzgerald Kennedy.

(Jimmy Breslin)[12]

On 26 November 1963, just a few days after John F Kennedy was assassinated and one day after his funeral, *The New York Herald Tribune* published 'It's an Honor', a column written by renowned journalist and author Jimmy Breslin. On the morning of John F Kennedy's funeral Breslin could have followed what every other American columnist was doing and go to the funeral, but instead he decided to seek out Clifton Pollard, a gravedigger at Arlington National Cemetery and tell the story of the funeral from his perspective. What resulted was arguably one of the most memorable newspaper columns of all time.

Breslin's astute piece of journalism is a great example of how taking a very different approach to what is expected can deliver truly exceptional results. Sometimes when the world zigs, it's better to zag. In the previous section I talked about how easy it is to get stuck in a process and to lose sight of the real outcome that we are seeking to achieve. In agile marketing, focused metrics are hugely beneficial in directing effort and aligning activity. Yet in the process of continuously optimizing against short-term measures we might easily miss an opportunity to rethink an approach in a way that will reframe a challenge or enable us to take a very different, less obvious path. In other words, a team can get stuck. Balancing short-term optimization with long-term vision and using a variety of inputs helps to avoid this. It's useful, for example, to continually consider the balance between claimed behaviour inputs (from market research, surveys and polls) with real behaviour measures (from interaction, customer behaviour and activity). On a regular basis, taking a step out from continual optimization around a focused set of metrics and using direct customer feedback (interviewing customers), qualitative inputs or new survey data can help a team to think differently about how they might better achieve their long-term goal.

Richard Shotton, author of *The Choice Factory: 25 Behavioural Biases That Influence What We Buy*[13] has written about how the danger of being too focused on singular metrics is that it can be overly reductive of a complex challenge:

> This process involves a trade-off: a loss of representativeness in return for simplicity... Problems arise when the trade-off is forgotten and tracking data is treated with reverence, as if it was the definitive answer rather than mere evidence.[14]

It's easy for a marketing team to become quite removed from customers. Looking at dashboards can be an excellent way of tracking behaviour and optimizing activity but sometimes you need to understand a problem in more depth, to see it from the customer's perspective and perhaps think differently about the course you are taking. Talking to real customers should be a habitual behaviour for an agile marketing team. Shotton gives an example from when Sir Terry Leahy was leading marketing at Tesco (he went on to become CEO of the company). Sales analysis of Tesco's small range of gluten-free products showed that customers who were buying from the range were not spending a lot on these products each time they visited the store. It looked as though the products were underperforming and might have understandably led him to conclude that there wasn't the demand and that they should be delisted. Yet rather than leap straight to this decision, he chose to interview some gluten-free shoppers. This revealed that these customers deliberately chose to shop in supermarkets that had a good range and availability of this type of product. So rather than delist the gluten-free range entirely, this insight led him in the opposite direction. Leahy introduced the Tesco 'Free From' range long before the competition and the range became very successful.

Every so often, everyone can benefit from reframing a challenge and questioning whether there is a better path to achieving our objective than the one that we are taking. Using a variety of inputs can help the agile marketing team to continually ensure that they are solving problems in the best way possible.

Valuing external perspectives

One of the critical strategies that can counteract complacency and that can help avoid process as a proxy and becoming stuck in a particular way of doing things, is the challenge that can come from external perspectives. This doesn't only come from consultants. There is huge merit in marketing teams adopting proactive behaviours and practices that bring the outside in and challenge assumptions and accepted norms. One of the best ways of doing this is to ask every new member of the team to proactively challenge accepted norms. Conduct a feedback session a month after a new team member has joined and encourage them to share examples of where working practices seem less than optimal or nonsensical. Make it clear that every assumption or method is open to challenge and every piece of feedback is valued.

Beyond this however, it's important that the marketing team systematically work to explore new territory and thinking, bringing a continuous flow of new perspectives in. This is harder than it seems. The pull within organizations is always internally facing. Overburdensome reporting, inefficiently run meetings and unnecessary bureaucracy can easily act as a time suck. Teams are rewarded for managing upwards rather than looking outside. Recognition comes from handling stakeholders well and producing comprehensive reports rather than spending time exploring and experimenting.

One of my favourite examples of the value of an external perspective from another industry is the unlikely collaboration between doctors at Great Ormond Street children's hospital and Formula One pit crew teams. The complex process to transfer children from surgery to the intensive care unit (ICU) typically took 30 minutes, with teams working in confined spaces to deal with a plethora of wires and tubes. The doctors knew that improving this process could have direct benefit for the children in their care and potentially even save lives. Following a 12-hour emergency transplant operation, Professor Martin Elliot, the heart surgeon at the hospital, and Dr Allan Goldman, the head ICU doctor, were watching a Formula One race in the staff common room. When the cars came into the pits for new tyres and more fuel, they noticed how seamlessly the pit crew worked to get the cars out on the track again in a matter of seconds, and this sparked an idea. They invited the Ferrari and McLaren racing teams to work with them to look at the hospital's own handover processes and the recommendations that the technicians came up with encompassed everything from equipment to process and even how staff were trained. The Formula One teams advised the hospital on how it should restructure procedures, manage key responsibilities and tasks during handover procedures, and they even provided diagrams for where each member of staff should be positioned and recommendations around rehearsals and implementation. A review of 27 operations following the intervention found that the number of technical and information handover errors had almost halved.

Fresh perspectives such as this can deliver both incremental improvements in efficiency and also big step-changes in capability. They can even help teams to see things that might be evident to an outsider but somehow hidden to the team themselves. It's easy to believe that the most obvious ideas will be readily identified and acted upon and yet somehow this is far from always being the case. The humble button, for example, is thousands of years old. The oldest button in existence is thought to be one made from shell found in Pakistan and is believed to be up to 5,000 years old. Given how common buttons became you may be forgiven for believing that it wasn't long before the invention of buttonholes followed. Yet for many centuries buttons were purely decorative and in medieval times clothing was still tied, toggled or fastened using brooches and clasps. It wasn't until the thirteenth century (thousands of years after the invention of the button) that reinforced buttonholes were invented and this dramatically changed how clothing was designed and worn.

FIGURE 14.1   A modern plough with the mouldboard

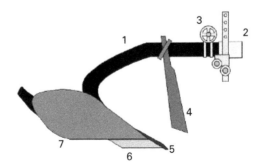

SOURCE Giancarlo Dessì (gian_d), Gian Luca Ruggero (aka Actam), CC BY 3.0, via Wikimedia Commons[15]

Similarly, one of the most obvious but also consequential inventions in the history of agriculture was missed for hundreds of years. The Chinese invented the mouldboard plough in the third century CE. The design of the plough incorporates a cast iron blade that is shaped like V, with two arms of the blade arching away like a bird's wings. This helped the blade to dig into the soil and turn the earth easily. In Figure 14.1, the mouldboard is marked with the number seven.

As Charles C Mann wrote in his book *1491: New Revelations of the Americas Before Columbus*[16] the design of the mouldboard plough seems obvious in its benefits, yet it wasn't until the mouldboard plough was imported in the seventeenth century that European farmers thought of moving on from the shapeless metal block that had been commonly used for hundreds of years. Where European farmers needed whole teams of oxen to pull their highly inefficient ploughs through the soil, the Chinese mouldboard plough needed only one. As Mann notes:

> European agricultural production exploded after the arrival of the moldboard plow. The prosperity this engendered was one of the cushions on which the Enlightenment floated.

For centuries, European farmers had been struggling with hard-to-use, extremely ineffective ploughs and no one had thought of how a relatively simple redesign might enable the task to be done in a much easier way.

The value of external perspectives can often be in challenging norms that commonly go unchallenged. These 'toxic assumptions' are the kind of beliefs that are embedded into processes and ways of thinking and remain unquestioned. Over time, toxic assumptions can accumulate and prevent new ideas from taking root. They can hamper innovation and keep teams fixed into inefficient or outdated ways of working.

PRACTICAL WAYS TO EMPOWER CURIOSITY

There are a number of strategies that leaders can use to amplify the opportunities that this essential attribute can bring:

- **Model inquisitive behaviour by asking questions:** When leaders ask a lot of searching questions, this not only models the right behaviour but it generates the need for answers, which encourages staff to explore. Be mindful in the response to questions that the team are asking.

- **Create learning goals:** Behavioural scientist Francesca Gino has written of the benefits in leaders specifying clear learning goals for teams, which can give them direction for exploration.[17]

- **Ask the right questions:** 'Why?', 'What if?' and 'How might we...?' are all powerful ways to open up new thinking.

- **Set time aside:** Even small amounts of time set aside for a team to experiment or learn together can be hugely valuable in creating space for curiosity.

- **Shifting gears:** Change the team environment (for example, having 'walking meetings' outside), reframe challenges and encourage the team to shift their perspective to look at potential opportunities or problems in a new way, bring in external inputs.

- **Building trust and psychological safety:** The right team environment helps people to speak up, learn together and not be afraid to ask challenging questions.

Creating space to learn

> The multitude of books, the shortness of time and the slipperiness of memory do not allow all things which are written to be equally retained in the mind.
>
> (Vincent of Beauvais, Dominican friar, 1255)[18]

One of the biggest challenges in catalysing team learning within organizations is the lack of time and space. Cal Newport's renowned book *Deep Work: Rules for Focused Success in a Distracted World*[19] describes one of the critical challenges in the modern corporate world – the ability to take time out from distractions to focus and make progress on cognitively demanding work. Many office workers' time is largely spent in a blur of meetings, emails and notifications, perhaps peppered intermittently by a quick scroll of social media or the news headlines. One of the curses of the modern working environment is the burden of context switching between different tasks, meetings and interruptions, which can easily sabotage productivity. Context switching was originally used in computing to describe how operating systems can switch processing power from one app to another by pausing the first one to enable the new one to utilize the processor capability. It allows multiple apps and processes to be run simultaneously. Yet while computer operating systems may be designed to be good at context switching, human brains are not. As a result, there is a hidden cost on time, focus and attention.

Sophie LeRoy from the University of Minnesota has described how context switching results in an 'attention residue', which can mean that a part of our attention remains on the previous task as we move on to the next one.[20] This can result in less attention being paid to the task at hand. Research from Microsoft has found that it can take an average of up to 23 minutes to fully regain focus on a task after a significant distraction.[21] Different parts of the brain are utilized each time a switch is made, which can mean that interruptions and distractions can have a significant impact on productivity. Yet research by the same team found that the modern knowledge worker typically spends the day bouncing between different tasks, screens, apps and tabs, and that the more switches that are made and the more time spent in emails and meetings the less productive people feel at the end of the day.[22]

Email can be one of the worst offenders at distracting our attention and creating inefficiencies through context switching. Every email that arrives is potentially about a different topic, meaning that going through a backlog in the inbox can involve successively jumping from one context to another. Research done by Dr Thomas Jackson at Loughborough University has shown that on average it takes over a minute (64 seconds) for us to recover our train of thought following even a relatively minor interruption like an email.[23] If staff habitually check their email inbox multiple times a day, this can add up to a significant amount of time that is spent getting back to where you were before the interruption. Unfortunately, the unpredictable way in which useful emails arrive has also been shown to encourage us to addictively check our inboxes. Email is characterized by what psychologists call a 'variable interval reinforcement schedule', which means that, rather like slot machines in a casino, the rewards (such as a positive or useful email) come intermittently and not in a predictable way. This encourages us to check our inboxes frequently. What arrives in our inbox is, of course, beyond our immediate control, which can mean that the inbox becomes a to-do list that anyone can add to at any time. Other communications tools (such as Slack, Teams and even WhatsApp) can be useful in reducing email overload but discipline, common practices and expectations are needed here too to avoid a similar problem, particularly when it comes to notifications.

Meetings can also provide their own set of challenges. Paul Graham, the founder of Silicon Valley incubator company Y-combinator, has written about the difference between what he calls a 'maker's' schedule and that which is typically used by managers and what can happen when these calendars collide.[24] If you're a 'maker' (a writer, programmer or someone that creates things for a living) then you'll likely need good blocks of dedicated time to make progress with something. Managers, however, will often segment their time into one-hour slots, and they are more likely to change what they're doing each hour. For the latter, a meeting can be simply a matter of finding a suitable one-hour slot, but dropping a one-hour meeting into the middle of a morning or afternoon can be disastrous for a maker since it breaks up that half day into time chunks too small to do anything productive with. Managers can inadvertently end up making everyone 'resonate at their frequency' and make it hard for anyone to keep blocks of time clear of calls or meetings. The challenge inherent in managers' schedules is that staff can easily find that they are spending their days moving from one call or meeting to the next and that there are no significant blocks of time to step back and think or really concentrate on a task for an extended period or to make meaningful progress towards outcomes without interruption. As designer Mike Monteiro has said, rather than a useful tool for managing time, calendars can simply become a 'record of interruptions'.[25]

In the modern work environment we have become used to this ongoing distraction and task-switching as part of the normal working day, and yet it reduces the ability to focus, to make meaningful progress towards outcomes, and it generates stress and the feeling that we are continuously being less productive than we are capable of. Context switching is exhausting. It can impact our motivation, productivity and creativity. Agile marketing teams and the individuals that work in them need space and time to focus in order to effectively progress towards outcomes. Constant distraction at the individual and at the team level can derail a team's progress, result in a heavy burden from context switching, poor attention on the task at hand and reduced productivity. Incorporating periods of deep work into the working week can result in higher levels of fulfilment and motivation and lead to better outcomes. Cal Newport defines four fundamental strategies that can help:

1 **Schedule time for deep work:** This is easy to say and far less easy to implement in the reality of demanding stakeholders, constant distraction and urgent tasks. It requires the discipline to carve out specific periods in the diary that are blocked out for deep work but also to push back on demands where possible in order to protect that time. Cal Newport draws an interesting distinction here, describing the need to schedule breaks from focus, rather than scheduling focused time. Most of us would approach this the other way around, but switching the emphasis like this

enables individuals and teams to compartmentalize periods that may be allocated to email and other potentially distracting or short-focus tasks.

Newport also makes the point that in those periods of deep work it's essential that teams and individuals focus on using blocks of time to progress with larger pieces of work and deliberately turn it off before moving on the next thing, rather than trying to multitask all the time. Practising this can support improved productivity but also creates good habits to increasing focus in the long term. This kind of calendar and diary management, whether at a team or individual level, needs explicit or tacit buy-in from leadership. It can help to coordinate regular slots in a week. Some teams run 'no meeting Fridays', for example, or deliberately create times of the day or week (for example, no meetings before 10 am or after 4 pm) to allow for more unstructured time. Leaders need to understand that response times may be different. However, it also requires team members to be disciplined about using these blocks of time to genuinely focus on deep work and not use it as a chance to catch up on email.

2 **Embrace boredom:** Newport mentions how important it is not to feel like we need to fill every moment of the working day with forwards progress towards goals. Progress is important, of course, but now and then we need to allow our minds to wander. Some studies have shown that engaging in undemanding tasks that allow the mind to wander can improve creative problem-solving.[26]

3 **Manage social media time:** Newport advocates the need to take a proactive approach to managing time spent engaging with social media. The constantly updated newsfeeds can prove to be a significant distraction and deliver the same kinds of intermittent but unpredictable rewards that make checking email so potentially addictive. It's key, therefore, to schedule time for it rather than reactively check it all the time.

4 **Deprioritize:** Earlier in the book I mentioned that a key principle within agile marketing is that the team should always be focusing on maximizing high-value work over low-value work. This means actively looking to deprioritize work that may not contribute much value but that takes valuable time and effort to complete so that capacity can be created for more high-value tasks. Taking this approach is one of the most valuable things a team can do to create space. It should become habitual behaviour, perhaps considered as part of the team retrospective, to regularly define how time and space can be created through a more ruthless deprioritization of low-value work.

It's important for agile marketing teams to avoid unnecessary distractions and context switching, which means taking a proactive approach to managing communication, notifications and time.

TECHNIQUES FOR CREATING SPACE IN AGILE MARKETING TEAMS

Building on Cal Newport's suggestions, there are a number of practical methods that teams and individuals can use to create space for more focused work and minimize context switching.

- **Pomodoro:** The Pomodoro Technique is a simple method of ensuring short, regular breaks in work, which can support improved focus. It involves breaking work down into half-hour chunks with 25 minutes of focused work followed by a 5-minute respite. It's useful to understand how much work is involved in a task and then to plan to minimize interruptions during focused time, set a timer to notify you to take a break and every four or five Pomodoros take a longer half-hour break.

- **Schedule email:** It can be a really helpful practice to schedule specific times of the day to dip into the inbox. Schedule the time for when works best for you but a focused half-hour of dealing with email or other communications at the start of the day, before lunch and at the end of the day can really help to avoid constant inbox checking, reduce context switching and allow for extended periods of focus.

- **Turn notifications off:** It's rare that anything is so urgent that it can't wait a few hours, but notifications are a major distraction so turn them off. Instead, take a more proactive approach to scheduling time to deal with emails and Slack messages, and if you really need to, agree with stakeholders a priority of communication that allows for only very urgent messages via a particular platform.

- **Send fewer emails:** The more emails you send the more you get so try to minimize volume by checking whether you really need to reply, avoiding unnecessary use of reply all and maybe consider picking up the phone or walking over to someone's desk.

- **If possible, avoid devices in meetings:** Taking phones and laptops into meetings can be useful, but it brings with it potential distraction. When looking at a device in a meeting, more of our attention is focused on the device than what is going on in the meeting, which hampers progress. Research has also shown that writing notes in longhand rather than a device results in us remembering more and having a deeper understanding of the topic.[27]

- **Work to narrative time:** The ancient Greeks had two ways of thinking about time. Clock time (or what the Greeks called 'Chronos') is based on fixed, measurable units of time that pass. Narrative time (what the Greeks called 'Kairos') is often used in storytelling and involves time being dictated more by how the story is told. Consultant Tom Critchlow has described how deadlines in companies are frequently set for legibility (control and measurement of work) rather than effectiveness.[28] Often, deadlines may well be set on a relatively arbitrary basis that is not necessarily reflective of the optimal way for progress to be achieved. Operating on shorter, faster feedback loops with stakeholders can help pivot the goal from creating specific deliverables against deadlines towards demonstrating progress and creating momentum and change. In other words, if a team can work more to narrative time rather than clock time it enables them to bring stakeholders on the journey with them but also to show momentum and progress, gain feedback as they go, rather than working to specific deliverables and deadlines, which may have been set in advance at a time when the work was not yet fully understood.

- **Schedule a cadence for updates:** Relating to this idea of using narrative time to show progress, utilizing agile ceremonies and tools can ensure a more inclusive approach to bringing stakeholders on the journey. Demonstrating the work shows tangible progress and enables for regular stakeholder input and reprioritization. Short daily stand-ups can be used to discuss barriers to progress and mitigate the amount of discussion that happens electronically, reducing email and notifications. Taking an inclusive approach like this can mitigate the kind of additional reporting that stakeholders request when they feel out of the loop.

- **Find your 'sacred hours':** Writing teacher Dickie Bush has described an approach for how to find chunks of time that can be blocked out for deep work.[29] These 'sacred hours' as he calls them are the distraction-free times when you are unreachable and where you can really move forwards with some focused work. In order to find the best slot to set this time aside you should ask yourself two questions: What time of day am I most productive? What time of day can I be least responsive? This may well be different for everyone but at least gives you the best chance of creating and protecting that time.

FIGURE 14.2 Sacred hours

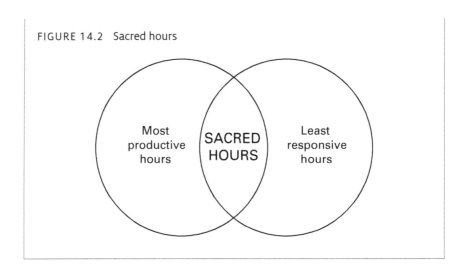

Endnotes

1 C Rovelli (2021) *Helgoland: Making Sense of the Quantum Revolution*, Riverhead Books, New York.

2 Chuck Close quote, Goodreads. www.goodreads.com/quotes/275483-the-advice-i-like-to-give-young-artists-or-really (archived at https://perma.cc/2UNP-YV62)

3 HBR. The business case for curiosity, September 2018. hbr.org/2018/09/curiosity#the-business-case-for-curiosity (archived at https://perma.cc/CZX8-UGA7)

4 S Harrison, E Pinkus and J Cohen. Research: 83% of executives say they encourage curiosity. Just 52% of employees agree, *Harvard Business Review*, 20 September 2018. hbr.org/2018/09/research-83-of-executives-say-they-encourage-curiosity-just-52-of-employees-agree (archived at https://perma.cc/48TE-YA4U)

5 Columbia Surgery. History of medicine: Dr Roentgen's accidental x-rays, 2021. columbiasurgery.org/news/2015/09/17/history-medicine-dr-roentgen-s-accidental-x-rays (archived at https://perma.cc/J9Q6-5TM5)

6 M Blitz. The amazing true story of how the microwave was invented by accident, Popular Mechanics, 2 September 2021. www.popularmechanics.com/technology/gadgets/a19567/how-the-microwave-was-invented-by-accident/ (archived at https://perma.cc/7T9C-69JG)

7 Velcro Companies. An idea that stuck: How Geroge de Mestral invented the Velcro fastener, 11 November 2016. www.velcro.com/blog/2016/11/an-idea-that-stuck-how-george-de-mestral-invented-the-velcro-fastener/ (archived at https://perma.cc/ZA3B-5XG8)

8   3M. About Post-It brand, 2021. www.3m.co.uk/3M/en_GB/post-it-notes/
     contact-us/about-us/ (archived at https://perma.cc/EF3A-596R)

9   S Levy. Google's Larry Page on why moon shots matter, Wired, 17 January
     2013. www.wired.com/2013/01/ff-qa-larry-page/ (archived at https://perma.cc/
     AMF8-EXAE)

10   J Bezos. Amazon letter to shareholders 2016. www.sec.gov/Archives/edgar/
     data/1018724/000119312517120198/d373368dex991.htm (archived at
     https://perma.cc/92L6-P73B)

11   J Bezos. Amazon letter to shareholders 2016. www.sec.gov/Archives/edgar/
     data/1018724/000119312517120198/d373368dex991.htm (archived at
     https://perma.cc/92L6-P73B)

12   J Breslin. It's an honor, Daily Beast, 2017. www.thedailybeast.com/its-an-honor
     (archived at https://perma.cc/4LGS-UQZK)

13   R Shotton (2018) *The Choice Factory: 25 Behavioural Biases That Influence
     What We Buy*, Harriman House, Pertersfield. www.harriman-house.com/
     choicefactory (archived at https://perma.cc/8R28-MQJ2)

14   R Shotton (2018) *The Choice Factory: 25 Behavioural Biases That Influence
     What We Buy*, Harriman House, Pertersfield. www.harriman-house.com/
     choicefactory (archived at https://perma.cc/8R28-MQJ2)

15   Mouldboard plough, Wikipedia, 2020. commons.wikimedia.org/wiki/
     File:Old_plough_schema.svg (archived at https://perma.cc/ZX3P-8M4J)

16   C C Mann (2006) *1491: New Revelations of the Americas Before Columbus*,
     Granta Books, London.

17   F Gino. The business case for curiosity, *Harvard Business Review*, September
     2018. hbr.org/2018/09/the-business-case-for-curiosity (archived at https://
     perma.cc/XX6H-QBUR)

18   A Blair. Reading strategies for coping with information overload ca. 1550–
     1700, *Journal of the History of Ideas*, January 2003. www.jstor.org/stable/
     3654293 (archived at https://perma.cc/98TU-DNXR)

19   C Newport (2016) *Deep Work: Rules for Focused Success in a Distracted
     World*, Piatkus, London.

20   S LeRoy. Why is it so hard to do my work? The challenge of attention residue
     when switching between work tasks, 2009. ideas.repec.org/a/eee/jobhdp/
     v109y2009i2p168-181.html (archived at https://perma.cc/Z8TA-NPSD)

21   G Mark, S Iqbal, M Czerwinski and P Johns. The cost of interrupted work:
     More speed and stress, 2008. www.ics.uci.edu/~gmark/chi08-mark.pdf
     (archived at https://perma.cc/TPH9-GYFH)

22   G Mark, S Iqbal, M Czerwinski and P Johns. Focused, aroused, but so
     distractible: A temporal perspective on multitasking and communications,
     2016. www.microsoft.com/en-us/research/wp-content/uploads/2016/10/
     p903-mark.pdf (archived at https://perma.cc/3TZJ-FT98)

23 T Jackson, R Dawson and D Wilson. Case study: Evaluating the effect of email interruptions within the workplace, 2005. repository.lboro.ac.uk/articles/online_resource/Case_study_evaluating_the_effect_of_email_interruptions_within_the_workplace/9404807 (archived at https://perma.cc/KU3E-KV5S)

24 P Graham. Maker's schedule, manager's schedule, 2009. www.paulgraham.com/makersschedule.html (archived at https://perma.cc/M4PS-Y3YF)

25 M Monteiro. The chokehold of calendars, July 2013. monteiro.medium.com/the-chokehold-of-calendars-f70bb9221b36 (archived at https://perma.cc/9YAV-NWFT)

26 B Baird, J Smallwood, M Mrazek and J Kim. Inspired by distraction: Mind wandering facilitates creative incubation, 2012. www.researchgate.net/publication/230786381_Inspired_by_Distraction_Mind_Wandering_Facilitates_Creative_Incubation (archived at https://perma.cc/XB39-JMAN)

27 C May. A learning secret: Don't take notes with a laptop, Scientific American, 2014. www.scientificamerican.com/article/a-learning-secret-don-t-take-notes-with-a-laptop/ (archived at https://perma.cc/M2UL-5ME5)

28 T Critchlow. The consultant out of time, 2021. tomcritchlow.com/2021/01/26/kairos/ (archived at https://perma.cc/AX8K-5BSB)

29 D Bush. Five steps to starting and sustaining an idea sharing habit, December 2020. www.dickiebush.com/articles/five-steps-to-starting-and-sustaining-a-writing-habit (archived at https://perma.cc/XJG5-XTUC)

15

Empowering high-performing marketing teams

Autonomy and empowerment

In agile marketing empowered teams are essential for moving fast. When teams need to make decisions rapidly it's tempting for leaders to step in and become directly involved in making those decisions on behalf of the team. In other words, to micro-manage. This becomes even more prevalent as situations become more complex or there is more at stake. Yet in agile environments micro-management carries with it some real risks:

- **Poor quality and slower decisions:** When the boss makes all the decisions the team are less likely to speak up, which results in a lack of open discussion and contribution. This in turn can easily lead to poor decision-making. The concentration of authority is also highly likely to slow the team down and prevent them from iterating, adapting and progressing in the way that they need to.

- **It creates a transactional environment:** When a leader is constantly checking numbers and metrics they are creating an environment in which numbers matter more than people and relationships. Metrics are important but such a granular focus can lead to the team spending too much time justifying numbers rather than focusing on how they can best solve the problem. It can hamper the sharing of ideas and innovation. It can result in an impersonal, even cold culture.

- **It can be demoralizing:** Having the authority to make decisions in the areas that you are responsible for taken away from you (or never having it in the first place) leads to poor motivation and disengagement. Over time this might even turn into resentment. Ironically, this can also lead to leaders having less control, not more.

- **It leads to a lack of trust:** Micro-management can erode trust, an essential ingredient for teams that need to move fast. A lack of trust can lead to politics and an unhealthy work environment, which may cause talented people to leave.

As I discussed earlier in the book, agile marketing teams need to be aligned, but this needs to be balanced with an environment of autonomy.

There's a valuable lesson that we can learn about the value of greater autonomy from the first modern organization chart that was ever created. Daniel McCallum took over running operations at the New York and Erie Railroad in 1854. It was a large, complex organization that oversaw almost 500 miles of track. You might be forgiven for thinking that in the 1850s one of the key problems in running a large railroad network would be a lack of information but in fact the reverse was true. The use of the telegraph had resulted in a surfeit of almost real-time data about everything from train delays to mechanical problems and broken equipment. With so much data coming in, attempting to organize it into useful information that could be used to improve the efficiency and working of the railroad proved extremely difficult. Failure to improve the railroad operations well would result in multiple delays to services (the trains ran on a single track meaning that a problem with one train might affect many others and perhaps even lead to accidents).

In response to this challenge McCallum wanted a way of understanding how decision-making could be distributed better through the organization. So he created the world's first organization chart. Yet, unlike today's static hierarchical pyramids, this design was modelled after a tree. In fact, it was a rather beautiful-looking model.

In this design the board of directors were the roots of the tree, chief officers were the trunk and the railroad's divisions and departments became the branches. The model helped McCallum and his company to understand how they could distribute decision-making more widely through the organization and in a controlled way to empower local supervisors. As Caitlin Rosenthal from McKinsey says:

> in McCallum's chart the hierarchy was reversed: authority over day-to-day scheduling and operations went to the divisional superintendents down the line, who oversaw the five branch lines of the railroad. The reasoning: they possessed the best operating data, were closer to the action, and thus were best placed to manage the line's persistent inefficiencies.[2]

FIGURE 15.1 Organizational diagram of the New York and Erie railroad, 1855

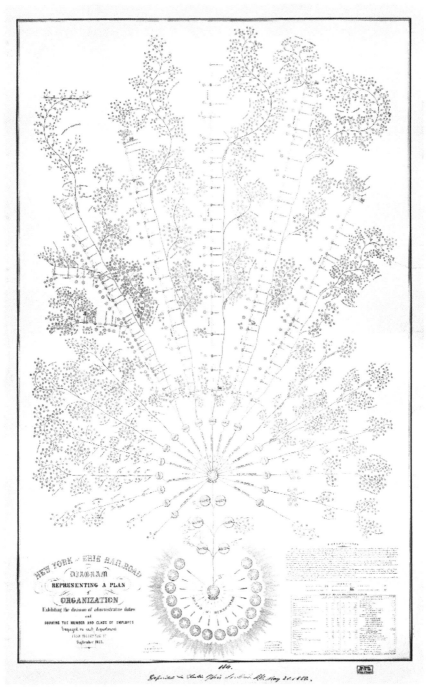

SOURCE Daniel McCallum & George Holt Henshaw, 1855, public domain, via Wikimedia Commons[1]

The chart helped organize how the railroad could use information in a better way but also empowered divisional superintendents with authority over day-to-day scheduling, giving them the authority to act on the information they were getting in real time and leading to a much more efficient system. The role of senior leaders became to support rather than direct operations. As Rosenthal notes, McCallum gained control by giving up control. He set up a system for targeted metrics to be reported back to the board of directors (flowing from the branches to the roots of the tree) where it could be repurposed into useful measures (like average load per car and cost per ton-mile) that could inform more strategic decisions around prioritization and long-term improvements and ensure that the directors spent their limited time in the most productive ways.

It's amazing to think that this all happened as long ago as the 1850s yet there are some clear parallels with the dilemmas faced by the modern marketing organization. A lack of information and data is rarely the real challenge for teams. Balancing authority with information means structuring the data flows and use in ways that both empower teams and inform senior oversight. In agile marketing teams need to have easy access to real-time data (perhaps through a dashboard) that is combined with the autonomy to pragmatically apply it in the ways that they believe will optimize outcomes. At the same time, leaders need to have oversight over a focused set of insightful measures that enable them to understand progress towards outcomes and make strategic decisions about prioritization and direction.

Let's think about this in a military context (after all, there are few domains where the stakes of decision-making are higher). In combat scenarios, you might be forgiven for thinking that micro-management of operations by senior military leaders is all important, but, again, the reverse is true. For hundreds of years military leaders have understood the fragility of rigid systems of leadership that dictate in detail what troops on the ground should do. Battle scenarios are highly unpredictable and change all the time, meaning that inflexible decision-making or responding to challenges with ever-more detailed plans restrict the soldiers on the front-line from responding rapidly to uncertain and emerging contexts. Mission command, for example, is a style of command that originated from Prussian military tactics that were conceived after their defeat at the hands of Napoleon in 1806. After that failure, the Prussians realized their need to be more flexible and adaptable in their military leadership and placed the emphasis on the outcome of a mission over specifying the exact means of achieving it.

Mission command brings a clear centralized intent together with decentralized execution and allows for greater autonomy of action by troops on the ground within defined constraints.

The German army used this principle to devastating effect during World War II with their concept of Blitzkrieg ('lightning war'). This was focused on generating a powerful operational tempo that combined the deployment of fast, highly mobile armoured units with a form of command that empowered front-line commanders to respond to changing situations faster. 'Schwerpunkt' (meaning the underlying goal or main emphasis) created clarity for front-line officers on direction and objectives. 'Fingerspitzengefuhl' (which translates as 'fingertip feel') allowed for greater autonomy for officers on the ground to respond to fluid situations and make fast decisions. This resulted in a powerful combination of sophisticated military capability with a greater autonomy and flexibility of command that enabled the German army to move fast both on the ground and in their speed of decision-making.

BALANCING DIRECTION WITH EMPOWERMENT

Mission command is built on three essential principles that provide a useful basis that leaders can use to achieve the right balance between alignment and autonomy:[3]

1 **Do not command more than is necessary. Don't plan beyond foreseeable circumstances.** Leaders should articulate the outcome that they need to achieve clearly and without ambiguity. After this leaders need to step back, let the team get on with execution and take decisions in the areas that they have responsibility for. Progress can be checked regularly through agile ceremonies such as demo and review, but stakeholders shouldn't be in the detail of decision-making or demanding updates more regularly (during the sprint, for example). While it's important to be clear on vision and outcomes, leaders need to allow the flexibility for teams to be emergent, adaptive and empowered in their execution.

2 **Communicate to every unit as much of the higher intent as is necessary to achieve the purpose.** Ensure that the specified outcome is well understood. It might be useful for example, to check back to make sure that the goal has been communicated well. Equip the team with access to the information and tools that they need to complete what is being asked of them.

3 **Ensure that everyone retains freedom of decision within understood boundaries.** Create and enable an environment that enables autonomy of decision-making within clearly defined guardrails. Be generous with the level of autonomy that the teams are given but don't leave the organization open to significant loss or risk.

Building on these basic principles, there are some useful additional tenets that were created by the US Army.[4] They describe the importance of creating shared understanding around the clear intent, but they also talk about building cohesive teams through mutual trust. It's far easier for leaders to empower teams to take on that responsibility when there is an atmosphere of trust between them. Within the freedom of decision-making both parties need to accept prudent risk, and the team should exercise 'disciplined initiative'.

Building a culture of collaboration

For all the talk about the value of collaboration in business, it is not always incentivized or rewarded well by organizations, which often prefer to focus merit on more tangible facets. The Peter Principle relates to the tendency in many organizations for employees to be promoted based on their success in previous roles until they reach a level at which they are no longer competent. Promoting staff that have specific functional expertise rather than staff that can effectively collaborate and inspire and lead teams can be costly. A 2019 study of the performance of over 50,000 sales workers at 214 companies by researchers Alan Benson, Danielle Li and Kelly Shue found that businesses systematically promoted the best salespeople into management positions even when those people end up being worse managers.[5] Salespeople who did not necessarily have the best sales figures but who were more collaborative (which the researchers measured through 'teamwork experience' or the likelihood of them passing leads on to colleagues or maintaining contacts passed to them) was a much better predictor of managerial quality but these people were less likely to get promoted. Put simply, the best salespeople did not always make the best managers and, in fact, pre-promotion sales performance proved to be negatively correlated with managerial quality (a doubling of pre-promotion sales corresponded with a 7.5 per cent decline in sales for those workers assigned to the new manager). Workers with more teamwork experience made better managers once promoted and the study found that if the best potential managers were promoted sales would go up by 20 per cent. The recommendation to come out of the study was that companies could manage the costs of the Peter Principle by placing less emphasis on functional performance and more on promoting workers with greater teamwork experience.

In agile marketing, the lesson is that effective team working and collaboration should be highly prized and that leaders should recognize and amplify the behaviours and attributes that can empower a culture that celebrates these qualities. It's very hard for teams to move quickly in environments that are characterized by low levels of trust, internal politics and poor cooperation. But what do we really mean by a culture of collaboration? Long-renowned for their studies and data-driven research in this area Google have conducted comprehensive multi-year studies that have run across hundreds of teams in their business in order to identify the attributes that are most meaningful in characterizing and contributing to high performance in teams. Surprisingly, the findings of this research are not what you might expect. One particular study that took in over 180 active Google teams and covered over 250 different attributes found that rather than team member skills, personality or even team longevity proving to be significant, there were actually five key dynamics that truly characterized high performance:[6]

- **Psychological safety:** It was Professor Amy Edmondson from Harvard Business School that first introduced the concept of psychological safety in her work in understanding how teams learn. She defined psychological safety as 'a shared belief held by members of a team that the team is safe for interpersonal risk-taking'.[7] This requires team members to feel comfortable in saying what they really think, to be able to have healthy debates and conversations and to feel safe to experiment and try new things out without feeling insecure.

- **Dependability:** Being able to rely on other team members to do high-quality work on time. Dependability is a critical element in building trust, along with transparency.

- **Structure and clarity:** Clarity around team and individual goals and responsibilities enables focus but also efficiency and reassurance.

- **Meaning of work:** It's really important that team members feel that the work that they're doing is important and personally meaningful.

- **Impact of work:** The feeling that the work being done actually creates impact and makes a difference.

FIGURE 15.2 Psychological safety in practice

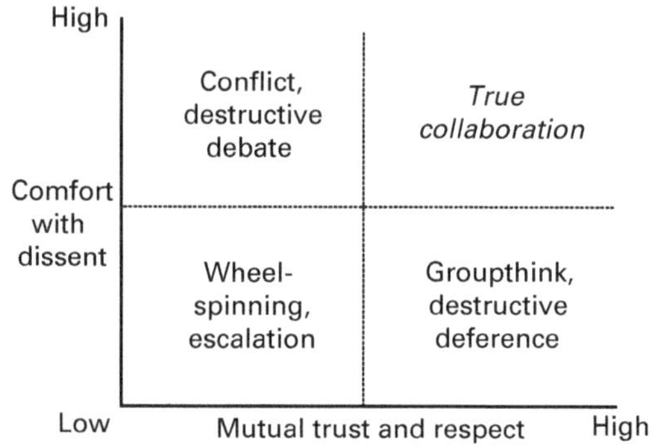

Adapted from Ben Thompson, The Uncanny Valley of a Functional Organization, July 2013. stratechery. com/2013/the-uncanny-valley-of-a-functional-organization/

Analyst Ben Thompson has a good take on creating a culture of true collaboration, describing it as the combination of mutual trust and respect with a willingness and freedom to disagree.[8] In many ways this is psychological safety in practice.

Let's dive deeper into each of these areas to understand how marketing leaders and teams can amplify behaviours that support them.

Building a culture of trust

There are many factors that contribute to the building of trusted relationships, but drawing on multiple academic studies, we might broadly set out these qualities and behaviours as:

- **Credibility:** Whether a person is credible in this domain and has the knowledge, experience, information or good judgement to support their opinions or advice. A sign that people trust someone's opinion or input is when they actively seek it out.

- **Dependability and reliability:** This may relate to a belief that people's actions match their commitments and the things that they say, the fact that they act in consistent rather than unpredictable ways, the fact that they will go out of their way to deliver or that there is a longstanding relationship in place.

- **Honesty and integrity:** When people are honest and act with integrity in accordance with stated beliefs and values, we are more confident that they care and more likely to share.

- **Openness and transparency:** Related to honesty, transparency helps to foster trust in organizational and team environments. We are far more likely to trust someone when they demonstrate that they are trusting us.

- **Safety and security:** The environment allows people to feel safe taking calculated risks and trying new ideas without fear of repercussion or ridicule.

- **Common, shared goals:** The feeling that people and teams are mutually aligned around shared objectives or outcomes can also foster greater trust.

- **Appreciation and acknowledgement:** Small things can go a long way in this area, particularly when it relates to recognizing individual or team contribution.

As an example of a business that has placed trust and transparency at the heart of their culture, social software business Buffer have not only articulated this in their stated company values but brought it to life through a clear expectation around the behaviours that support these values and also demonstrated it through their actions. The company values include cultivating positivity, showing gratitude, practising reflection, acting beyond yourself and improving continuously.[9]

Right at the top of the list is defaulting to transparency. As Joel Gascoigne, the CEO of Buffer, has said 'transparency breeds trust, and trust is the foundation of great teamwork'.[10] At an individual level they talk about this in terms of authenticity and honesty. At the team level they emphasize how important transparency is to effective working (particularly remote working). At the company level they describe the importance of avoiding 'big reveals' through clear communication, not making assumptions and by bringing staff into the decision process early. The company has long had a blog where employees post about ways of working, the culture at Buffer and where the senior team write about their strategies and even company finances. Since 2013 Buffer have openly shared their formula-based approach to compensation and even a list of employee salaries including those of the founders themselves.[11] This openness promotes trust in employees, investors and customers alike.

At the individual level, the practice of active listening can really help build trust. Listening is a critical yet often undervalued skill. In his famous book *The 7 Habits of Highly Effective People*,[12] Stephen Covey defines five levels of listening:

- **Pretending:** When someone looks like they might be listening to you, but you can tell that they aren't.

- **Selective:** When someone is listening according to their own agenda, perhaps picking out the parts that fit with their view.
- **Defensive:** When the listener is hearing everything but already has an intention to defend their view or defer someone else's opinion.
- **Attentive:** When the listener defers judgement, provides feedback, makes eye contact, observes non-verbal cues, as well as actively showing that they're listening and perhaps even repeating back what they have understood. This is active listening.
- **Empathic:** A stage beyond attentive, this is about truly empathizing with the other person and being able to place yourself in their situation to understand their context.

People can be very sensitive to how others are listening, even on the phone. When people listen in the wrong way it can make them seem controlling, selfish or not willing to take responsibility or ownership. Put simply, a lack of active or empathic listening can destroy trust.

Before I move on to the second dimension of psychological safety, comfort with dissent, it's worth considering what happens when trust is not evident within teams. In environments of low trust, decision-making can become overly hierarchical (as decisions go up the organization chart due to the failure of teams to collaborate well) or committee-driven as autonomy is eroded. A culture that emphasizes individual status among the hierarchy can lead to people becoming overly sensitive to perceived revisions in status and resistant to changes that may involve a shift in resource or budget. Negative office politics can impact morale, productivity and even staff turnover, but it can also slow teams down. Marketing leaders should actively work to reduce internal politics through the promotion of transparency, open feedback and a connection with what is happening through informal and formal networks within the team. Leaders shouldn't be in the detail of everyday decision-making but neither should they be isolated in ways that encourage negative power dynamics in the team.

The power of conformity

In the next section I'll take a closer look at how agile marketing leaders can support a culture of productive discussion and healthy disagreement and discussion in their teams. First, let's acknowledge just how powerful our desire for conformity is and how this can sometimes lead teams into poor-quality decisions.

FIGURE 15.3 Asch conformity test

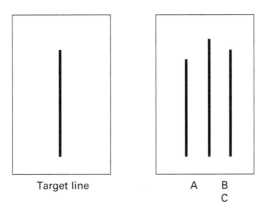

Target line   A   B
                                           C

In 1951, psychologist Solomon Asch conducted a renowned study that high-lighted the power of social pressure and conformity. He used a simple line judgement task and placed a naive participant in a room with seven other participants who had all agreed in advance what their answer was going to be.[13] The naive participant didn't know that the other seven people had been planted by the researchers. Each person in the group was then asked in turn to say out loud which comparison line from those presented (A, B or C) was most like the target line. The real participant sat at the end of the row and gave their answer last.

Despite the answer always being line C, Asch showed that a significant proportion of adults will change their opinions on objective facts in order to conform with the consensus of others. Over a series of trials only about 25 per cent of real participants never conformed even when the answer was plain to see. Asch's experiment was a good early example of what psychologists have since proven many times over – that our wish to conform is a powerful driver of behaviour. This is true because conformity helps us to feel validated and to gain social acceptance while non-conformity can cause confusion and anxiety. A study by social neuroscientist Vasily Klucharev from Radboud University in the Netherlands used functional magnetic resonance imaging (fMRI) to look at how our brains respond when we have an opinion that diverges from the group consensus.[14] The results showed that a brain region that is involved in detecting errors becomes very active and at the same time an area that anticipates rewards slows down. In other words, deviation from the group is regarded by the brain as a punishment, and this creates a desire to adjust our opinion to align with the consensus.

It's important for leaders to recognize how consensus and groupthink can influence decision-making. A key way to avoid this is to create an environment that enables healthy discussion and dissent.

Comfort with dissent

A key strategy in reducing team politics while also enhancing team communication and decision-making is enabling a culture within the team that supports a willingness and freedom to disagree. A culture that tacitly makes disagreement difficult makes the organization more vulnerable to petty office politics, abuses of power and errors of judgement. Comfort with dissent means that a team can solve challenges better since they are able to use a broader set of inputs and perspectives (and not just those from the loudest people in the room). It means that people are more likely to speak up and that a team is less likely to continue down a path that is not working. It means that more powerful ideas can emerge and take shape from the reasoning and discussion that the team has.

In his book *Conflicted: Why Arguments Are Tearing Us Apart and How They Can Bring Us Together*[15] Ian Leslie makes a powerful case for the value of healthy disagreement in helping us to find better solutions to problems. In Ancient Greece, Socrates attempted to establish an ethical system that was based on human reason rather than theological doctrine, and he believed that the best way to identify fallacies was through exchange of arguments (the so-called 'Socratic method' is named after him and utilizes cooperative argumentative dialogue between people and is based on asking and answering questions that can stimulate critical thinking and draw out ideas). Throughout history powerful ideas and innovations have come from a similar healthy exchange of honest views. The Wright brothers, for example, weren't engineers or scientists and never attended university, yet much of their extraordinary ideas and their eventual innovation was down to their capacity for productive argument. Wilbur Wright once wrote:

> No truth is without some mixture of error, and no error so false but that it possesses no element of truth. If a man is in too big a hurry to give up an error, he is liable to give up some truth with it, and in accepting the arguments of the other man he is sure to get some errors with it. Honest argument is merely a process of mutually picking the beams and motes out of each other's eyes so both can see clearly.[16]

Put simply, healthy debate and productive discord helps us to get to higher quality solutions and ideas, and draw from other people's expertise whilst contributing ours. Or as Ian puts it:

> Reasoning makes us smarter only when we practise it with other people in argument… the answers that emerge will be stronger for having been forged in the crucible of our disagreement.[17]

Ian gives an interesting example in his book on how depoliticizing a company culture and enabling healthy debate can ultimately lead to much better collaboration. Jody Hoffer Gittell, a management professor from Brandeis University, spent eight years studying the working culture of airlines in the 1990s. She found that there was often a culture of status-driven competition between the different staff involved in the various parts of the processes that an airline used.[18] The pilots often looked down on the cabin crew, who in turn looked down on the gate staff, who looked down on the baggage handlers and so on. Yet somehow one airline that Jody kept hearing about seemed to be different.

Southwest Airlines is one of the most successful airlines in the world. Pre-pandemic they had seen 46 consecutive years of profitability. One of the key focuses for competitive advantage and profitability throughout the airline's history has been on reducing turnaround times or the time that it takes for a plane to land, disembark passengers and baggage, clean the plane, embark the next set of passengers and baggage before taking off again. This was a matter of survival in their early years as they only had a few planes but as the effectiveness of their practices became more widely known, other airlines started to emulate them.

Since fast turnaround times needed all staff involved to work together in fundamentally new ways, Southwest Airlines put building a culture of collaboration and healthy dissent at the heart of their strategy. They encourage everyone to take ownership and work with the rest of the team regardless of their status or position around this shared goal to turn planes around faster. They ran so-called 'come to Jesus meetings', which proactively encouraged staff to air their frustrations in conflict resolution sessions. This reduced friction but also created a culture of open conversations and healthy respect.

In fact, the airline industry can teach us a lot about healthy disagreement. Comfort with dissent can be particularly tricky when the team believes that another team member or even a leader is making mistakes. Yet speaking up is vital in helping teams to avoid unnecessary errors. In their book *Meltdown: Why Our Systems Fail and What We Can Do About It* Chris Clearfield and

András Tilcsik use the example of how crew resource management (CRM) in the aviation industry revolutionized how teams can work well under pressure. CRM is a set of training procedures that are deliberately designed to minimize human error and improve aviation safety through better communication and decision-making in the cockpit. It acknowledges the fallibility of all humans (even airline pilots). It arose after a review of cockpit procedures following the 1977 Tenerife Airport Disaster, the worst in aviation history, in which two Boeing 747 airliners collided on the runway killing 583 people.

The key concept behind CRM is that while retaining a hierarchy of command, fewer errors will result from a less authoritarian environment in the cockpit where co-pilots are encouraged to question captains if they believe them to be making mistakes. This changed the whole culture of the airline industry and meant that it was no longer frowned upon to question the decisions of a superior but instead it was actively required. CRM training is based around a combination of approaches relating to situational awareness and analysis, self-awareness, assertiveness, leadership, adaptability and communication. It's focused on fostering a culture in which authority or actions may be questioned in the right way so that human errors or misjudgements may be minimized. Effectively, CRM taught aviation crews the language of respectful dissent.

CRM has arguably become one of the most valuable safety interventions that has ever been designed. Learning derived from accident investigations and aviation incident case studies have shown just how important and powerful it can be. In 2011 for example, a lack of CRM techniques was believed to be a significant contributory factor in the crash of First Air Flight 6560, a domestic charter flight that crashed on landing at Resolute, Canada. The Canadian Transportation Safety Board report described how the plane's Instrument Landing System and Global Positioning System both indicated that the plane was off course, but this contradicted a malfunctioning compass that was giving the crew misleading information.[19] The first officer made a number of attempts to bring the problem to the pilot's attention, but poor communication and a failure of CRM led to the pilot dismissing these warnings. This was exacerbated by how overburdened both pilots were in making preparations for landing, meaning that neither of them was able to pay full attention to the situation that was unfolding. Flight 6560 crashed into a hill enveloped in cloud near Resolute Bay, killing 12 of the 15 people on board.

In contrast to this, the response of the crew of Qantas Flight 32, a scheduled passenger flight from London to Sydney via Singapore in November 2010, is seen as a good example of how effective cockpit communication can manage an extremely dangerous situation. The Airbus A380 had just taken off from Changi airport when the crew heard two loud bangs and a number of warning signals flashed up in the cockpit related to serious system and structure problems. It turned out that the aircraft had suffered an uncontained failure in one of its four Rolls-Royce engines, which had then triggered multiple other problems. The crew decided to initiate a holding pattern while they assessed the situation and went through a number of initial responses and actions. There were so many warning messages coming in about different systems that the crew were in danger of being overwhelmed, but they systematically worked through an approach that would enable them to understand the status of the plane and get it back to Changi. Speaking at a flight safety seminar a year after the incident, Captain Richard de Crespigny said:

> We were getting pretty close to a [cockpit work] overload situation… It was hard to work out a list of what had failed. It was getting [to be] too much to follow. So we inverted our logic. Like Apollo 13, instead of worrying about what failed, I said, 'Let's look at what's working'. If all we could do is build ourselves a Cessna aircraft out of the rubble that remained, we would be happy.[20]

After holding for almost two hours to work through and assess the situation, the crew made a successful emergency landing at Changi airport.

These examples show how good team communication can make a huge difference in outcomes but also the importance of working through challenges as a team and having healthy, open communication around how best to solve problems. A failure to speak up, unheeded warnings, confusing communication and an inability to prioritize well in a potentially confusing situation can all create serious problems for teams and lead to poor outcomes. The pilot is in charge, but a culture that allows decisions to be questioned in respectful ways enables the avoidance of human errors. Dissent has no value unless someone listens. Leaders need to model active listening behaviours that demonstrate how contributions are valued. Thinking aloud and disagreeing with others but with the shared intention of finding the truth leads to better decisions and better progress. There is much that agile marketing teams can take from this approach.

APPLYING CREW RESOURCE MANAGEMENT TECHNIQUES IN YOUR TEAM

There are a number of fundamental skills and techniques that CRM teaches that are useful practices in creating a team environment that reduces errors while enabling everyone on the team to say when they believe mistakes are being made:[21]

1 **Communication:** Todd Bishop, a CRM expert, has defined a five-step process that can help crew members respectfully question a pilot's decisions.[22] It's a process that provides a pragmatic model for every team to apply:

   a. Start by getting the pilot's attention.

   b. State a concern (e.g. 'I'm concerned that we may not have enough fuel to fly around this storm system').

   c. State the problem as you see it ('we're showing only 40 minutes of fuel left').

   d. State a solution ('let's divert to another airport and refuel').

   e. Obtain buy-in or agreement ('does that sound good to you, Captain?').

   This provides a useful template for agile marketing teams to introduce helpful challenges and dissent. Bishop also states how language is also important. Using phrases such as 'red flag' rather than 'this is stupid' means that a leader is less likely to feel that their authority is undermined. Being aware of potential 'sender errors' (omission of information, omission of context for a message, inclusion of bias, being unwilling to repeat information) and 'receiver errors' (listening with prejudice, jumping ahead of the sender, ignoring non-verbal cues, failure to ask for clarification) can also be critical.

2 **Leadership and followership:** These will each be needed at different times. In CRM leadership is realized through ensuring mission safety, clearly defined goals and respectful, inclusive communication. Mission analysis, mentoring, building trust and effective conflict resolution are all a part of this. In CRM, followership is not a passive process but requires conscious effort. Staff should feel empowered to challenge a leader when it is right to do so, but alongside this staff must act responsibly, make success a higher priority than being right, use judgement, keep their egos in check, balance assertiveness with respect, be self-aware and publicly acknowledge mistakes themselves.

3 **Recognizing hazardous attitudes:** It's important to be aware of how some attitudes can get in the way of success and to take personal action to avoid them. These might include the impulse to always do things as fast as possible, the feeling that this won't happen to us or me, the desire to make everything look amazing (so-called 'airshow syndrome') or a fear of looking bad in front of others.

4 **Situational awareness:** As we learned from the examples above, a failure to understand what's going on around us can lead to disaster. Teams, and the individuals within them, need to maintain a constant state of situational awareness and an alertness to notice when things change. CRM lists a number of useful indicators of a lack of situational awareness including information that is open to multiple interpretations (ambiguity), unresolved discrepancies in information, focusing on one item at the expense of others (fixation), feeling overwhelmed or overloaded, being blind to risk (complacency) and where attention is drawn away from the key objective (distraction).

In organizations that are very hierarchical in their culture and structure, approaches like these can be challenging to introduce, so training around these communication norms can be helpful in evolving behaviours to better enable comfort with dissent. Teams need to understand how important communication is in solving problems well and avoiding errors, and how they can effectively challenge superiors or team assumptions. Leaders need to be open to change and understand that these practices are not threatening to authority but rather an improved way of enabling better outcomes. This touches at the heart of both personal and company habits, as well as team and organizational culture.

Taking ownership

Great team communication and healthy debate and conversation are essential prerequisites for a team being able to solve problems rapidly and in high-quality ways, but alongside this having a culture of ownership is essential. Ownership is critical in agile marketing since it results in teams taking responsibility for outcomes, being proactive in finding solutions and enabling a team to be truly empowered, utilize the autonomy and trust they have accrued to make faster decisions and to learn well. A team that talks endlessly about a problem without having team members that step up and say 'I don't know the answer but I'll go and find out' is a team that will become blocked, slow and overly reliant on others. A team that takes ownership seriously is more likely to solve complex problems well, to come up with more creative solutions, to become more resilient and deal with setbacks better and less likely to blame others when things go wrong. When teams are operating in fast-moving or complex environments where they need to experiment, learn fast from both successes and failures, explore new solutions and deal with unexpected challenges, taking ownership is imperative to success.

Leaders can't enforce a culture of ownership since it has to come voluntarily from the team members themselves but there is much that leaders can do to enable the right environment and encourage and reward the right kinds of behaviours to support it. In his book *Agile Leadership Toolkit: Learning to Thrive with Self-Managing Teams* agile practitioner Peter Koning sets out a useful model for ownership based on the balance between freedom and team maturity, which can help leaders to identify when intervention is necessary and when it is better to let go.[23]

FIGURE 15.4 Freedom and maturity ownership model

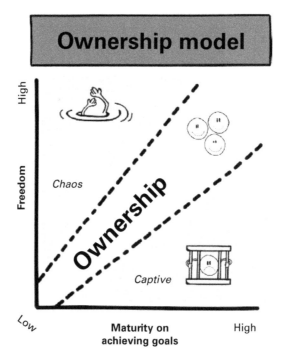

SOURCE Peter Koning

The key to this model is understanding when things are out of balance. If a team has a low level of maturity in solving problems and are given lots of freedom to do so, this may mean that they won't take ownership, resulting in chaos. In this situation a team may feel lost and lacking in the perspective they need to make effective decisions. If a team has a good level of maturity but lacks the freedom to take the initiative, they will feel frustrated, captive and unable to grow as a team.

Taking individual ownership and combining this with a clear vision and determination to succeed can result in great things. A good example of this is the story of the invention of (of all things) duct tape. Vesta Stoudt was a mum of two from Illinois who worked in an ordnance plant during World War II packing and inspecting boxes of ammunition. Both of her sons were in the Navy. At the time, ammunition boxes were sealed with paper tape that was dipped in wax and formed a tab to enable them to be opened, but Vesta noticed that the flimsy tab would often tear off meaning that soldiers in the field who would potentially be under fire at the time couldn't open them quickly.

Rather than consider this problem as someone else's job to fix, Vesta came up with the idea of creating a waterproof, tearable, cloth-based alternative tape and created and tested a version of it at work. Unfortunately, when she suggested this idea to her bosses, they didn't take her up on it. Yet Vesta could really see the difference that this would make and so she wrote a letter to President Franklin D. Roosevelt explaining the problem and offering up her solution.

The President liked the idea and forwarded it on to the War Production Board. They wrote back to Vesta:

> The Ordnance Department has not only pressed this idea... but has now informed us that the change you have recommended has been approved with the comment that the idea is of exceptional merit.[24]

Stoudt received a War Worker Award for her idea and her persistence with it, and duct tape has gone on to have all kinds of applications. It was even used by the astronauts in Apollo 13 to help them create a makeshift solution to adapt carbon dioxide filters when they had to transfer to the lunar module, which was not designed to carry three astronauts, for the 86 hours that they needed to safely get back to Earth. Vesta took ownership of wanting to solve a specific problem and found a creative way of making it happen.

ENABLING A CULTURE OF OWNERSHIP

There are some specific strategies that agile marketing leaders can use to empower greater ownership in their teams.

- **Manage intervention:** It can be hard for a leader to know when to intervene and when not to, but giving team members the space and time to solve problems themselves helps them to feel empowered to come forwards. Avoid stepping in too quickly in ways that will stifle or restrict, but also support where necessary to avoid people feeling lost.

- **Understand the maturity of the team:** Appreciating the level of maturity of the team is important in understanding the degree of support or intervention that they may need. Teams that are newly formed or staff that have recently joined will obviously need more support but it can be frustrating for a mature team when leaders intervene too much and they are not given enough autonomy and space.

- **Empower authority and autonomy:** It's important for leaders to not be down in the details of making the decisions on behalf of the team and this relates to getting the work done but also giving a team creative freedom to solve problems differently. It helps to advocate for team members to actively ask for feedback, encourage open communication and ensure they understand the impact that they can have in solving the problem.

- **Ask questions:** Setting expectations around ownership and asking incisive questions that challenge team members to find the answers themselves can help. Avoid trying to answer all the questions that the team has and instead turn them onto exploration and testing as a way to find the answers.

- **Encourage accountability:** Ensure that everyone on the team understands the goals and outcomes that you're going after, and remind them of their roles and responsibilities in achieving those outcomes. Hold people accountable for their work, and set an expectation around them realizing their full potential. Encourage them to stretch themselves.

- **Provide feedback:** Reward and recognize positive behaviour around ownership. Highlight it publicly in the team environment every time it happens.

A culture of ownership is essential to creating the environment in which agile marketing teams can thrive, and leaders play a critical role in setting the tone and enabling the norms that bring this to life.

Measuring psychological safety

It can be useful for leaders to place measures around the attributes that combine to generate psychological safety. A good place to start with this are the seven questions that Amy Edmondson defined in her original study. Richard McLean, a senior director at Elsevier, has suggested that a sensible and easy way to do this is to conduct a simple survey among the team, asking them how strongly they agree or disagree with seven statements aligned to the original research:[25]

1 If I make a mistake in this team, it is held against me.
2 Members of this team are able to bring up problems and tough issues.
3 People on this team sometimes reject others for being different.
4 It is safe to take a risk in this team.
5 It is difficult to ask other members of this team for help.
6 No one on this team would deliberately act in a way that undermines my efforts.
7 Working with members of this team, my unique skills and talents are valued and utilized.

Using a simple numerical scale enables leaders and team members to monitor levels of psychological safety and to identify areas that they might need to work on.

As I mentioned earlier in the book, agile is really a mindset that enables a process, so marketing leaders ignore the cultural and behavioural aspects of agile marketing at their peril. Psychological safety and the factors that support it can create an effective agile team environment that enables a team to generate trust, truly learn, adapt well and move fast.

APPLYING PSYCHOLOGICAL SAFETY IN AGILE MARKETING TEAMS

In her work and research on the topic Amy Edmondson set out three key strategies that leaders can adopt that can help generate an environment of psychological safety in teams:[26]

1 **Framing work as learning, rather than execution, problems:**
   Acknowledging the importance of learning helps teams to put the emphasis on collaboration, to value each member's inputs and to navigate uncertainty.

2 **Acknowledging fallibility:** It's important for leaders to recognize that they don't have all the answers and to demonstrate the value of different team inputs and perspectives in solving problems.

3 **Model curiosity by asking a lot of questions:** This helps generate the need to find answers but also encourages everyone on the team to have a voice.

Marketing leaders can adopt these strategies to generate the right environment for enabling high team performance and can combine this with simple measurement techniques such as the one mentioned earlier to monitor psychological safety and identify areas to improve.

Edmondson also stresses the importance of combining psychological safety with accountability. Too much of the former and the absence of the latter can create a comfortable environment for teams but can lead to complacency. Too much accountability and a lack of psychological safety, however, can lead to anxiety and not enough discussion around how best to solve problems.

FIGURE 15.5 Psychological safety and accountability

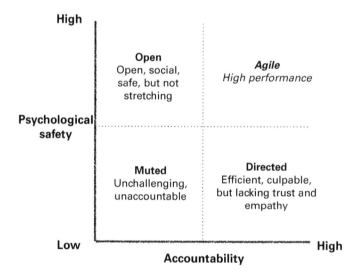

Establishing the optimal environment for teams to do their best work is hugely important in agile marketing. This requires marketing leaders to be cognizant of the behaviours that they can adopt, encourage and amplify to support good psychological safety and high performance.

FIGURE 15.6 Circle of concern, circle of influence

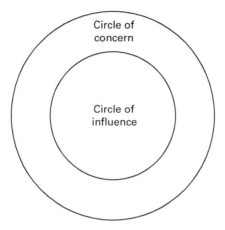

The circle of concern and the circle of influence

One of the key teaching points of Stoicism is to recognize what you can and can't control in life. According to *The Enchiridion*, a short manual of Stoic advice that originated in the second century:

> Things in our control are opinion, pursuit, desire, aversion, and, in a word, whatever are our own actions. Things not in our control are body, property, reputation, command, and, in a word, whatever are not our own actions.[27]

In a similar vein, in his renowned book *The 7 Habits of Highly Effective People*,[28] Stephen R Covey sets out a model based on two circles – our circle of concern and our circle of influence.

The former may include any number of things that may impact us in some way but are largely beyond our control. Examples might include the economy, the traffic on the way into the office, the weather, where we were born or even past decisions that we have made. These things are largely outside of our immediate sphere of influence and so there is likely very little that we can do about them. Spending energy on trying to change them may well be a waste of time.

Our circle of influence is likely to be smaller and include the things that we actually can influence or do something about. These might include factors such as other people's behaviours, our own productivity, how we work and what we prioritize. They might also include things within our direct control including what we think, our decisions, attitudes, actions and words. Our ability to change these things depend on the degree to which these elements are within our control and the level of influence that we have. Reactive people, says Covey, may well spend their time focusing on things that are beyond their control. This can be frustrating, lead to feelings of blame and victimization and to our circle of influence reducing. Proactive people, on the other hand, focus their energy on the inner circle and on changing the things that they can influence. This enables effective change to happen but can also lead to our circle of influence starting to widen.

The same is true of teams. An effective team understands how far its circle of influence extends. It recognizes when it may need external support (for example, from other teams or from senior leaders) in dealing with elements beyond its direct control and influence. It largely focuses its time and energy on the things that are within its circle of influence. In agile marketing, teams should always be focused on prioritizing high-value work and spending time and energy focusing on things that they have the ability to influence rather than things that are largely beyond their control.

INFLUENCING STAKEHOLDERS

Understanding and building influence is an important skill that can help agile marketing teams to mitigate dependencies and secure the autonomy and resources that they need to achieve their outcomes. There are a number of effective strategies that teams can deploy to improve the level of influence that they have with key stakeholders including emphasising the cost of not changing or making a decision, avoiding using jargon that can alienate, using the voice of the customer or data to support their arguments, making a challenge relatable, painting a picture of the future and making it easy for the stakeholders to say yes. A team can also use stakeholder mapping as a useful tool in understanding how to improve their influence.

FIGURE 15.7 Stakeholder mapping

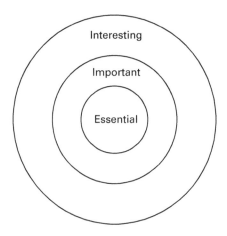

A good stakeholder mapping process may begin by clearly articulating the scope of the project or decision domain. It can then help to list all the stakeholders that may have influence on a decision or programme and to prioritize them into those that are essential to have on board, those that are important (but perhaps not essential) in this context and a wider group that may be useful or interesting. This framework can be set out on a virtual or real whiteboard and individual stakeholders can be mapped using Post-its or similar. It can then be useful to use arrows to map the value exchange between different stakeholders and define the relationship between them and what each gives to the other. A map can be done from different perspectives (for example, from the perspective of the team or from a customer), saved, used to understand how to best direct efforts to influence and revisited often.

At a more general level, understanding the key levers of influence can also be helpful for agile marketing teams. Robert Cialdini's book *Influence: The Psychology of Persuasion* defines six key principles of persuasion:[29]

- **Reciprocity:** People are often obliged to give back to others the form of a behaviour, gift or service that they have received first. It can therefore be useful for teams to network and be helpful, to look for the win-win, understand motivations and what they can do for the person or team that they are trying to influence.

- **Scarcity:** People want more of those things that there are less of. So it can be useful to frame the benefit as unique value, execution or advantage.

- **Authority:** People will follow credible, knowledgeable experts. This means that it's important for the team to build a reputation, demonstrate expertise and to use authoritative external data and advice.

- **Consistency:** People like to be consistent with things they have said or done. It can be useful to show how particular decisions align with a stakeholder's stated aims or previous actions.

- **Liking:** People prefer to say yes to those that they like. Teams can help themselves by looking for connection and avoiding alienating people.

- **Social proof:** When they are uncertain, people look at the actions and behaviours of others to determine their own. Showing how others are responding to something and building a wider consensus can therefore be a good strategy for influencing.

Getting good at influencing others can help an agile marketing team to secure the resources and empowerment that they need to achieve key objectives.

Growth mindset

> There are two kinds of people and organizations in the world: eaters and
> bakers. Eaters want a bigger slice of an existing pie; bakers want to make a
> bigger pie. Eaters think that if they win, you lose, and if you win, they lose.
> Bakers think that everyone can win with a bigger pie.
>
> (Guy Kawasaki)[30]

The concept of fixed and growth mindsets was originated by Stanford
Psychologist Carol Dweck through her research into how children and
students learn. It has become a key idea for organizations that are looking
to empower a culture of collaboration and learning, and is an excellent way
of capturing some key attributes of the team and organizational cultures in
which agile marketing can flourish. In her book *Mindset: The New
Psychology of Success*,[31] Dweck defines some key differences in how we
view our personality, learn and deploy strategies for success.

A 'fixed' mindset is founded in the view that our inherent capabilities set
the limits of our capabilities. Qualities such as intelligence and ability are
relatively fixed and static. Success serves to affirm these inherent qualities.
Those with a fixed mindset are more likely to stick to what they know, less
likely to enjoy being challenged and regard failure as a sign that they have
reached their limits. They tend to give up if frustrated and are more likely to
expect reward for little effort. For this reason they may well avoid failure at
all costs so that they can still feel accomplished, try to look smart at all times
and be afraid to try new things in case it reveals their inadequacies. They are
more likely to believe that if you have the inherent ability then you don't
need to try hard. Cultures that are characterized by fixed mindsets are more
likely to be highly political and competitive.

In contrast, a 'growth' mindset believes in the potential to always learn
new things and relishes challenges as an opportunity to learn and failure as
an opportunity to grow. For this reason people with a growth mindset like
to try new things, see feedback as constructive, are inspired by the success of
others and are determined in the face of setbacks. They also recognize the
need to put in effort, practice and work in order to improve. Their goal is to
learn at all times and at all costs. Cultures that are characterized by growth
mindsets are more likely to empower effective collaboration and learning.

Table 15.1 below captures some of the key differences between these very
different cultures.

TABLE 15.1 Fixed and growth mindset

	Fixed mindset culture	Growth mindset culture
Capabilities	inherent and fixed, intelligence is static	can be developed and cultivated
Failure	regard as reaching the limits of capability, discouraging, avoid at all costs	seen as an opportunity learn, setbacks are an opportunity to improve
Challenge	seen as a potential to fail, avoid where possible	seen as a learning opportunity so embraces them
Feedback	negative feedback is seen as personal criticism or ignored	values useful feedback whether negative or positive
Effort	effort is only required when you don't have the inherent ability; less willing to try new things	effort and work are needed to achieve successful outputs, progress and improvement
Collaboration	I win when you lose	win–win works best
Weaknesses	hides at all costs	acknowledges deficiencies, open about capabilities
Success	turns down offers of help and feels threatened by the success of others	seeks help when needed, enjoys working with smart people, inspired by the success of others

Growth mindset characteristics are fundamental to creating an agile marketing culture. Dweck talks about how these mindsets can be transmitted through words and actions, so it's important that marketing leaders model the right behaviours and set clear expectations around team demeanour, attitudes and actions. A key way in which leaders can do this is admitting that they don't have all the answers and framing situations as opportunities to learn and to progress together. This frees up staff to experiment more, test and learn, and see the opportunity in learning from both successes and failures. Choosing to praise trying new things and instances where a team has taken clear learning from doing so is another way to empower growth mindset. Every campaign, every test, every experiment, every piece of analysis is an opportunity to learn.

Cooperation over competition

> Competition has been shown to be useful up to a certain point and no further, but cooperation, which is the thing we must strive for today, begins where competition leaves off.
>
> (Franklin D Roosevelt)[32]

Good collaboration is a super-power for an agile marketing team. Yet in many organizations the belief persists that competitiveness between individuals and teams can drive performance and results. The thinking behind this posits that a competitive environment will challenge people and get the best work out of them. People and teams will feel compelled to try even harder to outperform their peers, to get better numbers, drive more impact and be more creative. As individuals we are taught that the way to get ahead in our careers is to compete with our peers. Yet there is a better way.

We can learn about the damaging effects of overly competitive environments from an unusual source. In the 1990s Dr William Muir, an evolutionary biologist at Purdue University, researched and championed a group-selection theory of livestock breeding.[33] He'd begun his research with the hypothesis that continually breeding the best egg producing hens (so-called 'super-chickens') over generations would result in higher numbers of eggs from the same number of chickens. The test for this hypothesis involved housing a control group of nine hens in one pen and allowing them to reproduce for six generations. A test group of 'super-chickens' was created from the individually most productive chickens (that laid the most eggs) from each generation. The simple measure was the number of eggs that the chicken groups produced.

After six generations his findings were somewhat surprising. The chickens in the control group were thriving, healthy and egg production had increased dramatically. Yet all but three of the super-chicken group had died. All the others had been pecked to death. Muir's conclusion was that competition among farm animals can have a dramatically negative impact on farm yield and productivity.

In her TED talk on the topic, entrepreneur Margaret Heffernan describes how the individually productive chickens had actually achieved their success by suppressing the productivity of the other chickens in the group and how our cultural obsession with individual success is threatening our potential for productivity and collaboration.[34] In organizations, leaders will often believe that the way to achieve optimal results is to allow teams to compete for resources and then to allocate those resources to the brightest superstars in their business. Yet the result can often be what Muir observed in his group of super-chickens: dysfunction, aggression and waste.

It's hard to move fast in business environments that are characterized by internal politics and/or aggressive competition. Instead, enabling the natural emergence of social connectedness and capital between individuals through psychological safety and productive communication norms creates a healthy, high-performing team. Extensive research conducted by the Human Dynamics Laboratory at MIT across a wide set of industries has shown that the most successful teams are those that establish good patterns of communication.[35] These teams performed better at solving complicated problems than those with the highest aggregate IQ or even those that had individuals with the highest IQs. A test for empathy and emotional intelligence called the 'reading the mind in the eye' test has shown that these high-performing teams typically exhibit high levels of social sensitivity to each other. The MIT Human Dynamics Lab research defined three key characteristics of team communication that really made a difference to team performance:

1 **Energy:** This is related to the number and nature of exchanges between team members. For example, face-to-face communication was more valuable than electronic communication. Team members face each other when they speak and connect with good energy.

2 **Engagement:** There was a more even distribution of energy among team members. Roughly equal time was given to each team member. No single voice was overly dominant and there were also no spectators. Contributions are kept short and sweet.

3 **Exploration:** High-performing teams have a good energy and relationship with other teams and actively seek more outside connections and perspectives.

Interestingly, MIT research has also shown that while there is little correlation between a group's collective intelligence and the IQs of its individual members, having more women in the team did increase a team's collective intelligence.[36] This, the researchers believed, could partly be explained by the fact that women tend to score higher on tests of social sensitivity. Since this is so key to group performance, having people that are high in this characteristic (whether they are men or women) is important in realizing high performance.

In agile marketing teams, establishing good communication norms is key to driving team performance. Teams that communicate well and show good social sensitivity to each other solve problems better, waste less time pursuing dead ends and make decisions faster. The concept of growth mindset that I wrote about earlier in this section is a powerful way of capturing all the behavioural attributes that can support good team collaboration and high performance.

HOW SATYA NADELLA REINVENTED MICROSOFT'S CULTURE: FROM 'KNOW IT ALL' TO 'LEARN IT ALL'

Satya Nadella took over as CEO of Microsoft in 2014. Born in Hyderabad, India, he held a number of senior positions at the company over a 22-year career before succeeding Steve Ballmer at the top of the company. As a young man, Bill Gates had been ferociously competitive, a trait that was also apparent in his friend Ballmer who took over from Gates when he stepped up to be chairman and who ran the company from 2000 to 2014.

A case study written by Herminia Ibarra and Aneeta Rattan from London Business School reveals how Nadella transformed the fortunes of the company by some smart strategic moves combined with a focus on cultural reinvention.[37] Under Ballmer, Microsoft had a very competitive company culture. As Ibarra and Rattan describe, when Nadella took over Microsoft was:

> plagued by internal knife fights, bickering and inertia. A culture of internal competition and a 'not-invented-here' mentality had focused employees on a narrow vision of performance over customers, crippling innovation.

As an example, so-called 'stack ranking' performance management techniques meant that, regardless of how much they had contributed, one in 10 employees would receive a poor review. Staff became protective over ideas, fearing that someone else would take the credit. They prioritized what would enable them to get the highest ranking over focusing on the quality of their contribution. The culture became one in which people played politics and tried to rise up the ladder rather than concentrating on doing their best work. Microsoft was in danger of fading into irrelevance.

When Nadella started as CEO, he placed empathy and customer obsession at the heart of his vision for how Microsoft should change. He wrote a letter to all employees saying that the company needed to get back to its original purpose of prioritizing innovation that is 'centred on our core value of empowering users and organisations to "do more"'. He described how he wanted a senior leadership team that would 'lean into each other's problems, promote dialogue and be effective... I don't mean yes-men and yes-women. Debate and argument are essential. Improving upon each other's ideas is crucial.' After a year of talking and listening to many staff members, Nadella spoke at a company conference about wanting to create a 'dynamic learning culture' that was based on a growth mindset. His wife had given him Dweck's book on growth mindset after finding it helpful for supporting their daughter who had learning difficulties. Nadella put Dweck's concept at the centre of their cultural reinvention. Working with his wider executive team enabled them to define three key areas of focus to empower this growth mindset: customer obsession (continually bringing the outside in, talking and listening to customers); diversity and inclusion (greater diversity but also greater inclusiveness and making it possible for everyone to speak to enable everyone's ideas to emerge); one Microsoft (removing silos, empowering collaboration). Stack ranking was abolished in favour of an approach based on continual feedback. Nadella signalled change by cancelling big internal quarterly reviews that consumed huge amounts of leadership time. Ongoing nudges helped embed positive behaviours. Managers began asking at the end of every meeting: 'Was that a growth mindset meeting or a fixed mindset one. Why?'

Growth mindset meant shifting from a culture of being 'know-it-alls' to one that celebrated 'learn-it-alls'. This empowered every employee to experiment, try out new ideas, learn from failure as well as success, and it transformed the company's fortunes. Nadella even modelled this behaviour himself, admitting in an all-company email how his own answer to a question at a Women in Tech conference could have been better. The humility of the CEO set a whole new tone for the organization that enabled collaboration and learning, accelerated innovation and resulted in a huge rise in Microsoft's value as a business. Suddenly, Microsoft was back building products that customers actually wanted rather than what Microsoft needed. When Satya became CEO in 2014 the share price had been stagnant for over a decade at around $38. At the time of writing, the share price has rocketed to $304. As technology writer John Naughton noted, Nadella 'liberated the company by getting it out of its own way'.[38]

Cognitive diversity

It makes intuitive sense that teams that are cognitively diverse should be able to solve problems better than those that are not, but the research also backs this up. Studies done by Alison Reynolds of Ashridge Business School and David Lewis of London Business School that analysed 150 senior teams found that cognitively diverse teams found solutions to problems faster than non-diverse teams.[39] Their research found that higher diversity in how people think and tackle challenges correlates with high performance, as measured by combining the level of knowledge processing (how much individuals in the team prefer to consolidate and use existing knowledge when facing new situations versus generating new knowledge) and perspective (the extent to which individuals in the team prefer to utilize their own expertise when facing new situations versus orchestrating the expertise and ideas of others).

The researchers make the point that this form of diversity is less visible than other types and also that there is often an inherent cultural barrier that comes from functional bias which can lead us to gravitate toward the people who seem to think and communicate in similar ways. Such functional bias can lessen the impact that teams can have, and teams can often believe that they are more cognitively diverse than they actually are. It's therefore important for leaders to actively be aware of how diverse their teams are in the way that they think and solve problems and the risk of self-selection or organization resulting in a lack of diversity in individual teams.

Interestingly, the researchers also noted that while cognitively diverse teams were effective in solving problems more quickly, not every team that was diverse succeeded. The real difference between success and failure in diverse teams came from combining cognitive diversity and psychological safety. A follow-up study by Reynolds and Lewis observed that teams high in both of these dimensions exhibited the kinds of encouraging behaviours, curiosity, determination and propensity to experiment that really helped to maintain momentum.[40] Conversely, teams that were low on psychological safety were too combative, even though they had high levels of cognitive diversity. And if the reverse was true the teams were prone to groupthink.

Multidisciplinary teams can naturally combine different approaches to solving problems through the bringing together of different specialist expertise (for example, more analytical approaches from data specialists combined with creative thinking from designers). However, it is also critical to empower these multidisciplinary teams through the cultural attributes and communication behaviours that can truly drive high performance. Bringing together qualities like growth mindset, cognitive diversity, psychological safety and environments that truly enable collaboration and trust can supercharge agile marketing teams.

External perspective from internal sources

In the previous chapter I looked at the value that external perspectives can bring to a team. Yet these inputs don't always need to come from outside the company or sector. Valuable fresh thinking or expertise can, of course, also come from within the business. Finding ways to amplify this can truly empower agile marketing teams.

Entrepreneur and management thinker Margaret Heffernan gives the example of when engineering business Arup were asked to build the equestrian centre for the 2008 Beijing Olympics.[40] One of the key problems faced by the engineers on the project was understanding how much waste that all the highly strung horses that had arrived on flights from all over the world would produce. It was a problem that none of the engineers had had to solve before. They could have spent countless hours speaking to vets and poring over spreadsheets to try and work through this conundrum and generate estimates. Instead, they took a very different approach.

Arup have over 12,000 people working around the world and have created a series of skills networks across the various engineering disciplines in which the business operates.[42] The skills networks enable improved collaboration and knowledge sharing across the wider business. If you're an engineer working on a challenging problem and need some help, there's a good chance that there will be someone in another region or area of the company that has relevant experience and can help. The engineers working on the equestrian centre posted their challenging conundrum up onto an Arup relevant skills network and within hours they had received a response from another Arup employee halfway around the world who had happened to design the Jockey Club in New York. This engineer had already resolved this issue and was able to give expert advice that saved the engineers working on the equestrian centre countless hours.

Arup skills networks are an excellent example of a collaborative platform that empowers a much improved level of knowledge sharing across teams and organizations. These platforms come into their own when they are designed well and used often by teams.

ESTABLISHING YOUR OWN SKILLS NETWORK

Skills networks can deliver exceptional value to businesses and staff alike. The larger the business and the more staff that use a skills network, the more potential value it can bring, as long as it is structured well. To provide real utility a collaborative skills network needs to be designed in such a way that it is broad enough to allow multiple teams to post a wide variety of challenges, while still being focused enough to connect individuals with particular knowledge domains to problems that can genuinely help. Arup's skills networks are effectively global communities across different disciplines and specialist expertise in the company. They have 45 such skills networks across disciplines as diverse as mechanical engineering, acoustics, fire engineering, architecture and transport planning.[43] There are a number of practical considerations that teams can use to build effective skills networks:

- Create clear guidance on the kinds of challenges that are suitable to post on the skills network. Complex or difficult to solve problems or solutions that require experience in specific knowledge areas are better than the kind of minor problems that teams may face on a daily basis.

- Skills networks work particularly well in enabling better problem-solving across communities of practice (discussed in the next section), since these bring together like-minded people with similar domain knowledge or interests.

- The platform that facilitates the skills network should be intuitive to use. Users should be able to post challenges in easy-to-understand formats and access the range of challenges to solve easily.

- A healthy skills network is one that is used often by staff. For this reason it can be useful for more senior leaders to model the right behaviours and use the platform themselves and for early successes to be celebrated.

Developing communities of practice

Communities of practice (CoP) can be enormously useful in sharing knowledge and learning broadly across a team and so can support agile marketing teams in both problem resolution and learning. They have been defined (by Etienne and Beverly Wenger-Trayner who expounded the original concept) as: 'groups of people who share a concern or a passion for something they do and learn how to do it better as they interact regularly'.[44]

Such CoP can form around problem or knowledge domains, around a focused goal or objective, or disciplines and shared interests. The communities may be formed in physical or virtual environments (digital tools have enabled a step-change in how virtual CoP can operate), but their purpose is always to progress learning and to share experiences and information. Some communities may be relatively diverse and come together via conversation around a hashtag on social media, and others may be more domain specific and use internal platforms and forums for discussion. Yet the elemental characteristics and purpose of these diverse communities remain the same: they are typically brought together around a common domain of knowledge or expertise, which can guide the learning; the community creates the social fabric and willingness to share; the practice provides the specific focus within the knowledge domain into which the community can contribute ideas and learn.[45]

These communities operate outside of formal and hierarchical organizational structures but are useful in bringing people together into more informal networks that can support improved organizational and team performance. As businesses and teams scale and become more complex, they can support more efficient and productive knowledge sharing and help teams to not only develop their learning but also to resolve challenges faster and in more informed ways.

In their paper on CoP, EL Lesser and J Storck define four key ways in which they can drive better business performance:[46]

1 They can ensure that teams are understanding changing customer needs and responding more effectively and quickly.

2 They can quicken the learning process for new staff.

3 They can reduce duplication of effort and prevent staff from repeating mistakes or work that has already been done, and they can coordinate effort to better solve a particular challenge in an efficient way.

4 They can help encourage and amplify new ideas and ensure that they gain momentum.

An early but powerful example of the value of a CoP was the community of Xerox customer service representatives that were responsible for repairing machines in the field. Reps began informally exchanging tips over breakfast and lunch, which led to the company forming the Eureka project. This brought together more than 14,000 service technicians and support centre staff across the world to share tips for fixing office equipment and has been estimated to have saved the business around $100 million.[47]

In their early work around how online communities shared knowledge Molly Wasko and Samer Faraj from the Department of Decision and Information Technologies at the University of Maryland defined three distinct types of knowledge: knowledge as object, knowledge that is embedded within individuals and knowledge that is embedded in a community.[48] Without more informal structures for knowledge sharing, teams are at risk of missing opportunities to develop wider learning and solve problems in enhanced ways. A CoP can be particularly valuable in sharing tacit knowledge or the kind of knowledge that is not explicitly codified but is instead learned and known implicitly by individuals through their experience. This can really help agile marketing teams to benefit from all the implicit knowledge that has been accumulated over time by team members, which ultimately can support better problem-solving and improved outcomes.

APPLYING COMMUNITIES OF PRACTICE IN AGILE MARKETING

In agile marketing teams, communities of practice (CoP) may be brought together in several key ways:

- **Discipline:** a CoP can be formed around discipline expertise that may be dispersed widely across a team. An example of this might be channel expertise (for example, specialists in SEO, CRM or social media that may be distributed widely across different marketing groups or global and regional teams) or functional expertise (for example, data and analytics specialists that may also be dispersed across areas of the organization). Similarly, a group may assemble around an interest area rather than a specific discipline.

- **Product or business focus:** a CoP can also come together around a product or service or another area of business-related focus. This may enable marketers to work in more informal ways with other functions outside of marketing around a focused objective or product.

- **Problem domain:** areas that are of strategic importance to a business may benefit from having a CoP form around them. This can help build momentum and shared experience and learning, which can result in more concurrent and faster problem-solving.

In a scaled application of small, multidisciplinary squads, CoPs can be very useful in bringing together functional and discipline expertise across multiple teams to enable shared learnings. A CoP may be gathered together regularly in more informal gatherings for this specific purpose. An example of this may be a CoP that has established regular learning sessions where volunteers from the group step forward to share specific solutions to problems, or what they have learned in solving specific challenges as a way to develop learning across the whole group. Drawing on Wenger's original principles for effective CoP, there are some useful practices that can enable a CoP to flourish:[49]

- **Natural evolution:** allowing and even proactively designing for a community to evolve naturally will help it to emerge in ways that are more likely to be sustainable. A CoP may also change its focus over time as the interests or needs change.

- **Varying participation:** supporting and allowing different levels of participation from practitioners can ensure that the community is useful whilst still enabling the critical feeling of ownership.

- **Establish a rhythm:** the community may be more informal but it may well be useful to create a clear rhythm around updates and gatherings that can set clear expectations and also maintain engagement.

- **Celebrating and sharing the value of the community:** amplifying stories of how the CoP has successfully contributed to better outcomes or solving problems can help widen its perceived value.

- **Different spaces and perspectives:** a healthy CoP can appreciate the different perspectives of its members but also bring in external viewpoints or knowledge that can also help develop learning. Open dialogue should be encouraged but private spaces that enable individuals to share knowledge can also be useful.

The role of coaching

As teams adopt agile practices it can be easy to drift back to more traditional linear ways of solving problems. Agile coaches can be very useful in marketing teams that have adopted agile principles in supporting staff through the transition to agile ways of working and in embedding key practices and beneficial habits and behaviours. The agile coach acts as a teacher of agile methodology and also as a champion for the values and mindsets that can support an effective deployment. This role can be fulfilled at an enterprise, team or individual level. Their goal is to enable better outcomes for teams through helping them to apply agile practices in the optimal way and employ the kinds of behaviours and ways of working that enables them to act as a cohesive, high-performing team. This goal may be achieved through a combination of professional coaching, facilitation and mentoring.

It can be easy for businesses and teams to ignore the value that coaching can bring or to regard it as a luxury. Yet the reality in practice is that teams will often need support in implementing agile practices in ways that can best support the achievement of the outcomes that they have been set. This can be particularly true when teams have recently moved from more traditional approaches to agile ways of working and team members are struggling to adjust or feeling uncomfortable about the level of autonomy they have been given or how they need to work differently with team members. Agile coaches can also deliver a valuable perspective that is external to the team and so can bring in new ways of solving challenges and help teams to become unstuck when progress is challenged. An example of this may be helping a team to mitigate dependencies by suggesting solutions that other teams have found to be beneficial. An agile coach can therefore provide critical support across multiple teams and ensure that agile practices are adhered to and embedded in operations but also championed more widely and applied in the most effective way.

Endnotes

1 D McCallum and G H Henshaw. Organization diagram of the New York and Erie railroad, 1855, public domain, Wikimedia Commons, 2021. commons. wikimedia.org/wiki/File:Organizational_diagram_of_the_New_York_and_Erie_ Railroad,_1855.jpg (archived at https://perma.cc/EV83-MPQ8)

2 C Rosenthal. Big data in the age of the telegraph. McKinsey Quarterly, March 2013. www.mckinsey.com/business-functions/people-and-organizational-performance/our-insights/big-data-in-the-age-of-the-telegraph (archived at https://perma.cc/2NEZ-EFBY)

3 J Gothelf and J Seiden. You need to manage digital projects for outcomes, not outputs, *Harvard Business Review*, February 2017. hbr.org/2017/02/you-need-to-manage-digital-projects-for-outcomes-not-outputs (archived at https://perma.cc/68WA-HYVA)

4 ADRP 6-0. Mission Command, Headquarters, Department of the Army, October 2012. irp.fas.org/doddir/army/adrp6_0.pdf (archived at https://perma.cc/PSS7-Y9GC)

5 A Benson, D Li and K Shue. Promotions and the Peter Principle, April 2019. voxeu.org/article/promotions-and-the-peter-principle (archived at https://perma.cc/J7HG-32UE)

6 J Rozovsky. The five keys to a successful Google team, Google ReWork, 17 November 2015. rework.withgoogle.com/blog/five-keys-to-a-successful-google-team/ (archived at https://perma.cc/ML93-NNJ8)

7   A Edmondson. Psychological safety and learning behavior in work teams, June 1999. journals.sagepub.com/doi/abs/10.2307/2666999 (archived at https://perma.cc/M47F-3P53)

8   B Thompson. The uncanny valley of a functional organisation, July 2013. stratechery.com/2013/the-uncanny-valley-of-a-functional-organization/ (archived at https://perma.cc/B3QP-8CKK)

9   Buffer. About us, 2021. buffer.com/about (archived at https://perma.cc/439T-PQRL)

10 K Lee. Why transparency in business matters (and how to get started), Buffer, 29 October 2018, buffer.com/resources/transparency-in-business/ (archived at https://perma.cc/XZ62-XCL5)

11 Buffer. Buffer salaries, 2021. buffer.com/salaries (archived at https://perma.cc/DSQ7-CK8X)

12 S Covey (2020) The 7 Habits of Highly Effective People, 30th anniversary ed., Simon & Schuster, New York.

13 S McLeod and S Asch. Conformity experiment, Simply Psychology, December 2018. www.simplypsychology.org/asch-conformity.html (archived at https://perma.cc/MR92-EENT)

14 V Klucharev, K Hytönen, M Rijpkema, A Smidts and G Fernández. Reinforcement learning signal predicts social conformity, Science Direct, January 2009. www.sciencedirect.com/science/article/pii/S0896627308010209# ! (archived at https://perma.cc/E9C8-SQWB)

15 I Leslie (2021) Conflicted: Why Arguments Are Tearing Us Apart and How They Can Bring Us Together, Faber & Faber, London.

16 I Leslie. Why disagreement is vital to advancing human understanding, Aeon, 2021. aeon.co/essays/why-disagreement-is-vital-to-advancing-human-understanding (archived at https://perma.cc/WTS9-QMM4)

17 I Leslie. Why disagreement is vital to advancing human understanding, Aeon, 2021. aeon.co/essays/why-disagreement-is-vital-to-advancing-human-understanding (archived at https://perma.cc/WTS9-QMM4)

18 J H Gittell (2005) The Southwest Airlines Way, McGraw-Hill Education, New York.

19 Transportation Safety Board of Canada. Aviation Investigation Report A11H0002, 20 August 2011. www.tsb.gc.ca/eng/rapports-reports/aviation/2011/A11H0002/A11H0002.html (archived at https://perma.cc/HLH4-C53Q)

20 L V D Arrubla. CRM at its best: Qantas flight 32, learning from the recent past, January 2017. livingsafelywithhumanerror.wordpress.com/2017/01/09/crm-at-its-best-qantas-flight-32-learning-from-the-recent-past/ (archived at https://perma.cc/DGG5-6ZN8)

21 Civil Aviation Authority. Methods used to evaluate the effectiveness of flightcrew CRM training in the UK aviation industry, 2002. publicapps.caa.co.uk/docs/33/CAPAP2002_05.PDF (archived at https://perma.cc/9CK7-HU6U)

22 T Bishop. Crew resource management, International Association of Fire Chiefs, 2003. www.nh.gov/safety/divisions/fstems/ems/training/documents/crewmgt.pdf (archived at https://perma.cc/W8XY-9MG7)

23 P Koning (2019) *Agile Leadership Toolkit: Learning to Thrive with Self-Managing Teams*, Pearson, Boston.

24 M Gurowitz. The woman who invented duct tape, Kilmer House, 21 June 2012. www.kilmerhouse.com/2012/06/the-woman-who-invented-duct-tape (archived at https://perma.cc/H3DC-B3RC)

25 Richard McLean, Measuring Psychological Safety, July 2019, https://mcleanonline.medium.com/measuring-psychological-safety-81dd1da91915 (archived at https://perma.cc/N4CW-XK58)

26 S Lebowitz. Google considers this to be the most critical trait of successful teams, Business Insider, 20 November 2015, uk.businessinsider.com/amy-edmondson-on-psychological-safety-2015-11 (archived at https://perma.cc/8WV7-VBZD)

27 Epictetus. *The Enchiridion*, translated by Elizabeth Carter. classics.mit.edu/Epictetus/epicench.html (archived at https://perma.cc/Q4PP-DL2Y)

28 S Covey (2020) The 7 Habits of Highly Effective People, 30th anniversary ed., Simon & Schuster, New York.

29 R Cialdini (2007) *Influence: The Psychology of Persuasion,* HarperBusiness, New York.

30 G Kawasaki (2011) *Enchantment: The Art of Changing Hearts, Minds and Actions*, Portfolio Penguin, New York.

31 C S Dweck (2007) *Mindset: The New Psychology of Success*, updated edition, Ballantine Books, New York.

32 T Nall. Cooperation versus competition, Odyssey Online, March 2016. www.theodysseyonline.com/cooperation-versus-competition (archived at https://perma.cc/5NEG-HH4D)

33 W Muir. Incorporation of Competitive Effects in Forest Tree or Animal Breeding Programs, Genetics, July 2005. www.genetics.org/content/170/3/1247 (archived at https://perma.cc/X8T9-NVY4)

34 M Heffenan, Forget the pecking order at work, TED, 2015. www.ted.com/talks/margaret_heffernan_forget_the_pecking_order_at_work (archived at https://perma.cc/9Z2K-KVYW)

35 A Pentland. The new science of building great teams, *Harvard Business Review*, April 2012. hbr.org/2012/04/the-new-science-of-building-great-teams (archived at https://perma.cc/6LDZ-K932)

36 A Woolley and T W Malone. Defend your research: What makes a team smarter? More women, *Harvard Business Review*, June 2011. hbr.org/2011/06/defend-your-research-what-makes-a-team-smarter-more-women (archived at https://perma.cc/8UFN-F2YT)

37 H Ibarra and A Rattan. Microsoft: Instilling a growth mindset, 2018. herminiaibarra.com/wp-content/uploads/2019/07/IBARRA_et_al-2018-London_Business_School_Review.pdf (archived at https://perma.cc/4APB-TAKQ)

38 J Naughton. How Microsoft reinvented itself, *The Guardian*, 12 May 2019. www.theguardian.com/commentisfree/2019/may/12/how-microsoft-was-resurrected-as-the-third-most-valuable-tech-company-1-trillion-dollars (archived at https://perma.cc/KXJ4-9LXB)

39 A Reynolds and D Lewis. Teams solve problems faster when they're more cognitively diverse, *Harvard Business Review*, March 2017. hbr.org/2017/03/teams-solve-problems-faster-when-theyre-more-cognitively-diverse (archived at https://perma.cc/LV4D-YE6L)

40 A Reynolds and D Lewis. The two traits of the best problem-solving teams, *Harvard Business Review*, April 2018. hbr.org/2018/04/the-two-traits-of-the-best-problem-solving-teams (archived at https://perma.cc/HTA8-RH7N)

41 M Heffenan. Forget the pecking order at work, TED, 2015. www.ted.com/talks/margaret_heffernan_forget_the_pecking_order_at_work (archived at https://perma.cc/9Z2K-KVYW)

42 Arup @4 Magazine, Issue 13. www.arup.com/perspectives/publications/magazines-and-periodicals/a4/at4-magazine-issue-13 (archived at https://perma.cc/4HV6-P8N5)

43 Arup @4 Magazine. www.arup.com/-/media/arup/files/publications/a/4issue13final.pdf (archived at https://perma.cc/J3TF-2ASJ)

44 W Trayner. Introduction to communities of practice. wenger-trayner.com/introduction-to-communities-of-practice/ (archived at https://perma.cc/5W3E-WXM7)

45 E Wenger, R McDermott and W Snyder (2002) *Cultivating Communities of Practice*, 2002, Harvard Business Press, Boston.

46 EL Lesser and J Storck, Communities of practice and organisational performance. web.archive.org/web/20110409160937/http://www.providersedge.com/docs/km_articles/CoP_and_Organizational_Performance.pdf (archived at https://perma.cc/Y2R2-EJJ9)

47 J S Brown and P Duguid. Balancing act: How to capture knowledge without killing it, *Harvard Business Review*, 2000. lymabe.edublogs.org/files/2007/04/balancing-act.doc (archived at https://perma.cc/A2PX-FEV7)

48 M Wasko and S Faraj. 'It is what one does': Why people participate and help others in electronic communities of practice, September 2000. www.sciencedirect.com/science/article/abs/pii/S0963868700000457?via%3Dihub#! (archived at https://perma.cc/26TF-T9AE)

49 E Wenger, R McDermott and W Snyder (2002) *Cultivating Communities of Practice*, Harvard Business Press, Boston.

PART SEVEN

The agile marketing transformation

16

Conclusion

A step-by-step guide

This book has made the case for applying agile principles in depth and at scale to marketing practice. This is about defining a new operating model for marketing that is fit for purpose for a rapidly evolving, technology-enabled, data-driven world. Transformation is rarely a journey with a defined beginning, middle and end. As marketers embark on this journey they need to plan for continuous evolution. The learning never stops and contexts never stand still, so it's key that this is seen as a journey towards a marketing organization that itself is characterized by continuous adaptation. In other words, we need to be agile in how we are implementing agile.

Bearing this in mind, we need to bake learning into the process of transformation. Even though change and transformation is rarely a linear process, we can define some critical steps that are helpful in deployment.

Situational awareness

As with any strategic process, this should start with a full understanding of contexts and situation. This might include understanding key customer behaviour shifts, the opportunity that new technologies can bring to the organization.

Creating a vision for the agile marketing organization

Leaders need to create a sense of urgency about the need for change. Why agile? Why now? Describing the contexts that compel the need for greater agility helps staff to connect and engage with the fundamental need to transform. The next step is to generate a compelling vision for the agile organization of the future. At this stage this does not need to be detailed plans or rigid organization design, but the vision should clearly articulate the key characteristics of the type of marketing organization that you want to become. This can help frame a direction, create an understanding of what good looks like and enable people to visualize the potential of the new way of working. Use of storytelling can help bring this vision to life and the importance of this vision should be communicated repeatedly by leaders.

Establish the foundation

This stage is about appreciating the foundational building blocks that can enable change to happen. This may involve everything from getting buy-in at the top of the organization, to identifying the technology, process and cultural enablers that will empower the change. For technology infrastructure this is about ensuring that a robust marketing technology stack can deliver the capability that the team will need to support a different operating environment. Remember the importance of data-driven and data-informed decision-making, of testing and experimentation, of feedback loops and access to metrics. Teams will need to be empowered to enact the behaviour change that is being asked of them, and access to the right tools and data is essential. For process this may well be about defining a foundational methodology and approach for how agile principles can be deployed by the team. For people, this is the plan that is created to bring the team on the journey and support teams in their knowledge building, mindset and behaviour change. This may be a plan for embedding agile thinking and understanding through the team via training and coaching (remember the need to 'be agile' and not just 'do agile'). It can be useful to create a vision for the key behaviours that will be expected of the wider team. There will inevitably be barriers and blockers to progress along the way. Be prepared to deal with them.

Start small to learn

It can be really useful to run a few pilot teams as a way of learning at the earliest opportunity. This learning may be about barriers that teams will come up against, about process blockers or dependency challenges, about how to align teams, about team composition, about the optimal agile methods and how to apply the principles in the best way, about the kinds of people that may be your early adopters and champions. All of these things can be enormously valuable in ensuring that a good foundation is created for a more scaled application of agile. Pilot teams should be small, cross-disciplinary groups that are as close as possible to the anticipated make-up of a squad, but it may be possible to experiment with slightly different team compositions. Teams can be focused on specific initiatives or campaigns, but it can be potentially useful to test different forms of alignment and as well as composition to learn about what will work best at scale. Aligning at least one team to key predicted areas of work (for example, a customer need state or segment) enables the organization to learn in a scenario that is as close as possible to a scaled application. Teams should be supported in their pilots to enable them the best opportunity to succeed.

Scaling fast and building momentum

Once the organization has a vision for what good looks like, and has learned from a few early pilots, it's time to scale fast. This means applying the learning that has been gained from the pilots to design an agile organization, with teams aligned and supported in the optimal way. Any learning around process should be applied to evolve methodology and practice. Learning generated around dependencies should inform the development of strategies to mitigate them as the number of teams grows. The creation of clear guidelines and standards can help scale good practices. A programme of supporting behaviour change through feedback and further training can help embed the right attitudes and approaches. Be prepared.

In physics, momentum is mass multiplied by velocity. In an agile marketing transformation mass is created through a growing scaled change. More people, more teams, more behaviour and mindset change. Velocity is speed with direction. This means that change should be scaled fast but also with a learning mindset that can enable adaptation and movement always in a positive direction.

Staying agile

Finally, it is important to make the change stick. Many transformations fail, let down by a lack of commitment, the absence of investment, or an overly rigid approach. Culture can take years to change but creating a movement can generate momentum behind both tangible and more intangible elements of transformation. Celebrate the early wins, build on them, see challenge and failure as an opportunity to learn, take that knowledge and apply it at scale without hesitation. Staying agile means always learning. Don't expect to get it completely right from the start. The process itself is one of continuous learning. Remember you need to *be* agile in how you transform to *become* agile.

INDEX

Note: Page numbers in *italics* indicate figures or tables

CPSIA information can be obtained
at www.ICGtesting.com
Printed in the USA
JSHW010024300322
24434JS00006B/25